DISABILITY, CULTURE, AND EQUITY SERIES

Alfredo J. Artiles and Elizabeth B. Kozleski, *Series Editors*

DisCrit—Disability Studies and Critical Race Theory in Education
DAVID J. CONNOR, BETH A. FERRI, & SUBINI A. ANNAMMA, EDS.

Closing the School Discipline Gap:
Equitable Remedies for Excessive Exclusion
DANIEL J. LOSEN, ED.

(Un)Learning Disability:
Recognizing and Changing Restrictive Views of Student Ability
ANNMARIE D. BAINES

Ability, Equity, and Culture:
Sustaining Inclusive Urban Education Reform
ELIZABETH B. KOZLESKI & KATHLEEN KING THORIUS, EDS.

Condition Critical—Key Principles for Equitable and Inclusive Education
DIANA LAWRENCE-BROWN & MARA SAPON-SHEVIN

DisCrit

Disability Studies and Critical Race Theory in Education

David J. Connor, Beth A. Ferri, and Subini A. Annamma

EDITORS

TEACHERS COLLEGE PRESS

TEACHERS COLLEGE | COLUMBIA UNIVERSITY

NEW YORK AND LONDON

Published by Teachers College Press, 1234 Amsterdam Avenue, New York, NY 10027

We gratefully acknowledge:

Taylor & Francis for giving permission to reprint our original article first published in the *Journal of Race, Ethnicity, & Education*. www.tandfonline.com, and excerpts from *The Colour of Class* by Nicola Rollock, David Gillborn, Carol Vincent, & Stephen J. Ball (2015, Routledge).

Lawrence Finney for permission to use his work, *City Girl, Red Braids* (2002), on the cover of our book, currently in the private collection of Mr. John D. Treadwell. Mr. Finney is represented by the UFA Gallery (ufagallery@aol.com).

Library of Congress Cataloging-in-Publication Data

Names: Connor, David J., 1961– editor of compilation. | Ferri, Beth A., 1961– editor of compilation. | Annamma, Subini A., editor of compilation.
Title: DisCrit : disability studies and critical race theory in education / edited by David J. Connor, Beth A. Ferri, Subini A. Annamma.
Description: New York, NY : Teachers College Press, 2016. | Series: Disability, culture, and equity series | Includes bibliographical references and index.
Identifiers: LCCN 2015032687|
   ISBN 9780807756676 (pbk. : alk. paper) |
   ISBN 9780807756683 (hardcover : alk. paper) |
   ISBN 9780807773864 (ebook)
Subjects: LCSH: People with disabilities—Education—United States. | African Americans with disabilities—Education—United States. | Disability studies—United States. | Racism in education—United States. | Discrimination in education—United States
Classification: LCC LC4031 .D57 2016 | DDC 371.9—dc23
LC record available at http://lccn.loc.gov/2015032687

ISBN 978-0-8077-5667-6 (paper)
ISBN 978-0-8077-5668-3 (hardcover)
ISBN 978-0-8077-7386-4 (ebook)

Printed on acid-free paper
Manufactured in the United States of America

In memory of

Ellen Brantlinger
&
Jeanette Klingner
&
Steve Taylor

Three exceptional teachers, scholars, mentors, and friends.
We stand on your shoulders.

Contents

A Truncated Genealogy of DisCrit

Subini Ancy Annamma
David J. Connor
Beth A. Ferri

The genesis of DisCrit, a dynamic framework through which to simultaneously engage with Disability Studies (DS) and Critical Race Theory (CRT), can be traced through an academic lineage of boundary pushing. This work is rooted in the work of intellectual ancestors such as James Baldwin, Anna Julia Cooper, Mary Church Terrell, W. E. B. Du Bois, Yuri Kochiyama, and Bayard Rustin. In naming these people in particular, the goal is not to create an exhaustive list but to trace the ancestry back far before the development of either Critical Race Theory or Disability Studies, to recognize those whose work made these critical theories possible. These theoretical frameworks were forged by people of color and people with dis/abilities respectively, each "grassroots" perspective purposefully designed to counter hegemonic knowledge-claims about the meaning of race and disability in society. (We utilize the term *dis/ability* to 1: counter the emphasis on having a whole person be represented by what he or she cannot do, rather than what he or she can, and 2: disrupt notions of the fixity and permanency of the concept of disability, seeking rather to analyze the entire context in which a person functions.) Our epistemological lineage exists outside and within the academy, built from the foundational work of activists, artists, and academics. There are many more whose work laid a foundation for DisCrit's beginnings, which is why the title of this introduction claims only a truncated genealogy. However, what is more important to our thinking than naming every contributor is that we were following a path laid by scholars of color, those with disabilities, those with intersecting marginalized identities, and their allies who were teaching us to move past simplistic and unidimensional notions of identity. Instead, to recognize humanity in a richer, nuanced, and more accurate sense, we acknowledge how the works of those before us broke open existing boundaries allowing us to recognize the multiple dimensions of individuals and the systems of oppression and marginalization in which they survive, resist, and thrive.

Chris Bell (2011) described the work of understanding raced and dis/-abled bodies as one of recovery and detection. Recovery is needed because raced bodies whose stories we are often quite familiar with (such as Harriet Tubman, Emmett Till, and James Byrd) are bodies also marked by dis/abilities that remain generally unacknowledged. As a result, these individuals are often (mis)constructed as unidimensional figures. Narratives of these individuals often insist on misrepresenting their bodies and neglecting their situatedness at the intersections of race and disability (along with others markers/shapers of identity). Their stories are presented in ways that gloss over their multiplicity. Additionally, recovery work requires detection in order to consider ways in which these raced and disabled bodies also "transform(ed) systems and cultures" (Bell, 2011, p. 4). Most important, this work "requires a willingness to deconstruct the systems that would keep those bodies in separate spheres" (Bell, 2011, p. 3).

For me (Subini), the journey to dismantle systems that regulate children's bodies into separate categories was deeply impacted when I was sitting in the office of my mentor, Janette Klingner. She handed me a book called *Urban Narratives: Portraits-in-Progress—Life at the Intersections of Learning Disability, Race, and Social Class* by David Connor. She had been asked to comment on Connor's tenure dossier, and because she knew that I was deeply interested in the intersections of race and disability, she thought we could read the book together. From the moment I picked it up, I knew Connor was someone I wanted to emulate. Drawing from Disability Studies and Critical Race Theory, he situated his work with youth of color with dis/abilities within a framework that was responsive to their lives. Connor's work led me to the scholarship of Beth A. Ferri. Her deep commitment to intersectionality from a Feminist and Disability Studies perspective was awe-inspiring. (*Intersectionality* is a widely used concept in contemporary scholarly inquiry, addressing the question of how multiple forms of inequality and identity are interrelated across different contexts and over time, such race, gender, class, dis/ability, and so on.) In both their joint and separate writing, Connor and Ferri have been motivated to study the intersections of race, disability, gender, and other identity markers.

Building on the foundations of Connor and Ferri (along with many other scholars including those listed above) within my own work, I sought to expand the conversation to build a framework that was responsive to the social location of the students of color with disabilities with whom I had worked as an educator. These students, "forged in the crucibles of difference" (Lorde, 2007, p. 112), were brilliant yet floundering in schools and were seemingly being ignored by the academy at large. I found this absence even more troubling, given the centrality of students of color in entrenched inequities in education (for example, overrepresentation of students of color in special education, the achievement gap, the school-to-prison pipeline). To render the links between perceptions of race and dis/ability more visible, I coined the term *DisCrit*. DisCrit afforded the opportunity for the recovery and detection work Bell (2011) refers to, in this case recovering the bodies of my students, and the detection of how their lives transformed the systems and cultures of which they were a part. This rhetorical move allowed for the development of a new branch on the CRT tree that explicitly rejected what Bell called "White Disability Studies" (Bell, 2006).

From our mutual interests in the intersections of race and dis/ability, we contemplated the possibility of formalizing a framework that could encapsulate our collective research interests. The result was a collaboratively written paper, "Dis/ability Critical Race Studies (DisCrit): Theorizing at the Intersections of Race and Dis/ability," which took almost a year to write in our quest to "get it right," as we were fully aware of the responsibility involved in attempting to forge something new. During the writing process, we each brought unique perspectives, interests, and areas of expertise to the paper. Furthermore, we were all deeply committed to intersectionality in our own work, particularly to better understanding the mutually constitutive nature of race and ability.

The publication of the article in the United Kingdom–based *Journal of Race, Ethnicity, and Education* and subsequent interest by a small but influential number of scholars in both fields of CRT and DS led us to consider further developing our initial article. In sum, this book grew out of our belief in the potential for DisCrit to expand our capacity as scholars to analyze some of the most entrenched educational inequities from an intersectional lens. We decided to organize the book both thematically and intersectionally. We began with our original article, which serves as the "touchstone text." Thematically, contributors—leading scholars in race and/or dis/ability studies—were asked to engage with DisCrit by addressing the following entrenched inequities in education: perceptions of race, class, and ability (Part I); the achievement/opportunity gap (Part II); the overrepresentation of children of color in special education (Part III); the school-to-prison pipeline (Part IV); school reform (Part V); and race, ability, and the law (Part VI). Our primary goal was to create a polyvocal dialectic in a multidisciplinary text that would ultimately expand, critique, and push DisCrit forward. These thematic and intersectional sections are intentionally porous, interanimating race and ability from various theoretical, methodological, and analytical standpoints.

The collection opens with "The Black Middle Classes, Education, Racism, and Dis/Ability" by David Gillborn, Nicola Rollock, Carol Vincent, and Stephen J. Ball. The authors use intersectional qualitative research to capture the experiences of middle-class Black parents within special education processes and practices. This empirical study uncovers ways that racism and ableism function qualitatively differently for young people of color with disabilities and their families, disputing the assumption of a universal dis/ability experience.

The second chapter, written by Alicia A. Broderick and Zeus Leonardo, is titled "What a Good Boy: The Deployment and Distribution of 'Goodness' as Ideological Property in Schools." This theoretical piece accounts for ways that discipline systems relegate the property of goodness to normative (for instance, White, male) bodies. Using the embodied educational experiences of Broderick's son, the authors recognize how compliance is conflated with goodness and how goodness, in turn, perpetuates the concept of smartness for some children. Additionally, the authors recognize how White complicity is subtly groomed into the White body, including how children are taught from a young age to rationalize the inequitable distribution of "property" based on skin color.

Elizabeth Mendoza, Christina Paguyo, and Kris Gutiérrez approach the discussion of race and ability through a cultural historical activity theory (CH/AT) perspective in Chapter 3, "Understanding the Intersection of Race and Dis/Ability: Common Sense Notions of Learning and Culture." The authors illustrate how critical theories and theories of learning can be interwoven to utilize the strengths of both in an empirical study surrounding a teacher education course. Recognizing the processes by which racism and ableism occur through common sense, non-tensions, and mediating artifacts, the authors also identify ways to disrupt these inequities by creating intentional places for growth.

The fourth chapter, "Expanding Analysis of Educational Debt: Considering Intersections of Race and Ability," by Kathleen A. King Thorius and Paulo Tan, expertly weaves an intersectional analysis onto Ladson-Billings's concept of education debt. The authors examine how race and dis/ability mutually construct the historical, economic, sociopolitical, and moral debt that we know as the education debt.

Chapter 5, "Reifying Categories: Measurement in Search of Understanding," by Elizabeth B. Kozleski, highlights how data collection systems, presumed to be accurate, are nonetheless quite fallible. Kozleski examines the measurement tools of large-scale data and highlights the assumptions on which these instruments are based, which serve to maintain inequities. She concludes that because these tools impede intersectional analyses, they limit opportunities to accurately quantify problems and produce viable solutions.

Edward Fergus, in Chapter 6, "Social Reproduction Ideologies: Teacher Beliefs About Race and Culture," analyzes quantitative and descriptive survey data. He utilizes social reproduction theory to connect microlevel teachers' beliefs about children of color to macrolevel outcomes, such as overrepresentation of children of color in special education.

In Chapter 7, "Shadow Play: DisCrit, Dis/respectability and Carceral Logics," D. L. Adams and Nirmala Erevelles draw on an empirical qualitative study to explore the processes of dis-location via the mechanism of dis/respectability politics in teacher discourse. In other words, the authors link ways Black and Brown people with dis/abilities have been criminalized in society through extrajudicial killings, but also in less violent (and therefore less visible) normalized practices in schools. Adams and Erevelles reveal ways that teachers justify removing unwanted bodies through what they term "carceral logics"—schooling processes affiliated with deeply rooted historical associations of punishment and removal from mainstream life settings.

In Chapter 8, "The Overrepresentation of Students of Color with Learning Disabilities: How 'Working Identity' Plays a Role in the School-to-Prison Pipeline," Claustina Mahon-Reynolds and Laurence Parker explore the process of criminalization of Black males. The authors suggest how racial working identity is very much a school-based practice that plays a significant role in perpetuating the pipeline.

Sally Tomlinson, in Chapter 9, "Race, Class, Ability, and School Reform," uses an intersectional lens to link how social hierarchies are built and maintained in school. Broadening the view to international contexts, Tomlinson uses historical analysis to explore ways in which nations structure normalcy around race, class, and ability.

In Chapter 10, "Toward Unity in School Reform: What DisCrit Contributes to Multicultural and Inclusive Education," Susan Baglieri explicitly links school reform to the economic industry of co-constructing race and ability through individual pathology. Baglieri calls for inclusive education, multicultural education, and other progressive forms of education to form a critical alliance to resist economics of marginalization.

Kathleen M. Collins seamlessly weaves the personal and political in Chapter 11, "A DisCrit Perspective on *The State of Florida v. George Zimmerman*: Racism, Ableism, and Youth Out of Place in Community and School." In this chapter, Collins juxtaposes the killing of Trayvon Martin and the trial of George Zimmerman against her own biracial sons' education experiences and her perspective as a mother. Using media analysis and narrative storytelling, Collins explores how children of color are constituted as raced and abled in ways that position them "out of place" geographically, socially, and discursively.

Chapter 12, "Disability Does Not Discriminate: Toward a Theory of Multiple Identity Through Coalition," by Zanita E. Fenton, examines the legal construct of equal protection, particularly in terms of its protection of marginalized groups. Fenton traces historical parallels and contemporary intersections of race and disability from a legal standpoint. This chapter provides important links to CRT's roots in legal studies and illustrates the continued relevance to Disability Studies.

In the concluding chapter, "Critical Conversations Across Race and Ability," we select important contributions by contributing authors, draw connections within each Part, and illuminate tensions and possibilities for future work. Recognizing that DisCrit is not a singular answer to entrenched educational inequities, we discuss its limitations—alongside its possibilities—with equal verve and commitment.

We close this introduction with two points. The first is about language. As editors, we situate ourselves in deeply critical epistemologies around race and ability and have committed to using particular language. However, we have accepted that other authors utilize different language for distinct purposes. Our job is not to police their choice of words but instead to explicitly address how we use language as a tool. Therefore, we have left it up to the authors to use the terms they feel most comfortable with and to address how and why they use particular terms when they feel it necessary. We will include some of the terms here that we use and why we use them:

1. Most authors use "person first" language such as "*a student with a dis/ability*" or "*a student of color*" to emphasize the individual over the disability. At the same time, authors sometimes use "*disabled people*" to emphasize disability as a valued identity as well as to show how people are actively (dis)enabled by society's commitment to physical and psychological barriers. In other words, in the latter usage, *disabled* is both a verb and an adjective.

2. We refrained from using the term "*color-blindness*," which equates not seeing with not knowing. In other words, the phrase likens lack of vision to ignorance. We regard both blind and sighted people as holders and generators of knowledge. The term *blindness* is also regarded as a passive characteristic or something static that one is born or "struck" with—this common sense notion of blindness is not only false, as environments impact sight, but it is a rhetorical move. The passivity it suggests disregards the active avoidance of racial issues that "*color-blindness*" implies when describing racial inequities. Alternatively, Frankenberg (1993) suggests and Stubblefield (2005) expands on the term *color-evasiveness*, which both refuses to position people who are blind as embodying deficit and recognizes the active evasion involved in people's refusing to discuss race in the face of racial inequities.

3. We deliberately use the term dis/ability instead of disability in our own work to call attention to ways in which the latter overwhelmingly signals a specific inability to perform culturally defined expected tasks (such as learning or walking) that come to define the individual as primarily and generally unable to navigate

society. We believe the slash in the word dis/ability disrupts misleading understandings of disability, as it simultaneously conveys the social construction of both ability and disability. We have maintained the use of disability when referring to its official or traditional use within classification structures and organizations.

Finally, we want to acknowledge all those who have worked to make this book possible.

Subini's acknowledgments: The original DisCrit article would not have been possible without the support of Darrell Jackson, who encouraged me to take the lead in writing it, especially when I doubted myself. Additionally, the support of Ruth Lopez, Elizabeth Mendoza, and Christina Paguyo was and continues to be instrumental. Thank you to my two coauthors, David and Beth, for being open to collaborating with me, and allowing me to grow DisCrit from an idea to reality. Finally, I would like to thank my advisor and mentor, Janette Klingner, who always encouraged me to create what was not there, assuring that such creations are needed to help fill the sometimes discomforting gaps evident in our field of education. Janette passed away in March 2014, but her memory lives on through her work and her loved ones.

Beth's acknowledgments: Collaborating with David and Subini on this project has been invigorating and sustaining. We each brought such different things to the table, and it is those differences that really moved this project along at crucial moments. I also want to thank our contributors who offered such compelling, carefully argued, and nuanced papers. Finally, I wish to thank my partner, Vivian, for all the big and little ways she makes my life better.

David's acknowledgments: Thanks to my collaborators on this project— Subini for starting the ball rolling with the very concept of DisCrit, and Beth for coming on board. In addition, I'd like to thank all the contributing authors, both seasoned and emerging scholars, who have helped begin the dialogues that we sought.

As a group, we wish to thank Teachers College Press personnel: Brian Ellerbeck, Executive Acquisitions Editor, for his patience and guidance in bringing this project into fruition; Noelle DeLaPaz for her support during the entire process; David Strauss, for his assistance in creating the cover; Karl Nyberg, for his help in production; and Tara Tomczyk for her careful editing of the entire text. We would also like to thank Alfredo J. Artiles and Elizabeth B. Kozleski for the opportunity to contribute to their much-needed book series. In addition, we would like to acknowledge David Gillborn, editor of the *Journal of Race, Ethnicity, and Education,* for his encouragement in transforming a conference presentation on intersectionality into a fully developed article that has become, in turn, the touchstone text of this edited volume. We also thank the contributors who have gone far beyond the call for chapters to create a book that expanded the conversation around race and dis/ability more than we could have hoped. In closing, we thank our many and intersecting intellectual communities who have welcomed this work, have pushed our thinking, and have added to our own understandings of the necessity of forging connections and nurturing dialogues. Finally, thank you—the reader—for coming to this book and being willing to build upon DisCrit, further developing it in the context of your own expertise.

Dis/ability Critical Race Studies (DisCrit)

Theorizing at the Intersections of Race and Dis/ability

Subini Ancy Annamma
David J. Connor
Beth A. Ferri

In this article, we combine aspects of Critical Race Theory (CRT) and Disability Studies (DS) to propose a new theoretical framework that incorporates a dual analysis of race and ability: Dis/ability Critical Race Studies, or DisCrit. We first examine some connections between the interdependent constructions of race and dis/ability in education and society in the United States and why we find it necessary to add another branch to Critical Race Theory and Disability Studies. Next, we outline the tenets of DisCrit, calling attention to its potential value as well as elucidate some tensions, cautions, and current limitations within DisCrit. Finally, we suggest ways in which DisCrit can be used in relation to moving beyond the contemporary impasse of researching race and dis/ability within education and other fields.

> For a century or more it had been the dream of those who do not believe Negroes are human that their wish should find some scientific basis. For years they depended on the weight of the human brain, trusting that the alleged underweight of less than a thousand Negro brains, measured without reference to age, stature, nutrition or cause of death, would convince the world that Black men simply could not be educated. Today scientists acknowledge that there is no warrant for such a conclusion. (W. E. B. Du Bois, 1920)

INTRODUCTION: RACIALIZING ABILITY, DISABLING RACE

Drawing on tools of scientific racism, including post-mortem studies of human brains, scientists have attempted to prove the inferiority and lower intelligence of African Americans in order to justify segregation and inequitable treatment within the United States and beyond. In his essay, *Racial Intelligence*, Du Bois (1920) highlighted some of these attempts to align ability with racial classification. These attempts included comparing skeletal and cranium sizes without regard to age or developmental conditions, and giving tests that required individuals to fill in details of pictures depicting things they had never seen before such as tennis courts or bowling alleys. Du Bois chronicled what is now widely recognized as a continued attempt throughout history to "prove" people of African descent possessed limited intelligence and were therefore not quite fully human. This notion had been reified throughout the nineteenth century in the fields of phrenology and racial anthropological physiognomy that claimed physical attributes were the basis of intellectual, social, and moral growth. Black and brown bodies were viewed as less developed than White bodies, more "primitive," and even considered sub-species of humans (Trent, 1998). This historical conceptualization of human differences was used to justify the slavery, segregation, unequal treatment, harassment, violence and even murder of Black and brown bodies (Menchaca, 1997; Valencia, 1997).

Unfortunately, the legacy of historical beliefs about race and ability, which were clearly based on White supremacy, have become intertwined in complex ways that carry into the present day. Segregated special classes have been populated with students from non-dominant racial and ethnic groups, from immigrant populations, and from "lower" social classes and status since their inception (Erevelles, 2000; Ferri & Connor, 2006; Franklin, 1987). A disproportionate number of non-dominant racial, ethnic, and linguistic continue to be referred, labeled, and placed in special education, particularly in the categories of Learning Disability, Intellectual Disability (formerly called Mental Retardation), and Emotional Disturbance or Behavior Disorders (Harry & Klingner, 2014; Losen & Orfield, 2002). These categories, often referred to as high incidence categories, are the most problematic in terms of diagnosis because they rely on the subjective judgment of school personnel rather than biological facts. Although it is perhaps easier to conceptualize dis/abilities that are "clinically determined" (i.e., based on professional judgment) as subjective, all dis/ability categories, whether physical, cognitive, or sensory, are also subjective. In other words, societal interpretations of and responses to specific differences from the normed body are what signify a dis/ability. Indeed, notions of dis/ability continually shift over time according to the social context. Thus, dis/ability categories are *not* "given" or "real" *on their own*. Rather, dis/abilities such as "autism, mental retardation, and competence are what any of us make of them" (Kliewer, Biklen, & Kasa-Hendrickson, 2006). Moreover, even dis/abilities that might seem self-evident are largely determined by relatively arbitrary distinctions between, for instance, what is considered poor eyesight and what constitutes blindness. Of course, while disability and ability are seen as either/or categories, how well someone can see or hear is largely influenced by the context—such as the existence of light and color and the degree of background noise and tone. Likewise, the definition (and even the terminology) of intellectual dis/ability has been revised continually, most notably when the AAMD (American Association of Mental Deficiency) revised the definition of mental retardation in 1973 from those with a measured IQ score of 85 to an IQ score of 70. In the stroke of a policy change, many people who had been labeled as mentally retarded were essentially "cured" of their condition. This monumental change was largely the result of special education coming under fire for the over-representation of students of color in programs for students with intellectual dis/abilities.

Despite this change in definition, however, African American students continue to be three times as likely to be labeled mentally retarded, two times as likely to be labeled emotionally disturbed, and one and a half times as likely to be labeled learning disabled, compared to their White peers (Parrish, 2002). African American students, in particular, are at risk of being over-represented (Fierros & Conroy, 2002), but Latino, American Indian, and Native Alaskan students are also disproportionately represented, particularly in states with large numbers of students from these groups (Losen & Orfield, 2002). Over-representation of students of color is much less likely in dis/ability categories that are sensory or physical in nature such as blindness, deafness, or physical impairments. This fact alone is evidence that race and perceived ability (or lack thereof) are still connected within educational structures and practices today albeit in much more subtle ways (Harry & Klingner, 2014).

As critical special educators whose work involves challenging commonly accepted notions of dis/ability, we are most interested in researching the ways that race and dis/ability intersect. However, to date we have found very few theories that sufficiently examine the ways these two markers of identity interact with each other. Several scholars have noted that many in Disability Studies (DS) leave race unexamined (Bell, 2006; Blanchett, 2006; Connor, 2008b). Some critical special educators employ DS on its own and mention race as a mitigating factor (Reid & Knight, 2006). Others have begun to find points between DS and Critical Race Theory (CRT) with a view to showing CRT how this intersection can offer more nuanced readings of the way race and ability are deployed in schools and in society (Erevelles, 2011b; Erevelles, Kanga, & Middleton 2006; Ferri, 2010; Leonardo & Broderick, 2011; Watts & Erevelles, 2004). These efforts have contributed greatly to our understandings about how race and ability interact in complex ways, yet some of these attempts still seem to leave one identity marker foregrounded, while the other is an additive and subsequently defaults into the background. In the field of CRT, for instance, it has been noted that the topics of dis/ability and special education are not sufficiently represented or simply omitted, despite many overlapping interests and concerns that hold the promise of potentially strong allegiances between researchers (Connor, 2008a). Similarly, there remains a vital task of fully accounting for race and critiquing the deployment of Whiteness within the field of DS (Bell, 2006; Blanchett, 2010; Leonardo & Broderick, 2011). Given the ways that race has figured so prominently in special education status, we would argue that it is nothing short of irresponsible to leave race out of dis/ability-related research in special education.

Recently, scholars have begun to examine the intersection of race and dis/ability in more complex ways. For example, Erevelles and Minear (2010) illustrate the value of intersectional approaches to race and dis/ability, while specifying three differing approaches used in current scholarship "on the constitutive features of multiply minoritizing identities" (p. 127). They outline these approaches as follows:

1. Anticategorical frameworks that insist on race, class, and gender as social constructs/fictions;
2. Intracategorical frameworks that critique merely additive approaches to differences as layered stigmas; and
3. Constitutive frameworks that describe the structural conditions within which social categories in the above models are constructed by (and intermeshed with) each other in specific historical contexts.

It is clear that intersectional work on race and dis/ability is complex by nature. Perhaps this is, arguably, what has drawn a small but growing constellation of scholars in CRT to engage with dis/ability. At a recent conference on CRT, for instance, several researchers addressed the intersectionality of race and dis/ability in diverse areas such as mainstream films (Agosto, 2012), teacher–student verbal interactions (Davila, 2012), and notions of normalcy (Watson, Oyler, Schlessinger, & Chako, 2012). The keynote presentation titled *Intersectionality and the Primacy of Racism: Race, Class, Gender and Disability in Education* (Gillborn, 2012) fully accounted for the intersections of race and dis/ability. While arguing that race can unapologetically be positioned at the front and center of intersectional work, Gillborn incorporated dis/ability as a marker of identity and social location, alongside the more widely accepted classifications of social class and gender. In other words, Gillborn recognizes that it is fine for a primary interest to drive a researcher, but imperative that other dimensions must be taken seriously within the work, rather than giving a cursory nod before moving on. Thus, by analyzing multiple dimensions within a specific context, researchers are able to see how they can mesh, blur, overlap, and interact in various ways to reveal knowledge, such as Gillborn's research on Black children identified as dis/abled in the UK revealing how perceptions of race can trump social class status. The product of deeply entrenched racism embedded within educational and societal structures, Gillborn's research shows how students who are positioned as Black and disabled experience myriad educational and social inequalities.

Given the small but growing interest in ways that race and dis/ability are co-constructed, we argue the time is right to propose Dis/ability Critical Race Studies (DisCrit). DisCrit explores ways in which both race and ability are socially constructed and interdependent. As scholars working within DisCrit, we seek to examine the processes in which students are simultaneously raced and dis/abled. Culling from the work of Solorzano and Bernal (2001) in which they illustrated how "Chicana and Chicano students live between and within layers of subordination base on race, class, gender, language, immigration status, accent, and phenotype" (as cited in Johnson, 1998) so that these students do not "fit" neatly into a single category" (p. 335), we believe that students of color who have been labeled with dis/abilities live in this same complex world where they do not fit neatly into any one category. However, for students of color, the label of dis/ability situates them in unique positions where they are considered "less than" White peers with or without dis/ability labels, as well as their non-disabled peers of color. In brief, their embodiment and positioning reveals ways in which racism and ableism inform and rely upon each other in interdependent ways.

In order to examine the connections between the construction of race and dis/ability, we have separated this article into three parts. In the first section we explicitly name our rationale; why we believe it is necessary to add another branch to CRT and why the location of being both a person of color *and* a person labeled with a dis/ability is qualitatively different for students of color than White students with a dis/ability (Crenshaw, 1993; Solorzano & Yosso, 2001). In the second section, we outline the tenets of DisCrit. Finally, in the third section, we elucidate some tensions and cautions within DisCrit.

RATIONALE FOR DISCRIT

Scholars outside Dis/ability studies might see an article about dis/ability and think, "This is a special education issue so I do not have to concern myself." However, we believe that issues of perceived dis/ability constitute issues of equity that involve all people. Like Du Bois before them, many critical scholars outside the field of special education have recognized that the social construction of dis/ability depends heavily on race and can result in marginalization, particularly for people of color and those from nondominant communities (Gutiérrez & Stone, 1997; McDermott, Goldman, & Varenne, 2006; Oakes, 1995; Rubin & Noguera, 2004). Given the racial gap in graduation, incidents of discipline, and incarceration rates, along with vast over-representation of students of color in special education and the lackluster achievement rates within many of these special education programs, we must critically examine why so many students labeled with a dis/ability, particularly students of color, are either experiencing failure or being perceived as failing and on what grounds.

We introduce DisCrit as an exploratory conversation wherein we ask, "How might DisCrit further expand our knowledge (or understanding) of race and dis/ability?" We seek to add important dimensions to CRT analysis by considering the ways race and dis/ability are co-constructed. Our goal is not to replace or replicate CRT, but to recognize what it both enables and constrains and then propose the necessity of considering ability within the framework. Indeed, we are indebted to CRT, LatCrit and FemCrit (as well as Feminist Legal Studies), along with Disabilities Studies theorists, for laying the groundwork and stimulating our thinking in this endeavor (Bell, 1987; Berry, 2010; Brantlinger, 1997; Crenshaw, Gotanda, Peller, & Thomas, 1995; Delgado Bernal, 2002; Delgado & Stefancic, 2001; Erevelles et al., 2006; Ladson-Billings & Tate, 1995; MacKinnon, 1998/2011; Reid & Valle, 2004; Solorzano & Bernal, 2001; Solorzano & Yosso, 2001). We draw on many of these works, not to co-opt them, but rather to illustrate points of connection between and among dis/ability and the various social locations theorized by these scholars with the intent to further develop theory that will be of service in understanding the lived realities of people. DisCrit is an attempt to recognize a confluence between fields that are profoundly connected but are, for various reasons, often unable or unwilling to engage in joint thinking and efforts to solve issues faced by people of color. The aim of DisCrit is to push DS and CRT to academically and practically bridge commonalities utilizing the tensions between the theories as places for growth instead of resistance and separation. Ultimately we want to extend CRT and DS in ways that are useful and thoughtful to better understand how concepts of race and ability are intertwined.

We believe, for instance, that racism and ableism are normalizing processes that are interconnected and collusive. In other words, racism and ableism often work in ways that are unspoken, yet racism validates and reinforces ableism, and ableism validates and reinforces racism. For students of color, race does not exist outside of ability and ability does not exist outside of race; each is being built upon the perception of the other (Crenshaw, 1993). However, because racism and ableism are "so enmeshed in the fabric of our social order, [they] appear both normal and natural to people in this culture" (Delgado & Stefancic, 2001, p. 21). Our goals, then, align with Delgado and Stefancic's (2001) desire to unmask and expose the normalizing processes of racism and ableism as they circulate in society.

A DisCrit theory in education is a framework that theorizes about the ways in which race, racism, dis/ability and ableism are built into the interactions, procedures, discourses, and institutions of education, which affect students of color with dis/abilities qualitatively differently than White students with dis/abilities (Crenshaw, 1993; Solorzano & Yosso, 2001). The qualitatively different experiences of students of color labeled with the same dis/ability in comparison to White peers in education settings is illustrative. For example, students of color tend to be educated in settings segregated from the general population more often than their White peers with the same dis/ability label who were more likely to receive support in the general education classroom and learn alongside their general education peers (Fierros & Conroy, 2002). In other words, dis/ability status justifies segregation and unequal treatment for students of color compared to their White counterparts. Additionally, African American students are "67% more likely than White students with emotional and behavioral problems to be removed from school on the grounds of dangerousness and 13 times more likely than White students with emotional and behavioral problems to be arrested in school" (Meiners, 2007, p. 38). Dis/ability status works somewhat differently within higher education. For example, although there has been an increase in students with Learning Dis/abilities (LD) entering college, the majority of students are White and from families whose annual income exceeded $100,000 (Reid & Knight, 2006), signaling that being White *and* possessing economic means allows a student with LD to gain access to higher education. The experiences of students of color with dis/abilities, such as where they are educated, with whom they are educated, and their access to college, tend to be qualitatively different than the experiences of their White peers with the same label (Blackorby & Wagner, 1996). The role of the liberal, White middle class in maintaining structures and practices of privilege within education has been documented by Brantlinger in her study of social class and race interlock (2003).

Using DisCrit, we seek to address the structural power of ableism and racism by recognizing the historical, social, political, and economic interests of limiting access to educational equity to students of color with dis/abilities on both macro and microlevels (Connor, 2008b). We recognize that ability and dis/ability are perceived and created based on ideologies of race and located within social and institutional structures as well as personal attitudes. As Collins (1990) notes:

> First, the notion of interlocking oppressions refers to the macrolevel connections linking systems of oppression such as race, class, and gender. This is the model describing the social structures that create social positions. Second, the notion of intersectionality describes microlevel processes—namely, how each individual and group occupies a social position within interlocking structures of oppression described by the metaphor of intersectionality. Together they shape oppression. (p. 492)

DisCrit seeks to understand ways that macrolevel issues of racism and ableism, among other structural discriminatory processes, are enacted in the day-to-day lives of students of color with dis/abilities.

Additionally, we find Crenshaw's (1993) work on intersectionality useful for theorizing the ways in which race and ability are likewise intertwined in terms of identity. Similar to Crenshaw's articulation of race and gender, students of color labeled with a dis/ability likewise "have no discourse responsive to their specific position in the social landscape; instead they are constantly forced to divide loyalties as social conflict is presented as a choice between grounds of identity" (Crenshaw et al., 1995, p. 354). Although Crenshaw does not speak directly to dis/ability, Watts and Erevelles (2004) contend that students of color labeled as disabled, like women of color or gay and lesbian people of color, must also choose where to stand in social conflicts with groups that do not fully share their identities. Moreover, in terms of dis/ability identity, dis/abled students are often positioned such that they are likely (and even encouraged) to reject identifying as disabled as something that is inherently negative or shameful (Connor, 2008b) rather than a potentially politicized identity or critical consciousness (Peterson, 2009; Shakespeare, 1996). The consequences of simply being labeled as disabled, even if one does not claim that identity, can result in rejection from cultural, racial, ethnic, and gender groups (Goodwin, 2003). Moreover, unlike race and ethnicity, individuals who are disabled, like individuals who are lesbian, gay, bisexual, or transgender (LGBT) typically do not share this social status with their immediate family members (Morris, 1991; Shakespeare, 1996). DisCrit draws on insights from Dis/ability Studies to provide a discourse responsive to the social positioning of students of color with a dis/ability, reframing dis/ability from its subordinate position to a positive marker of identity and something to be "claimed" (Caldwell, 2011; Linton, 1998a).

The ways in which over-representation of students of color in special education currently works reinforces the racial hierarchies the U.S. subscribes to, namely: (1) the under-representation of Asian Americans, which problematically allows them to be seen as a homogenized "model" minority (Lee, 2009); (2) the exclusion of Native Americans in almost all research and continues to emphasize their invisibility in education and larger societal discourse even though they are vastly over-represented in many categories of special education, particularly in states with large numbers of Native American students (Brayboy, 2006; Fierros & Conroy, 2002); (3) the over-representation of Latinos/Latinas in some regions of the country where their population is high and the ways those who speak a second language intersects with notion of ability. Additionally, emerging bilinguals are more likely to be over-represented in middle and high school and this timing may coincide when they are exited or graduated from segregated ESL or bilingual programs (Artiles, Rueda, Salazar, & Higardea, 2005); and (4) and the continual over-representation of African Americans across the United States, regardless of social class, positions them as the continual problem in American education (Erevelles et al., 2006). Each of these trends in over-representation must be examined in relation to race and ability. In this case, an additional consideration would include gender, given that most of these statistics represent males; at the same time, females of color are also disproportionately represented in disciplinary actions, special education, and the juvenile justice system compared to their White female peers (American Bar Association and National Bar Association 2001; Losen & Skiba, 2010; Mendez & Knoff, 2003; Oswald, Coutinho, & Best, 2002).

As we frame our discussion of DisCrit, we draw on research that relies on the statistical categories of ability and race because these categories result in socially constructed inequities, not because we believe they are necessarily biological realities. This is essential to state explicitly as we do not want to impose identity categories upon any one individual or group of people. Instead, we seek to highlight how the process of structural racism externally imposes identities on individuals by applying socially constructed labels. We also hope to illustrate how specific consequences are associated with labeling. We therefore acknowledge that while ability and racial categories are socially constructed, they continue to have real material outcomes in terms of lived experiences.

DisCrit problematizes the ways that binaries between normal/abnormal and abled/disabled play out in a range of contexts, from the physical layout of K–12 schools, where special education is often relegated to separate hallways or even buildings removed from the rest of the students, to universities where departments of Special Education are often detached from Curriculum and Instruction in schools of education (Young, 2011). Thus, in symbolic and material ways dis/ability occupies quarantined spaces (Foucault, 1977; Graham & Slee, 2007). Similar lines are drawn in such diverse contexts as film and media, to publications on dis/ability, to sports and recreation.

Where particular kinds of texts get published and circulated is another salient example of this line between able/disabled. For example, articles that focus upon the over-representation of students of color are often published in special education journals, whereas articles that are perceived as general education topics are published in journals that are specific to general education. Thus, rarely do these topics of race and dis/ability intersect. When those of us in special education attempt to write for a "general education" journal audience, editors respond that we must give explicit explanations for why our work should be read by those who do not work within the field of special education. This is a professionally enforced line between special compartmentalization of these two artificially separated domains, instead of seeing and sharing the same field of education. Furthermore, the separation of research reifies the differences between ability and disability, emphasizing divisions among educators and the students we serve.

We see this general–special dividing line being drawn in K–12 schools, teacher education programs, teacher certification, education research, and society at large. It is a line that is focused upon what children with dis/abilities cannot do, instead of emphasizing what their strengths are and what unique abilities they possess. It also reifies some students as "regular" or normative and others as so different that their instruction should be left to specialists. DisCrit questions how this line is drawn, how it has changed over time for a variety of types of dis/abilities, who has the control over this line, and what effects the line produces in education and in society. In other words, DisCrit recognizes the shifting boundary between normal and abnormal, between ability and disability, and seeks to question ways in which race contributes to one being positioned on either side of the line. Like Whiteness as a social construct or the phenomenon of differential racialization, which both expand and contract racial categories to include and exclude different people in order to limit and extend benefits of being labeled as such, ability and disability changes throughout history in similar ways and are deeply impacted by perceptions of race (Banks, 2002; Delgado & Stefancic, 2001; Leonardo, 2007). In order to understand this phenomenological "line," it will be necessary to examine ways in which differential minority groups have become racialized in various regions of the country throughout different periods of time—and how beliefs about dis/ability affect those occurrences.

Encountering the social construction of dis/ability, many people pose the question, "Are you arguing that there are no physical or mental differences in abilities?" In response, we would acknowledge that there are, of course, corporeal differences among humans though those differences are rarely, if ever, as fixed and obvious as generally assumed. However, we *are* most interested in human *responses* to those differences we currently call dis/abilities. We do not see the benefit of drawing what is inevitably an arbitrary (and unstable) line, where certain differences are not perceived as part of normal human variation, but rather become a "thing" so different that we must call them disabled. Moreover, the very notion of difference relies on something else being normative. We are all different from one another. In other words, a person who is perceived as having a dis/ability is no more or less different from someone who is considered nondisabled than that nondisabled person is different from him/her. Yet, the person with the dis/ability is perceived as the one who is inherently different. However, there can be no difference without a norm, upon which difference is measured. We agree, therefore, with Baglieri and Knopf (2004), who state, "The question is not whether we perceive differences among people, but, rather, *what meaning is brought to bear on those perceived differences*" (p. 525, emphasis added).

In the remaining portion of this article we put some of these ideas into specific tenets and then elaborate on each tenet. We do so not to be prescriptive, but rather to try to operationalize what kinds of specific questions and issues can be illuminated from a DisCrit approach.

TENETS OF DISCRIT

For DisCrit to be useful, we propose the following tenets:

1. DisCrit focuses on ways that the forces of racism and ableism circulate interdependently, often in neutralized and invisible ways, to uphold notions of normalcy.
2. DisCrit values multidimensional identities and troubles singular notions of identity such as race *or* dis/ability *or* class *or* gender *or* sexuality, and so on.
3. DisCrit emphasizes the social constructions of race and ability and yet recognizes the material and psychological impacts of being labeled as raced or dis/abled, which sets one outside of the western cultural norms.
4. DisCrit privileges voices of marginalized populations, traditionally not acknowledged within research.
5. DisCrit considers legal and historical aspects of dis/ability and race and how both have been used separately and together to deny the rights of some citizens.
6. DisCrit recognizes Whiteness and Ability as Property and that gains for people labeled with dis/abilities have largely been made as the result of interest convergence of White, middle-class citizens.
7. DisCrit requires activism and supports all forms of resistance.

Tenet One

DisCrit focuses on the ways race and dis/ability have been used in tandem to marginalize particular groups in society. In other words, DisCrit focuses on the interdependent ways that racism and ableism shape notions of normalcy. These mutually constitutive processes are enacted through normalizing practices such as labeling a student "at-risk" for simply being a person of color, thereby reinforcing the unmarked norms of Whiteness, and signaling to many that the student is not capable in body and mind (Collins, 2003; Ferri, 2010; Ladson-Billings & Tate, 1995). Neither institutional racism alone nor institutional ableism on its own can explain why students of color are more likely to be labeled with dis/abilities and segregated than their White peers with and without dis/abilities; instead, it is the two working together (Beratan, 2008). Like Watts and Erevelles (2004), we argue that "any discussion of racial and dis/ability oppression must necessarily, at the same time, engage with a critique of structures of "normativity" that are produced in an ableist and racist society" (p. 292). As Ladson-Billings (1998) notes, when traits such as Whiteness and ability are seen as normal, "everyone is ranked and categorized in relation to these points of opposition" (p. 9). Said differently, DisCrit recognizes that normative cultural standards such as Whiteness and ability lead to viewing differences among certain individuals as deficits.

Moreover, DisCrit seeks to reject the commonly held assumption that those who are perceived as deviating from standards of Whiteness or ability necessarily want to achieve those standards (Erevelles, 2000). Many individuals who identify as having learning or other differences that we might perceive as dis/abilities, for instance, talk about the strengths they have because of their unique perspective in the world. They insist that they would not give up their so-called dis/ability to "achieve normality" (Kunc, in Habib, 2008; Mooney, 2008). Yet, purposely "falling short" of cultural standards, in addition to being seen as irresponsible and unintelligible, can be sanctioned if viewed as a burden to society. In an extreme example of this, a school district in Michigan worked to legally compel a deaf mother to get cochlear implants for her two deaf sons arguing that it was best for the boys and society in terms of their future employability and economic opportunities (Shapiro, 2002).

Tenet Two

DisCrit emphasizes multidimensional identities (Solorzano & Bernal, 2001) rather than singular notions of identity, such as race, dis/ability, social class, or gender. Central, too, is a consideration of how certain identity markers, which have been viewed as differences from normative cultural standards, have allowed teachers, other school personnel, and society to perceive particular students as deficient, lacking, and inferior (Collins, 2003). Therefore, DisCrit foregrounds issues that have previously not been given prominence in CRT and recognize how these other markers of difference from the norm, in addition to race, contribute to constructing dis/ability (e.g., culture, sexuality, language, immigration status, gender, class). Additionally, DisCrit acknowledges how experiences with stigma and segregation often vary, based on other identity markers (i.e., gender, language, class) and how this negotiation of multiple stigmatized identities adds complexity.

Tenet Three

DisCrit rejects the understanding of both race and dis/ability as primarily biological facts and recognizes the social construction of both as society's response to "differences" from the norm (Mirza, 1998). Race and ability are socially constructed in tandem, the perception of race "informing" the potential abilities of a student and the abilities "informing" the perceived race. Simultaneously, DisCrit rejects what Crenshaw (1993) has called the vulgarization of social construction, where critics claim that if race is considered a social construction then it should be seen as insignificant and be ignored. In other words, while recognizing the social construction of particular identity markers, such as race and ability, DisCrit acknowledges that these categories hold profound significance in people's lives, both in the present and historically. The error, however, made by those who make a false distinction between race as a social construction and dis/ability as a biological fact, distinguishing dis/ability from aspects of identity that are seen as culturally determined "differences," continues to justify the segregation and marginalization of students who are considered dis/abled from their "normal" peers. As stated above, this phenomenon is particularly true for students of color with dis/ability labels who are more likely to be segregated than their White peers with the same dis/ability label (Fierros & Conroy, 2002). Segregation, particularly of Black and brown students labeled with a dis/ability, would be illegal if based upon race, but is allowed because dis/ability is seen as a "real" rather than a constructed difference (Beratan, 2008; Kim, Losen, & Hewitt, 2010). DisCrit renounces the uncritical assumption that segregation is a necessary or rational approach to dis/ability any more than it would be a necessary or rational approach to other identity markers. Moreover, simply "fixing" over-representation of students of color is insufficient if by doing so, we still leave segregation based on dis/ability intact—something that DisCrit finds unjustified and problematic.

Tenet Four

DisCrit empathizes with John Powell's words, "I feel like I've been spoken for and I feel like I've been spoken about, but rarely do I feel like I've been spoken to" (cited in Dalton, 1987). A similar mantra in dis/ability rights circles, "Nothing about us, without us" (Charlton, 2000, p. 3), also speaks to this tenet. DisCrit, therefore, seeks to disrupt the tradition of ignoring the voices of traditionally marginalized groups and instead privileges insider voices (Matsuda, 1987). DisCrit invites understanding of ways students respond to injustices (i.e., being constructed as deficient, or being segregated and stigmatized) through fostering or attending to counter narratives and explicitly reading these stories against the grain of master narratives. Attending to counter narratives encourage us to learn how students respond to injustice, not through passive acceptance, but through tactics such as strategic maneuvering. In one study, for instance, young women labeled with an invisible dis/ability would physically or verbally deflect or avoid being identified by peers as being in special education not simply to pass as "normal," but to counter easy assumptions about who they were as young women (Ferri & Connor, 2010). In another study of young woman with intellectual dis/abilities, Erevelles and Mutua (2005) illustrate how the claiming of subjectivity can even entail the acknowledgment that one *is* in fact a woman, because others, including family members, may fail to acknowledge the adult status of individuals with dis/abilities and see them instead as perpetual children.

We emphasize that DisCrit does not purport to "give voice," as we recognize that people of color and/or those with dis/abilities already have voice. Research that purports to give voices runs the risks of speaking for or in place of people of color with dis/abilities, which can reinforce paternalistic notions. Although the perspectives and insights of historically marginalized populations have been ignored in traditional research and education reform, we argue, instead, that it is imperative for readers to listen carefully and respectfully to counter narratives, and for researchers to use them as a form of academic activism to explicitly "talk back" to master narratives. Matsuda (1987) highlights the benefits of contrasting counter narratives with the master narrative, "When notions of right and wrong, justice and injustice, are examined . . . from the position of groups who have suffered through history, moral relativism recedes and identifiable normative priorities emerge" (p. 325).

Tenet Five

DisCrit considers legal, ideological, and historical aspects of dis/ability and race and how both have been used separately and together to deny the rights of certain citizens. The root cause of this denial of rights is the belief in the superiority of Whiteness, wherein a racial hierarchy was created with Whiteness at the apex, Blackness at the base and all other races falling in between (Bonilla-Silva, 2006). To be clear, this hierarchy had only two permanent fixtures, Whiteness and Blackness; differential racialization meant that other races could shift in their positions, but none could match the superiority of Whiteness (Delgado & Stefancic, 2001).

Salient is that pseudo-scientific knowledge emerged not as objective findings, which is what they were presented as, but as ways to reinforce the belief of Whiteness as superior (Valencia, 1997). Through the "science" of phrenology, craniology, and eugenics among others, it was "proven" that people of color had less capacity for intelligence than Whites and laws, policies, and programs were created that discouraged reproduction of particular types of people, particularly the poor and people of color, along with racial mixing (Menchaca, 1997). We must acknowledge differential racialization, however—in other words, that race is an ever-shifting category. For example, Whiteness was not always the property of poor Whites or certain immigrant groups (Roediger, 1991). Forced sterilization in parts of the United States was directed not just at people who we would now recognize as people of color, but also poor Whites and Eastern European immigrants who were thought to be feebleminded (Selden, 1999).

DisCrit, therefore, offers the possibility of a more complicated reading of the basis of White supremacy. Without racialized notions of ability, racial difference would simply be racial difference. Because racial difference has been explicitly linked with an intellectual hierarchy, however, racial differences take on additional weight. Historically, scientific knowledge in the form of phrenology coupled with anthropological physiognomy did not simply reinforce racial hierarchies; it created their possibility. Today, various notions of dis/ability (identified through what are assumed to be objective clinical assessments or responses to "evidence-based" interventions) reinforce similar race and ability hierarchies. Said another way, dis/ability and race first became equated and molded through pseudo-sciences, but later further cemented through seemingly "objective" clinical assessment practices. The dis/ability–race nexus was then reified through laws, policies, and programs until these concepts became uncritically conflated and viewed as the natural order of things (Baynton, 2001). DisCrit consequently challenges beliefs about the inferiority of the intelligence and culture of people of color, born within pseudo-sciences and later upheld by contemporary assessment practices.

Legal policies also worked to "racialize" dis/ability both historically and currently (Schweik, 2009). Black codes were used against freed slaves after Reconstruction that criminalized vagrancy or laziness in a way that implied African Americans refused to work due to mental illness or dis/ability instead of refusal to work due to unfair and dangerous labor practices (Alexander, 2010; Davis, 2003). These codes criminalized actions such as vagrancy, absence from work, and insulting gestures only when the person was Black. In 1974, the *Lau vs Nichols* case, along with the Lau remedies, established the need for bilingual education and attempted to end the practice of finding limited English proficient speaking children disabled through English-only instruction (Baca & Cervantes, 2004; Baker, 2001). Currently, the Individuals with Disabilities Education Improvement Act (IDEIA) has made racial disproportionality in special education one of the three priorities for monitoring and enforcement (Kim et al., 2010). Overall, we see how legal policies have racialized dis/ability and therefore made students of color with dis/abilities the beneficiaries of a double-edged sword wherein they receive specialized services due to the dis/ability label but endure segregation, stigmatization, and "debatable quality of educational outcomes" (Hart, Cramer, Harry, Klingner, & Sturges, 2009). Thus, DisCrit renounces imposed segregation and promotes an ethic of unqualified belonging and full inclusion in schools and society.

Finally, the focus on over-representation can deflect concerns about the lack of special education supports in under resourced schools that students of color are more likely to attend. Kim et al. (2010) note:

> For minority children, there is a tension between the misuse of special education identification, placement, and discipline as a means of school exclusion, and another equally troubling phenomenon, the failure to identify poor and minority students with disabilities who need high-quality special education and the related procedural protections. (p. 54)

Additionally, DisCrit is interested in ways that race and ability shape ideas about citizenship and belonging. Race and dis/ability figure into who is perceived as an ideal citizen, including who is allowed to represent or signify a nation, how nations pursue "building" a strong, healthy population that is ready for competition in work and war, and ways nations seek to reproduce and expand. We acknowledge that dis/ability plays out contra to these notions—triggering stereotypic associations with weaknesses, including fears of individuals seen as unhealthy, unable to adequately compete in work and war, with their reproductive potential questioned, feared or even forcibly managed (Terry & Urla, 1995). It is important to make these connections—not just historically, but also in the current context of immigration restrictions, punitive policies, and the changing demographics of schools (Caps, Fix, Murray, Ost, Passel, & Herwantoro, 2005). Furthermore, DisCrit acknowledges ways that marginalization in schools flows in multiple directions at once—illustrating how English Language Learners, for instance, are also marginalized and generally perceived from a deficit lens, which leads to their citizenship and belonging also being questioned (Olivos & Quintana de Vallidolid, 2005).

Tenet Six

DisCrit recognizes Whiteness and Ability as "property," conferring economic benefits to those who can claim Whiteness and/or normalcy (Harris, 1993) and disadvantages for those who cannot lay claim to these identity statuses. For years, populations fighting for civil rights, such as women and people of color, have been positioned as disabled, or unfit in some way that justified their exclusion from the rights of others who fit the norm (Kudlick, 2003). In addition to the denial of basic rights of life, liberty, and the pursuit of happiness, society also diverted economic resources to those within the dominant class, which kept marginalized groups economically fettered by not providing access to fully participate in all aspects of society. In turn, those being denied rights often claimed to be deserving of civil rights by claiming membership within the categorization of Whiteness or able-bodiedness, thereby denying membership in the categories of being "colored" or disabled (May & Ferri, 2005).

Some who advocate for a strong deaf culture argue they should be categorized as not disabled (Baynton, 2001; Lane, 2002), but as a linguistic minority. Early suffrage posters, advocating the right of women to vote, often relied on juxtaposing visual images of the educated and cultured White woman with images of men of color and men who were visually coded as insane or feebleminded (Ferri, 2011). We recognize that individuals who resist labels of color and/or dis/ability are making strategic attempts to partake in the benefits of being perceived within the normative cultural standards of able bodied and White. These benefits of passing for White and/or able bodied in some extreme cases could literally mean survival, while for others it might simply afford opportunities to benefit from the economic and social privileges enjoyed by dominant groups. However, these attempts ultimately reify binaries of able/disabled and White/Black and solidify property and other rights as only accessible to some (Harris, 1993).

Due to a societal subscription to Whiteness and ability as property, DisCrit holds that the political interests of oppressed groups have often been gained only through interest convergence. Interest convergence, a concept Derrick Bell (1980) put forth, holds that "the interests of Blacks in receiving racial equality will be accommodated only when it converges with the interests of Whites" (p. 22). Bell uses the example of the legal ruling of *Brown vs Board of Education*, which was passed at a time when it was in the best interests of Whites, who were working to defeat communism and needed to win the hearts and minds of those in the Third World and, for that matter, African Americans in the United States, to end segregation. Laws protecting people with dis/abilities, such as the Americans with Disabilities Act (ADA) of 1990, sought to extend many of the same protections to people with dis/abilities that were extended to people of color in the Civil Rights Act of 1965, such as access to public accommodations and protection from discrimination. Thus, resistance to even basic accessibility provisions and efforts to remove disabling barriers from society must be marketed as good for all (Asch, 2001; Guinier & Torres, 2002). The common example of curb cuts and wider sidewalks, which were useful for parents with baby strollers and people pulling wheeled suitcases, helped to justify the time and expense of making sidewalks accessible for people in wheelchairs.

Moreover, as schools face budget crises, fewer students may get dis/ability labels or be placed in segregated special education classes, not because teaching is becoming more responsive to their needs or because segregation is wrong, but because these may be seen as saving money. However, DisCrit does more than identify when just the interests of dominant groups align with those who are of color *or* those who are labeled disabled; DisCrit also makes visible the ways in which the same labels provide different opportunities to students of different races. For instance, labeling a White student with a learning disability may lead to more support in the general education classroom and extra time on high-stakes tests, which can ensure access to college, whereas for a student of color, the same disability label can result in increased segregation, less access to the general education curriculum, and therefore, limited access to post-secondary education.

Tenet Seven

DisCrit supports activism and promotes diverse forms of resistance. Many Critical Race Theorists call for activism that links academic work to the community. This avoids sterile ideas being handed down from the ivory tower without practical application as well as "studying the natives" wherein people who know nothing about the community suggest ways to fix it based on deficit perspectives (Dixson & Rousseau, 2005; Stovall, 2006). DisCrit acknowledges the need for activism and the reasons behind it, but recognizes that some of the activities traditionally thought of as activism (e.g., marches, sit-ins, and some forms of civil disobedience) may be based on ableist norms, which may not be accessible for those with corporeal differences. Those with admirable equity-based goals can inadvertently maintain and perpetuate inequity for other groups. In other words, to suggest that activism cannot occur from behind a desk may be missing a larger point about what it means to resist forms of domination. If theory can be violent, that is, if theory can erase large portions of the population by ignoring their needs and realities, we also believe that theory can be emancipatory, offering oppressed groups a language of critique and resistance (Leonardo, 2004). DisCrit supports diverse expressions of resistance that are linked to and informed by the community, whether that be academic or theoretical, pedagogical, or activist.

To summarize, each of the tenets we put forth shares the desire to reject forces, practices, and institutions that attempt to construct dis/ability based on differences from normative cultural standards. We reject attempts at the containment of people of color with dis/abilities due to their perceived divergence from normative cultural standards. Instead, we encourage society to become more encompassing of diversity and perceived difference, at the same time we question the very norms that create difference. Becoming more encompassing includes removing the policing and enforcement of normality, dissolving barriers that actively dis/able people, and focusing instead on learning from those that have historically been uniquely positioned as having what Baker (2002) terms "outlaw ontologies" (p. 663). As Matsuda (1987) plainly states, "Those who have experienced discrimination speak with a special voice to which we should listen" (p. 63).

TENSIONS AND CAUTIONS

There are several tensions between DS and CRT that may have previously kept some theorists from forging a coalition or engaging in dialogue. We see these tensions as productive sites for furthering knowledge, with the potential to transform current inequities in our education system. People of color have been historically positioned as dis/abled and inferior in order to justify limited rights. During slavery some would try to restrict African Americans' bid for citizenship rights by stating that they were feeble-minded and lacked intelligence—in other words, too flawed to participate in self-governance. A common response from African Americans (and other people of color) was to argue that they were not dis/abled and, therefore, deserving of their rights (Baynton, 2001). Although we recognize that dis/ability has long been associated with deviance and lack of intelligence and that this might explain why people of color would fiercely fight against labeling themselves as dis/abled, we also believe this ideology is grounded in hegemonic notions of normalcy. Unfortunately, subscribing to the binary of abled/disabled pits marginalized communities against each other and ignores the fact that rights should not be taken away from anyone, dis/abled or not.

We believe that dis/ability must be primarily understood as a political and social category. As Erevelles and Minear (2010) note:

> Unfortunately, rather than nurturing an alliance between race and disability, CRT scholars (like other radical scholars) have mistakenly conceived of disability as a biological category, as an immutable and pathological abnormality rooted in the "medical language of symptoms and diagnostic categories." (p. 132)

Other marginalized groups have, to date, largely failed to recognize dis/ability as a socially constructed identity. Instead, relying on hegemonic notions of normality, they view dis/ability as purely biological fact that is apolitical, asocial, and ahistorical. In other words, when deaf activists insist that they are not disabled—they are more than likely subscribing to a medical model definition of dis/ability rather than a social model one. Similarly, people of color who argue that the problem of over-representation is the *inaccurate labeling* of kids of color as dis/abled still see special education labeling as appropriate, even necessary, for those children with "real" dis/abilities. To complicate matters further, Gillborn's (2012) study mentioned earlier reveals how racism can also impede the opportunities for people of color in accessing reasonable accommodations for impairments. In sum, in addition to giving labels, racism can withhold them.

Some DS scholars ignore or minimize racial dimensions that affect the social construction of dis/ability or include only a cursory mentioning of race. A lack of or limited discussion of race focuses on only one dimension of a person, dis/ability, and ignores multidimensional identities. Other DS theorists take up gender, yet many leave it out (Jean & Samuels, 2002; Wendell, 1993). Those who focus on this singular dimension of a person often claim that dis/ability creates a universal experience, that it is an essential or primary identity marker. However, we would ask, "What is universal about dis/ability experience—is there really one dis/ability experience or isn't it mediated by the particular social, historical, and political context?" (Ferri, 2010, p. 141). There are a variety of dis/ability labels and each can be experienced differently depending on cultural contexts, social class, race, and gender. Resisting essentialism, we recognize that having a dis/ability is not universal and, in fact, is qualitatively different for individuals with the *same* dis/ability depending on cultural contexts, race, social class, sexuality, and so on. Likewise, *dissimilar* dis/abilities are experienced in various ways as they intersect with these and other markers of identity.

We also recognize that intersectionality, or "the need to account for multiple grounds of identity when considering how the social world is constructed" (Crenshaw, 1993, p. 1245), can be, and often is, co-opted or misused (Delgado, 2012). As Jones (2010) notes:

> The ubiquitous use (or misuse) of the respective frameworks can sometimes leave the impression that a scholar's most important objective is to "test" the respective theoretical approaches—spotting gender or difference here, there, and everywhere—not, instead, to use these frameworks to illuminate the complicated and sometimes contradictory ways in which situated interaction is linked to structural circumstances. (p. 91)

We want to consider how race and dis/ability are built together in order to recognize that boundaries of only racism or ableism leave out a wealth of experiences without forgetting that other social locations affect how the social world is constructed.

Along with productive tensions, there are also explicit cautions that should be noted. DisCrit recognizes that we cannot conflate race and dis/ability; they are not interchangeable (Ferri & Connor, 2006). This is not to say that those of color who are labeled dis/abled should be ashamed of their race or their dis/ability label. Instead, it recognizes that to be of color does not make one dis/abled and to be labeled dis/abled does not make one of color. Moreover, we must resist the urge to assume that all types of oppression result in the same or equivalent experience (Spelman, 1990). We must not assume that because an individual has experienced oppression of one type (e.g., ableism) that that person knows what it is like to have experienced oppression of other types (e.g., racism). A recent example of this occurred during the Occupy Wall Street protests when a Slutwalk sign, held by White feminists, quoted John Lennon by saying, "Woman is nigger of the world." The sign implied that positions of subordination are exactly the same, when, in actuality, they are quite different (Simmons, 2011). To be a woman is not equal to being Black, to be a Black woman is not equal to being a White woman, and to be a Black woman with a dis/ability is different than being a White woman with a dis/ability. Moreover, there is a diversity of experience within any of those categories based on social class, culture, nation, and so on. Additionally, this is an example of how traditional activism (e.g., protesting and marching) with an equity aim can have unintended consequences as it does not guarantee equity. Instead, DisCrit attempts to address ways in which race and dis/ability, as socially constructed and maintained systems of oppression, have been used in tandem to justify limiting access.

Additionally, DisCrit acknowledges that if we are not careful, dis/ability can be assumed to refer to every type and degree of dis/ability. As mentioned earlier, we are wary of any attempts to suggest universal experiences, or essentializing one identity marker of a person. DisCrit rejects any attempt to offer an account of the life and experience of all people with dis/abilities without their voices. Instead, it encourages understanding about ways in which society limits access and embodiment of difference. While Berry observes, "Commonality of race does not produce commonality of self-identity" (Berry, 2010, p. 24), we believe this to also be true of dis/ability. Therefore we respect any movement in which people take up the label that has been a point of oppression and rework into a point of pride. Crip culture reclaims the dis/ability label similar to gay communities reclaiming queer (Warner, 1999), and the Black pride movement of 1960s and 1970s (VanDeBurg, 1992). We believe that oppressed individuals and groups have the rights to name themselves, in contrast to privileged individuals and groups creating norms that perpetuate their privilege and labeling others in contrast to that norm. This work is not neat, tidy, or simple. As the late poet Laura Hershey (1991) stated, "You get proud by practicing."

CONCLUSION

In this article, we have articulated the need for simultaneously keeping race *and* dis/ability at front and center in our research. We have put forth DisCrit as valuable both as a theoretical framework and as a methodological tool to help investigate intersectional positionings to reveal what has been, to date, missed, dismissed, hidden, or purposefully unacknowledged within educational research. We believe that this shared branch of CRT and DS holds great potential for inter-animating, expanding, and deepening what is understood about the interconnectedness of race and dis/ability. Its scope can encompass critiques of structures and systems, historical movements, contemporary practices, and how they relate to current education reforms. Connecting macro levels of analysis to on the ground explorations of how systems of race and dis/ability are experienced at micro level, DisCrit foregrounds communities that are impacted by their position at these (and other) interstices that influence the degree of access to all aspects of life, including education, housing, health, transportation, public services (libraries, parks, stores), wealth, culture, supportive and community services. DisCrit, however, does not seek to simplify our understanding of oppression; rather, it seeks to complicate notions of race and ability by recognizing ways they are intertwined.

It is imperative that in an age of mass standardization within education as a result of *No Child Left Behind*, institutionalized sorting mechanisms such as *Response to Intervention*, privatization of public educational services, the imposition of the Common Core Standards, and the accountability of teachers tied to student test scores, that we do not lose sight of the most vulnerable population of dis/abled students of color. These students have historically be been among the first to fall through the cracks, as they do not and cannot fit rigid norms imposed upon them, and are now even considered a "liability" for teachers (Ball & Harry, 2010; Danforth, Taff, & Ferguson, 2006; Dudley-Marling & Gurn, 2010; Ferri & Connor, 2006; Slee, 2011; Smith, 2009).

We believe that DisCrit can be used to help push past the impasse experienced in researching the perpetual over-representation of children of color within dis/ability categories that trigger more restrictive environments. It is obvious that responses to address over-representation are inadequate, serving too often as lip-service to one of the United States's most longstanding problems. Many institutional attempts at rectifying over-representation are pro forma and are not taken seriously. For example, Voulgarides (2012) describes how in one suburban district, disproportionality was simply referred to its official designation within State Education Quality Assurance reports as "indicator nine," instead of examining the practices that led school officials to be cited for noncompliance yet simultaneously state, "We don't have a problem here." In another example, Artiles (2011) studied the U.S. Department of Education's relative risk ratio thresholds for disproportionality, noting the ineffectiveness of states determining and self-monitoring their own ratios, some with ratios of 5:1 (p. 439).

In a fitting nod to CRT, Artiles, Kozleski, et al. (2010) cull from the work of Tate, Ladson-Billings, and Grant's (1996) analysis of *Brown vs Board of Education's* implementation, to conclude that researchers cannot "Mathematize social problems with deep structural roots because such calculations are not likely to unearth historical precursors and ideologically laden processes that constitute them" (p. 296). Artiles, Kozleski, et al. (2010) also connect disproportionality to resistance within educational research to acknowledge cultural influences. They write, "The reluctance to frame disproportionality as a problem stresses technical arguments that ignore the role of historical, contextual, and structural forces" (p. 282). Furthermore, they note, "Similarly, this position has ignored the notion of culture and its impact on professional practices" (p. 282).

In her work on how systems construct ability and create disproportionality, Kozleski (2011) urges the research community to go beyond its self-imposed boundaries and embrace what have been "found to be powerful allies: activity theory, systems thinking, and complexity theory" (p. 5). It is clear that by researching the situatedness of people in different environments and how they function within those contexts, *cultural* practices can be contrasted with *institutional* practices. As Arzubiaga, Artiles, King, and

Harris-Murri (2008) point out, it is incumbent on researchers to understand "not people's cultures, but how people live culturally . . . [and therefore become able to] reimagine communities, particularly those historically marginalized and construed as culturally deprived, devoid of resources, and/or culturally stagnant" (p. 314).

In their analysis of classroom-based research, Artiles, Kozleski, et al. (2010) noted the deliberate sidestepping of cultural locations, including those of the researcher, the researched, and the context in which the research occurs. Their work reveals the inadequacy of traditional models of inquiry in furthering knowledge of cultural differences among children and the professionals who research them. Arzubiaga et al. (2008) note that

> Systematic analysis of empirical studies published over substantial periods of time in peer refereed journals in psychology, special education, and school psychology show that researchers have neglected to ask questions, or to document and/or analyze data that would shed light on the role of culture in human development and provide alternative explanations for student achievement and behavior other than student deficits, which are often assumed with minority group status. (p. 311)

The critique of traditional research methods (particularly within special education), the ineffective responses to reducing disproportionality, and the movement by some scholars toward more culturally focused understandings of how difference is constituted are all movements compatible with DisCrit. At the same time, influenced by the collaborative work of White Studies theorist Zeus Leonardo and DS scholar Alicia Broderick (Leonardo & Broderick, 2011), DisCrit problematizes the very notion of over-representation. After all, what would be the correct "representation" of children of color in dis/ability categories? According to whom? Based on what rationale? In many ways, the exploration of these questions can be seen as the tip of the iceberg in terms of how DisCrit has the potential to deepen our understanding about complicated issues.

This article is a beginning. We acknowledge that DisCrit is a theoretical framework that is very much a work-in-progress. We have endeavored to make the case for expanding the fields of CRT and DS by engaging with each other through an intersectional approach to understanding ways in which society configures notions of ability and disability both in and out of schools. DisCrit contends that a non-intersectional approach to research, one that attempts to side-step particularized contexts and the dynamic forces of culture manifest within them, provide limited—even misleading— conclusions that do not necessarily serve the people being studied, despite claims to the contrary. Much of the limited work within the field of special education is a major case in point (Brantlinger, 2006).

In closing, by contributing to broadening ideas about how research is conceptualized and carried out, DisCrit holds great potential for looking at old, seemingly intractable problems through a new lens. Ultimately, its purpose is to contribute by pushing past current theoretical and conceptual limitations within several fields, including CRT, DS, special education, and multiculturalism, among others. In going forward, we invite other researchers to engage in conversations around the promise of DisCrit and partake in related difficult discussions linking race and dis/ability to education, laws, civil rights, human rights, in the quest for a more socially just society.

Part I

RACE, CLASS, AND ABILITY

CHAPTER 1

The Black Middle Classes, Education, Racism, and Dis/ability

An Intersectional Analysis

David Gillborn
Nicola Rollock,
Carol Vincent
Stephen J. Ball

Who Draws the Line?

We see this general–special dividing line being drawn in K–12 schools, teacher education programs, teacher certification, education research, and society at large. It is a line that is focused upon what children with dis/abilities cannot do, instead of emphasizing what their strengths are and what unique abilities they possess. . . . DisCrit questions how this line is drawn, how it has changed over time for a variety of types of dis/abilities, who has the control over this line, and what effects the line produces in education and in society? (Annamma, Connor, & Ferri, 2013, p. 10)

Below the Line

Quite a lot of Black people were what they called, in [my secondary school], "below the line." And "below the line" was a term [used] not by the kids, but by the teachers. The teachers called it "Man and Mongo." Like Mongolians. Mongo. . . . [Out of five hierarchically ranked teaching groups] four was the cutoff point at which they'd allow you to take maths, English, and a science if you wanted to go to an exam. "Below the line" you weren't taking any exams. You could go to school; you could cut out of the catalogs; they'd do a lot of sticking and gluing. They might get the sex talk . . . it was like "Man in the Environment." It was to teach them how to live, basically. That's all they were doing. Those people, they weren't gonna take any exams. . . . A lot of the Black kids were doing "Man and Mongo." (Patricia, resources manager)

Patricia is a 45-year-old divorced mother of three, who grew up in the north of England. She is one of 62 middle-class Black parents we interviewed as part of a study exploring race/class intersections in contemporary education (Rollock, Gillborn, Vincent, & Ball, 2015). In this chapter, we draw on our findings to address some of the key questions raised by Annamma, Connor, and Ferri (2013) in their groundbreaking exposition of the essential shape and problematics at the heart of Dis/ability Critical Race Studies (DisCrit). We begin by outlining the research project as the empirical foundation for the chapter and situate it within the wider field of critical intersectional research. Subsequent sections explore interviewees' experiences as they navigated the educational system and, in particular, the processes that surround the assessment of dis/ability and schools' reaction to those assessments. We conclude by considering the relationships between the findings and some of the core tenets of DisCrit.

RESEARCHING DIS/ABILITY-RACE-CLASS-GENDER INTERSECTIONS

We should note from the outset that our research with Black middle-class parents did not set out to focus equally on every possible dimension of identity and inequality—indeed, we doubt that any project and team of researchers could possibly do justice to *every possible* intersectional dynamic. Intersectionality is a widely used (sometimes misused) concept in contemporary social science. The term addresses the question of how multiple forms of inequality and identity interrelate in different contexts and over time and originated in the work of U.S. critical race theorist Kimberlé Crenshaw (1995). It has also been deployed widely across the social sciences to the point where it is viewed as a "buzzword," whose frequent iteration sometimes disguises an absence of clarity and specificity (Davis, 2008). Richard Delgado (2012), one of the founders of CRT, has warned that intersectionality can be taken to such extreme positions that the constant subdivision of experience into more and more identity categories can eventually shatter any sense of robust analyses because identity categories are, potentially, infinitely divisible. Despite the frequency with which it is used, therefore, the term intersectionality does not have a clear single meaning and does not necessarily denote a critical and progressive perspective. Indeed, different scholars approach intersectionality from different places, often privileging one set of identities and issues in their analysis (Bhopal & Preston, 2012). Our project began with an explicit focus on how *race* and *class* intersect in the lives of Black middle-class parents. This focus arose from our desire to speak to the silences and assumptions that have frequently shaped education research, policy, and practice in the United Kingdom, where middle-class families are generally assumed to be White, and minoritized families—especially those who identify their family heritage in Africa and/or the Caribbean—are assumed to be uniformly working-class (Rollock, Vincent, Gillborn, & Ball, 2013). By interviewing Black parents employed in higher professional and managerial roles, we hoped to gain a more nuanced and critical understanding of race/class intersections.

We limited our sample to parents who identified as being of Black Caribbean ethnic heritage. We chose to focus on the Black Caribbean group because, like African Americans in the United States, they are one of the longest established racially minoritized groups in the United Kingdom, with a prominent history of campaigning for social justice, and yet they continue to face marked educational inequalities; for example, Black Caribbean students are less likely to achieve national benchmark levels of success than White counterparts of the same gender and social class background, but around three times more likely to be permanently expelled (Gillborn, 2008; John, 2006; Sivanandan, 1990; Warmington, 2014). At the time of our interviews (2009–2010), all the parents had children between the ages of 8 and 18, a range that spans key decisionmaking points in the English education system. As is common in research with parents, most interviewees were mothers. Because we also wanted to redress common deficit assumptions about Black men (McKenley, 2005; Reynolds, 2009), we ensured that a portion of the sample was made up of fathers. All the parents were in professional/managerial jobs and most lived in Greater London (although we also included parents from elsewhere across England). Parents volunteered to take part, responding to advertisements placed in professional publications and on the web. Once our initial round of 62 interviews had been completed, we identified 15 parents for a second interview to explore in further detail some of the key issues emerging from our analyses, for a total of 77 interviews.

Our interviews explored parents' experiences of the education system (both as students themselves and as parents), their aspirations for their children, and how their experiences were shaped by race/racism and social class. Because we are a team of three White researchers and one Black researcher, we asked all of our respondents to indicate in advance whether they preferred a Black interviewer, a White interviewer, or had no preference. Their preferences were met accordingly. Following the interviews, around half of the participants (55%) felt that interviewer ethnicity had made a difference and almost all of these felt that rapport with a Black researcher had been an advantage.

In addition to race/class intersections, a key theme that emerged in the study was gender—in particular, the greater surveillance and control that parents reported being experienced by their sons (see Gillborn, Rollock, Vincent, & Ball, 2012; Rollock et al., 2015). We anticipated that gender would play a key role because, in common with the United States, historic patterns of racist exclusion and injustice in the United Kingdom are highly gendered (McKenley, 2005; Mirza, 1998; Warmington, 2014). However, we were initially less certain that dis/ability would play a major role in the research. We were, of course, aware of the historic and continuing overrepresentation of Black children in particular categories considered special educational needs (SEN) on both sides of the Atlantic (Artiles & Trent, 1994; Artiles, Trent, & Palmer, 2004; Beratan, 2008; Tomlinson, 1981). In the United States, Harry and Klingner (2014) have noted that African American students face much higher "risk rates" in categories "that depend on clinical judgment rather than on verifiable biological data" (p. 2). Similarly, in the United Kingdom, Black students are twice as likely to be defined as displaying behavioral, emotional, and social difficulties (BESD) (Lindsay, Pather, & Strand, 2006, Table 5a)—a category that depends upon the subjective judgment of (mostly White) professionals and results in students being placed in segregated settings. In fact, research on labeling and segregating Black children in behavioral units (colloquially known as sin-bins) and in schools for the "educationally subnormal" (as they used to be called) provided the foundation for UK scholarship on racism in education (Coard, 1971/2005; Tomlinson, 1981). Nevertheless, although two members of the research team have declared dis/abilities, we did not anticipate that dis/ability would feature as a key issue in the study. We were wrong: Fifteen of our interviewees (around a quarter of the total) mentioned dis/ability or disability-related issues during their interviews, and some important and disturbing patterns became clear. For instance, Linda described trying to help her 12-year-old son understand why he'd been placed in an SEN group with no formal assessment and no consultation:

> This was the first time I had to have this conversation with [him] about being a Black child in Britain. And I said to him, "This is your first lesson on what it means to be a Black boy in Britain." And I said, "You've got a number of choices; you *either* accept what they're telling you about yourself, that you're not very good and you can't do stuff—even though you know that you can be, you know, and you shouldn't be in that class. You've got a choice; you either feel bad about it, accept what they say, and just feel like crap. Or, you remember who you are and what you're able to do and you work hard and prove them wrong, or you just get angry, act out, and fulfill another stereotype of Black boys. That's the choice you've got and this is . . . you're going to get more of it later on in life, so you might as well learn *now*, that you've got to fight that, you know." (Linda, an academic in higher education)

It is revealing that Linda's understanding of her son's experiences makes explicit reference to the gendered nature of racism where "judgmental" SEN labeling is applied with disproportionate frequency to Black Caribbean boys and young men:

> Boys were 2.5 times more likely to be identified than girls. . . . Black Caribbean, mixed White and Black Caribbean, and Black other students in the English sample were overrepresented by about 2:1 relative to White British students for BESD, comparable with U.S. findings for Black American students and emotional disturbance. . . . (Strand & Lindsay, 2009, pp. 180–184)

As our data illustrate, however, it would be a mistake to imagine that these processes only impact Black boys and young men. Although the overrepresentation of Black girls and young women is less pronounced, there is no doubt that, to some extent, similar processes of labeling and exclusion operate across gender boundaries. Nevertheless, it is clear that the particular constellation of negative stereotypes that attach to Black masculinity in White supremacist societies (such as the United Kingdom and United States) lead to a situation of extreme danger in relation to the hyper-surveillance, labeling, and control of Black male bodies, a situation recognized by the parents in our project:

> I think as a Black *guy* and not a *small* Black guy, you know, the instant perception is of, in the street, is of someone who might be dangerous, might be a little bit violent, might be a little bit angry. I am not the first person people come up and ask the time. (Richard, director, voluntary sector)

The particular strength of qualitative research arises from the detail and complexity that the data reveal about the *processes* that construct and police dis/ability in a classed and racialized context. In the following sections we explore, first, how certain students came to be assessed in relation to particular categories of dis/ability, and second, how schools and teachers reacted when these lines were drawn by someone other than themselves. Our findings highlight the contested nature of dis/ability in education where Black students find themselves denied access to categories that might provide for additional resources and instead labeled with behavioral/emotional diagnoses—a category that cements a deficit reading of the child and protects the White racist status quo.

Our focus in this chapter, however, is not on questions of over- and underrepresentation, as if there were some objective *real* notion of dis/ability into which Black students should gain rightful admittance or avoid wrongful categorization. Rather, we are interested in how and in whose interests understandings of dis/ability are made, asserted, and contested in schools. In particular, we seek to understand the experiences of Black middle-class parents and their children as they encounter labels being used against them or alternatively how they attempt to use labels to access additional resources. In so doing, we seek to build upon and extend DisCrit by further exploring the co-constitutive nature of racism and ableism:

Racism and ableism are normalizing processes that are interconnected and collusive. In other words, racism and ableism often work in ways that are unspoken, yet racism validates and reinforces ableism, and ableism validates and reinforces racism. (Annamma et al., 2013, p. 6)

ASSESSING "SPECIAL NEEDS": BY WHOM? FOR WHOM?

I didn't necessarily want her to be labeled as special educational needs. I just wanted her to get the support that she required to get through secondary education. (Maud, university administrator)

The troubled history of "race" and SEN is well-known within the Black community, and middle-class Black parents are only too aware of the potential dangers of being negatively labeled in school (Gillborn et al., 2012). The decision to pursue a formal SEN assessment, therefore, is not one that parents take lightly. Indeed, sometimes parents view the label as too great a risk. In Maud's case, above, she studiously avoided her daughter being formally labeled, preferring to work closely with teachers, including the school's head teacher (principal), to build knowledge of her daughter's condition and encourage greater understanding:

> I was very much involved with anything (whether it was things going smoothly or things weren't going so well) and I was *always* involved. . . . My approach wasn't so defensive with the school. I became more engaging. So, rather than saying "You shouldn't be doing it this way," I said, "Let's work together and see how we can make [my daughter's] education more productive." (Maud, university administrator)

Many of the parents in the study consciously adopted strategies aimed at smoothing their children's path through school (Vincent, Rollock, et al., 2012), but few enjoyed the level of success that Maud describes. For parents who believe their children need additional support, a more formal assessment of their needs is often seen as a vital step in the process. In England, the official government advice for parents of children with dis/abilities (Department of Children, Schools and Families [DCSF], 2010) imagines a mutually supportive process that typically involves the following:

1. The parents and/or school identify that the child is having problems.
2. An assessment is arranged through the school or the local authority (state).
3. The nature of the child's needs is identified and adjustments are recommended.

4. The school acts on the recommendations, and the student is better able to fulfill his or her potential.

The official guide includes advice on appeals procedures but tends to envisage a constructive and trusting relationship between parents and teachers:

> If you think your child may have a special educational need that has not been identified by the school or early education setting, you should talk to your child's class teacher, to the SENCO (this is the person in the school or preschool who has a particular responsibility for coordinating help for children with special educational needs) or to the head teacher straightaway. . . . Working together with your child's teachers will often help to sort out worries and problems. The closer you work with your child's teachers, the more successful any help for your child can be. (DCSF, 2010, p. 9)

In our data, there was only one other instance that comes close to this model of mutually supportive and proactive parent/school interaction. Matthew was extremely positive about the help and support that his son's primary (elementary) school supplied, confirming his own worries about his child's development and helping to identify professional support:

> It was the school that picked up on it actually; they realized that he wasn't developing very fast. . . . The school brought in a speech development person to look at [him] and then they noticed that he was way behind age-wise and so we went along, they said maybe he's got ADHD [attention deficit hyperactivity disorder] so we started that process of going to psychologists all instigated by the school. . . . (Matthew, company director)

As is characteristic of many middle-class parents, Matthew and his partner soon mobilized their considerable social class capital (personal networks and research skills) to find out as much as possible about the issues and determine the best ways of proceeding. They pushed for a formal and officially recognized "statement of special educational needs" as a means of securing a binding commitment to the resources and support that their son should receive from school:

> The moment that was mentioned, ADHD, we . . . went [out] and got educated. We read everything, we bought the books, we spoke to certain people who were experienced, and we started to understand what was going on. And then at that point, we knew we had to fight for statementing [eligibility], again with the help of the school. And I felt the school gave us that help. (Matthew, company director)

Matthew's experience with his son's school stands out in our data as the *only* case where a positive experience came anywhere close to the kind of process envisaged in the official SEN guidance. Contrary to the official expectation of school–parent *partnerships*, our interviewees mostly reported negative experiences as they dealt with schools whose reactions ranged from disinterest to outright disbelief and hostility.

The reaction of teachers (including senior leaders) emerged in our data as a considerable barrier to parents' attempts to access supports. In almost every case, it was the parent (rather than the school) who took the initiative to explore whether the child had an impairment that could be positively addressed. This typically involved parents deploying a range of class-related resources, for example, utilizing their *economic capital* (to finance expensive specialist assessments) and also their *cultural and social capital* (using friendships and professional networks to help them negotiate a complex system). For instance, because of her own professional education, Paulette, a psychologist, viewed a sharp discrepancy in a child's performance on different types of tasks as a possible sign of a learning disability (Developmental Adult Neuro-Diversity Association, 2011). Yet, when she brought this to the school's attention, she was informed that her daughter's *true* level of attainment was the *lower* level and her concerns were unwelcome:

> A discrepancy was emerging, in that she would get a B for a piece of work that she had spent time doing [at home] and then she would get a D or an E even [for timed work in class]. So I then contacted the school and said, "Look, there's a problem here." And they just said, "Well, she needs to work harder." So they were actually not at all helpful and I ended up having a row with the head of sixth form because she accused me of being "*a fussy parent*." And what she said was that my daughter was working to her level, which was the timed essay level, she was working to a D. (Paulette, psychologist)

Paulette was frustrated that her parental concern and professional knowledge was dismissed so readily by the school. In a further manifestation of low expectations that characterize so much of Black parents' experiences of the education system, she discovered that the school viewed her daughter's *higher* levels of achievement as at best anomalous, and at worst suspicious:

> I felt really frustrated and actually very angry that they wouldn't listen. Because I could see that, yes, okay, in a class of 30 you could overlook that, but if someone's actually pointing out to you the difference [between timed classwork and homework] and you are still saying, "Well, actually, you know, we don't see that," and "Is someone

actually helping her with her homework?" Which is what I was asked, because she is getting better grades when she is producing work from home, so it got really unpleasant. (Paulette, psychologist)

Paulette paid for a private assessment, which resulted in a diagnosis of dyslexia, and she eventually moved her daughter to a private school that honored the recommended adjustments. Subsequently, her daughter's performance in advanced-level examinations, when taken at age 18, improved dramatically: from three failing grades before the adjustments and change of school to three passes.

Black parents and students encounter low academic expectations almost routinely within schools (despite their middle-class status). Conveyance of such expectations takes numerous forms. For example, in many ways Vanessa's son was well liked by his teachers, but their lack of academic ambition for him meant that they were unconcerned by his relative passivity in class. She lamented that *years* had been wasted:

Each time I went to school, or if I passed the window, [he] would be sitting looking out the window and I was convinced that he was somewhere on the autistic spectrum . . . but because [he] could sit for an entire lesson silent and not be disruptive, all they ever said was [in a patronizing tone] "He's so handsome" and "He's so quiet" and I said, "Yes, but that's not normal is it?" . . . So when he actually saw the psychologist he was just about to leave [elementary] school—so he was about 11. So all the support that he could have had, the learning plan, *nothing* was done at all. So we wasted a lot of time that he could have been supported. (Vanessa, community development officer)

As noted, Matthew's experiences stood out from our data as the only positive case of mutual support between parent and school. There were two further occasions where the impetus for an SEN assessment came from the school, rather than the parent, but these cases were much less positive. In both cases, the Black student was a boy who had been racially harassed by White peers. And in both cases, the schools' actions served to divert attention from accusations of White racism and refocused attention onto a supposed individual deficit within the Black child.

Simon, a 37-year-old teacher, describes how his son was expelled for reacting violently to racist harassment. In a situation that echoes previous UK research on the overrepresentation of Black students in expulsions (Blair, 2001; Communities Empowerment Network, 2005; Wright, Weekes, & McGlaughlin, 2000), it seemed that the school refused to take account of the violence that the young man had experienced at the hands of racist peers and, instead, chose to view his actions in isolation:

Someone called him a "'Black monkey"' and he responded by
beating him up. . . . I just don't think the school really understood
the impact, or how isolated pupils can feel when they stand out
physically, and that's just something that I don't think they get.
(Simon, teacher)

The process culminated in Simon's son being labeled as having "behavior and anger management" problems. In a strikingly similar case, Felicia
discovered that her son was experiencing racist bullying. Initially, she was
encouraged by the school's reaction:

I started being concerned about his performance and then the little
things, like he'd be coming home and his shirts were ripped and he'd
say he'd been playing rugby, but his shirt was completely torn in
two. . . . Eventually he said about the comments and what had been
going on and how they'd been behaving toward him and essentially
the racism he had been tolerating. So I contacted the school and
arranged to see the head of his year. . . . The head of year was quite
shocked and quite encouraging in terms of our conversation; calling
and saying, you know, "Really sorry. We've let you down; we've
let [your son] down; we didn't know this was happening." (Felicia,
senior solicitor)

Unfortunately, the school's reassuring words did not translate into action, and when Felicia sought additional information, the situation deteri-
orated further:

Nothing happened. I'd asked them about what policies they have for
bullying and racism, they said they have got a policy and I said I'd like
to see it. This is a school with loads of money, [but they said that] all
the computers were down during our meeting. [She laughs, signaling
disbelief.] The place has got hundreds of computers. So [they said]
they couldn't print it off for me to take with me that morning but they
would send it to me. And I waited for 2 days and didn't get it; third
day, I sent an email saying, "I was promised this." "Oh, it's coming."
When it finally came, it said *draft* on it. So I wrote back to them
saying, the fact that it says draft suggests that (a) it's not in place and
more importantly the parents don't know about it. . . . My son's class
teacher had said to my son that I'm asking *too much* but not to tell
me. (Felicia, senior solicitor)

The situation hit rock bottom when Felicia unexpectedly received a phone
call:

I got this telephone call out of the blue one Sunday afternoon, from his class teacher, suggesting that he have some *test*—I can't remember exactly how this conversation went because it was such a shock; it was five o'clock on Sunday afternoon—that there might be some reason for his underperforming; not the racism at the school that I told them about, but there might be some reason, that he might have some *learning difficulties*. (Felicia, senior solicitor)

Both Simon and Felicia sought to resist the schools' actions and to insist that the racism experienced by their children be addressed. Neither was successful. Instead, they met with an escalating insistence that their child was in the wrong:

I wrote and explained [to the head teacher] I'm concerned that nothing has really been done and, having been told that it was accepted that he'd been let down, that nothing was being done and that perhaps he ought to, you know, [the head teacher] needs to talk to the boys [responsible] and their parents. And I had a stinker of a letter back from him essentially suggesting that my son was some sort of latent gangster . . . that he talked to some of his peers, who said they found him *an intimidating presence*, all sorts of things! If you'd looked at his school reports for those 4 years, there's never been any suggestion of bad behavior; in fact, most of the teachers say he's a nice boy. That his peers found him an intimidating presence, that something about the *rap culture*, he talked about specifically about *bling* . . . basically telling me off about this monster I've produced. (Felicia, senior solicitor)

Our data, therefore, reveal that from the very first stage in SEN procedures our Black middle-class interviewees overwhelmingly experienced uncertainty and problems—despite their considerable middle-class capital. In almost every case, when parents believed that their children might have a learning disability that should be addressed, it was the parents themselves—not the school—who took the initiative in seeking advice and arranging a formal assessment, often in the face of suspicion or explicit resistance from the school. In our sample, there were only three exceptions to this pattern: One parent had a positive experience, and the other two reported that the school initiated SEN assessments following incidents of racist bullying against their Black children. The schools failed to support the children by taking action against the racist attackers and instead invoked SEN proceedings against the victims of White aggression—actions that the Black students and their parents experienced as signs of the schools' reluctance to address White racism.

SCHOOLS' REACTIONS TO SEN ASSESSMENTS

> I don't think they want to know. And as long as they think academically
> she's doing okay, that's where they're concerned. I'm concerned with her
> performing to the best of her ability, which I don't think she does, and I think
> they're concerned with her reaching their target grades, which is I think a
> different thing. (Lorraine, researcher in the voluntary sector)

Having negotiated the first stage in the SEN process (usually by paying
for a private assessment in the face of official inaction), Black middle-class
parents then faced the task of presenting the assessment to the school. In
principle, the assessment should indicate actions that should be taken by
the school and/or local authority to better support the child. In some instances, the assessments suggested fairly basic adjustments—for example, to
accommodate an identified specific learning disability, such as dyslexia, recommendations might include the use of a laptop computer or provision of
additional time on examinations. In some cases, the assessments pointed to
more profound issues that required more far-reaching changes. Regardless
of the nature of the issues that were identified, however, our interviewees
overwhelmingly reported that schools' reactions were at best slow and uncertain, and at worst they were actively hostile and obstructive. Nigel, for
example, was advised that his son should use a laptop in class. Ready to buy
the machine himself, Nigel was stunned when the school refused permission:

> So we have gone up, we thought it would be a *fait accompli*, we
> thought we would get the laptop. We were going to buy the laptop,
> the school wouldn't have to *buy* it, you know, we would do all of
> that, and they said no. So we had a long conversation with the head
> [principal], who we were very friendly with, and they said that it
> would set a precedent. (Nigel, human resources manager)

The school's rejection of Nigel's approach was unusually direct. Much
more common was an initial reaction that *seemed* positive and constructive;
only later, after months (and sometimes years) of inaction did the schools'
actual lack of concern become apparent. Despite their supportive rhetoric,
the schools' inaction sometimes felt like deliberate obstruction. Lorraine's
experiences illustrated this pattern. As a trained researcher, Lorraine was
able to use her professional contacts to access information and wider support networks in order to explore possible ways of supporting her daughter.
Unfortunately, the school's positive early reactions and promises remained
unfulfilled:

> I have a daughter who now has been diagnosed with autism. I
> actually do want to get much more involved in the school and how

they deal with her. But I think for the school it's easier if they don't get involved with me. So, for instance, going in and having meetings; her head of year says, "Oh, you know, I understand now, we'll do this, we'll do that" and then that just doesn't happen. (Lorraine, researcher)

Attempts to follow up promises by telephone or email frequently prove fruitless. Government advice, noted earlier, informs parents that "Working together with your child's teachers will often help to sort out worries and problems" (DCSF, 2010, p. 9); yet, in reality, it can take up to a month to simply *meet* the relevant member of school staff:

It's almost impossible to talk to the head of year on the phone because she's always teaching or "somewhere else." It may well be *a week* before she gets back to me. And then it may be another 2–3 weeks before a meeting is scheduled. (Lorraine, researcher)

Repeated visits, and even enrolling highly trained support, did not guarantee success:

There were *constant* visits to try to get them to take some kind of action to help. . . . You know, at first I thought it was me not being forceful enough, but as I said, I was accompanied by a clinical psychologist who tried to get them to help as well and *they* failed. . . . I went in with the clinical psychologist who has experience of autism; what we were saying to the school was that [my daughter] needs this particular kind of intervention and we felt very strongly that *all* her teachers should know about this. The head of year's response was, "None of us know anything about autism." So the psychologist wrote to them, she wrote *three times* offering to come in and do a day with staff about autism, and they never responded to that at all. (Lorraine, researcher)

Even when parents succeeded in securing an assessment *and* having a formal action plan agreed with the school, they typically encountered patchy or nonexistent follow-up. This pattern emerged regardless of whether the assistance was sought within the state system or in private schools. For example, Rachel described her constant vigilance at her daughter's private school:

I went to a parents' evening recently. I went round to see all of the teachers individually. And I said, "Have you seen her [agreed-upon plan]? Have you read it?" Not all of them had. Some of them didn't even have it. . . . I went immediately and complained to the headmistress—who was there—because I thought why—don't advertise and promote yourself as a school that is good at pastoral care and being supportive if, when you have a child who has learning needs and you have an [agreed-upon plan], and the staff can't be bothered to read it. It's not good enough. She said, "Oh, which teachers were you talking to?" and "I'm going to get on to it and I'll get back to you." And I haven't heard from her since. (Rachel, senior solicitor)

The failure to circulate accurate information among staff (about students' needs and how their impairments might present in class) can have serious consequences—not only leading to conflict and distress but, in one case, meaning that a child was denied access to an important examination:

[There are] two or three teachers who have got very annoyed with [my daughter] because she has done things which they don't like, but which I think are because of her autism. And so they have thrown her out of lessons, made her stand in the corridor. So this particular teacher threw her out of a class in which everyone else was informed of when they had to submit their work. So [she] didn't know and when she *did* submit it, it was too late and she wasn't allowed to submit her coursework. Absolutely unbelievable. . . . I said to her when she got her results, "How did you manage to get a U [ungraded result]?" Because I had seen some of the work she had done . . . and then she explained to me that she wasn't allowed to submit the work. (Lorraine, researcher)

DISCRIT AND THE BLACK MIDDLE CLASSES

In this chapter, we have reviewed how the intersections of race–class–gender–dis/ability featured in our research with Black middle-class parents in England. The limits of space prevent a detailed engagement with every aspect of the relevant data, but several key issues emerged from our findings that connect with some of the core tenets of DisCrit outlined by Annamma et al. (2013):

1. DisCrit focuses on ways that the forces of racism and ableism circulate interdependently, often in neutralized and invisible ways, to uphold notions of normalcy.
2. DisCrit values multidimensional identities and troubles singular notions of identity such as race *or* dis/ability *or* class *or* gender *or* sexuality, and so on. (p. 11)

Our data show how the coming together of particular identities of race (Black Caribbean), class (middle-class professional occupations), and dis/ability (the construction and regulation of particular dis/ability labels) operates in a volatile and contested way. The results cannot be predicted in any simple linear fashion. The parents' relatively privileged middle-class status and class capital might be predicted to put them in a prime position to make use of certain labels to the advantage of their children. Christine Sleeter (1987), for instance, has famously posited that the notion of learning disabilities (LD) emerged specifically to protect the privileged position of children from White elite backgrounds:

> Rather than being a product of progress, the category [learning disabilities] was essentially conservative in that it helped schools continue to serve best those whom schools have always served best: the white middle and upper-middle class. This political purpose, however, has been cloaked in the ideology of individual differences and biological determinism, thus making it appear scientifically sound. (p. 212)

More than 20 years after Sleeter's original article, Wanda Blanchett (2010) revisited these issues, and drawing on a range of U.S. research, she concluded that there are important race inequalities in the quality and nature of provision that students experience despite having the same official designation of "learning disabilities":

> Middle- and upper-class white students with LD receive accommodations and modifications within the general education classroom setting while students of color with the same labels are educated in self-contained [i.e., segregated] settings. (p. 4)

For Black students, the correlations between race and SEN placement appear to be relatively stable on both sides of the Atlantic, with minoritized students being overrepresented in particular categories that often lead to segregated provision and lower attainment. Existing research is less plentiful, however, when the issue of social class is added to the mix. Although Sleeter's original argument addressed race, dis/ability, and class simultaneously, later work has tended to deal with dis/ability and *either* race *or* class. Blanchett, for example, describes work that looks at socioeconomic factors and work that looks at race, but none of the studies (neither quantitative nor qualitative) deals simultaneously with race, class, and dis/ability. In the United Kingdom, education policy and research typically emphasize the primacy of *social class* as the key determinant of achievement levels and future life chances. But our data strongly suggest that the *racist* processes that result in labeling and segregating working-class Black students also operate to the disadvantage of middle-class Black students and their parents.

"Race does not exist outside of ability and ability does not exist outside of race" (Annamma et al., 2013, p. 6). This insight is powerfully confirmed by the experiences of the Black middle-class parents and their children in our research. LD categories, such as autism and dyslexia, are mostly treated in contemporary England as a property right for the benefit of White middle-class students—a property right to which our Black interviewees' social class profile does not grant access. Even armed with the supposedly "scientific" warrant of a formal assessment (a certification meant to credentialize and medicalize the "condition"), Black middle-class parents' claims were rejected. Within an educational competition where particular LD dis/ability labels *can* become a valuable asset, therefore, this asset is denied to the Black parents and their children. Their greater social class capital is rejected, their claims denied, and their motives questioned. In contrast, however, schools seem content to mobilize certain dis/ability labels, especially negative *behavioral* categories, in all too familiar ways *against* the parents and their children—a finding that relates to a further DisCrit tenet:

3. DisCrit emphasizes the social constructions of race and ability and yet recognizes the material and psychological impacts of being labeled as raced or dis/abled, which sets one outside of the western cultural norms. (p. 11)

At the particular nexus of identities and locations (England in the early 21st century, wherein Black racial identity, middle-class social status, and a range of dis/ability labels collide) the outcomes follow a pattern that privileges White supremacy and the racial status quo. Although a dis/ability label might be a useful resource (providing additional resources or supports), it is generally denied by White power holders. Yet, dis/ability labels that serve to exclude, stigmatize, and control (emotional or behavioral disabilities) are applied without regard to national guidelines or formal procedures. This can clearly be seen in the cases of Simon and Felicia, whose sons' experience of racist violence at the hands of White peers prompted moves on their schools' part to label the Black children with deficits and point to them as the cause of problems:

4. DisCrit privileges voices of marginalized populations, traditionally not acknowledged within research; and (5) DisCrit considers legal and historical aspects of dis/ability and race and how both have been used separately and together to deny the rights of some citizens. (p. 11)

Our mostly White research team reflects the institutionalized patterns of inequality that pervade the academy on both sides of the Atlantic. However, by putting the experiences and perspectives of minoritized people at the heart of the project, we acknowledge the social construction and contestation of these issues at a day-to-day level and as a historical fact. Indeed, the professional expertise and life experience of our interviewees meant that they had witnessed many of these processes at work in multiple contexts, in addition to those encountered in their own schooling and the education of their children. Paulette, for example, worked as a psychologist, and sometimes her role required her to visit schools. Profoundly disturbed by what she described as the "brutalization" of Black boys in segregated provision in a state secondary school, Paulette observed a group that had been created as a result of the school's decision to selectively group students in hierarchically ranked teaching "sets"—similar to tracking in the United States. This form of so-called "ability grouping" is known to generate problems for particular groups of students who are consistently placed in the bottom groups, denied a full curriculum, and taught by less experienced teachers. Black students and their White peers from poor backgrounds are typically overrepresented in the bottom sets (tracks) (Araujo, 2007; Ball, 1981; Commission for Racial Equality, 1992; Gillborn, 2008; Gillies & Robinson, 2012; Hallam, 2002; Hallam & Toutounji, 1996; Sukhnandan & Lee, 1998; Tikly, Haynes, Caballero, Hill, & Gillborn, 2006; Wiliam & Bartholomew, 2004):

> The bottom set has been written off as boys who are just not going to get anywhere. . . . And I just felt that there was something that that school—you know, it sounds crazy—but something that that school did, actually *did*, to particular Black boys. I'm not saying that Black boys go there and they don't achieve because many do, but there is *a particular group of boys* perhaps underachieving—you know the type that I'm describing—who perhaps have an unidentified need—not doing so well at school. The school *does* something to them because they don't—literally, the deputy head said to me when I made the complaint [about what I have seen in the class], "Well, you know, what do you expect, they are in bottom sets?" . . . And I just think, I just thought that what it is, is that maybe the school just brutalizes those children *unintentionally*. Am I making sense? (Paulette, psychologist)

Paulette's experiences testify to the contemporary reality of a problem that was first identified in the earliest English antiracist educational research by the Caribbean scholar and political activist Bernard Coard in the 1970s. The co-constitution of race and dis/ability has become so normalized that even when Paulette described the processes to an interviewer of the same gender, class, and minoritized group, the reality sounds almost nonsensical. As critical scholars working at the intersections of multiple inequities, we know that Paulette *is* "making sense" and we remain committed to challenging the assumptions that reproduce and legitimize these inequities.

CONCLUSIONS

Oppression is a bundled set of relations that reinforce one another, so there
is little to suggest that advantages in terms of one relation necessarily
contradict the enforcement of another relation. (Leonardo & Broderick, 2011,
p. 2224)

"Race" and "disability" are socially constructed categories of difference
and exclusion that have a long history of complex intersectional relations. Some of the most important early work on the racist operation of
the English education system exposed how particular notions of dis/ability
(concerning supposed "educational subnormality") operated to segregate
Black British students from mainstream classrooms, with disastrous consequences for their subsequent educational achievement. Understandings of
dis/ability have changed over the years, but the racialization of these issues
continues. On both sides of the Atlantic, there is a longstanding pattern of
Black overrepresentation in categories that rely heavily on the judgment of
White teachers, who perceive an "emotional" or "behavioral" aberration in
the actions of Black students. Recently, however, there have been growing
calls for studies that deal with race–dis/ability intersections in more detail,
particularly through the development of DisCrit as a theoretical framework
that gives equal weight to these fundamental axes of oppression (Annamma
et al., 2013; Ferri & Connor, 2014). In this chapter, we sought to contribute
to these developments by exploring the intersections of race, class, gender,
and dis/ability in the lives of middle-class Black parents in England.

Despite the relatively advantaged socioeconomic profile of the parents
in our research, our findings powerfully demonstrate that dis/ability continues to operate as a racialized barrier to equity in English schools. Indeed, an
intersectional analysis reveals new dimensions that illuminate the simultaneously raced and classed nature of particular understandings of dis/ability
in education.

Fifteen of our 62 respondents, around a quarter, mentioned dis/ability-
related issues during their interviews. Only one reported an overwhelmingly
positive experience, in which the systems operated as they are envisaged
in official guidance, with a mutually respectful and supportive relationship
between home and school. In all other cases, there was a degree of tension
and mistrust, sometimes leading to conflict and a complete breakdown of
home–school relations. Our interviewees' professional status and income
meant that they could draw on considerable class resources, including economic capital (for example, they can afford private specialist assessments)
and social and cultural capital (enabling them to mobilize extensive social
and professional networks that provide support). Despite these resources,
however, Black middle-class parents in England encounter all-too-familiar
patterns of racist exclusion and labeling. For instance, when two of our

interviewees, Simon and Felicia, discovered that their sons had been the victims of racist bullying, they expected the schools to provide help and support. Instead, their sons were deemed to be the problem and subjected to negative dis/ability labeling that assumed a deficit on the child's part. On the other hand, when our interviewees believed that their children might benefit from accessing additional resources following an LD diagnosis, as has been afforded to White middle-class students (Sleeter, 1987), they found their advocacy blocked. Teachers appeared content to accept poor academic performance from Black students as an inevitable outcome of their assumed lesser "ability," regardless of the child's social class background. Even when parents paid for specialist assessments, they encountered a system that reacted with little interest, ranging from slow responses to open antagonism and refusal.

We noted earlier that our goal was not to make judgments about the ontological status of dis/ability labels or truth claims. Our intent was not to pronounce on the supposed "accuracy," or not, of labeling processes, but rather to understand how notions of dis/ability are constituted and show the significance of race/class intersections in those processes. Sleeter (1987) proposed that learning disabilities emerged as a category "created by white middle class parents in an effort to differentiate their children from low-achieving low income and minority children" (p. 210). Similarly, our data suggest that learning disabilities (such as dyslexia and autism) are policed by schools in ways that position Black parents' claims as illegitimate, *regardless* of their class status. In all but one case, because of school resistance, our respondents had to seek private assessments outside the state system. Once armed with the requisite assessments (and even when physically accompanied by specialists), they continued to face resistance to having their claims addressed. Thus, parents' enhanced socioeconomic standing did not seem to alter schools' approaches to dis/ability labels and processes. Instead, particular labels were used to deflect accusations of White racism and to segregate Black students from the mainstream. Meanwhile, attempts to access additional resources for Black children on the basis of particular LD claims were resisted by schools at virtually every stage.

In conclusion, we hope not only that our analysis adds to the growing body of critical intersectional research in DisCrit, but that it has consequences for a praxis of resistance. We believe that DisCrit has the potential to better inform collaborations with the people at the heart of these processes as they seek to resist dis/abling practices and achieve social justice. In particular, there may be numerous practical payoffs from academic work that reveals that these issues are structured in racialized oppression. Moments of exclusion and racism are not idiosyncratic one-off events involving teachers who are too overworked or too uninterested to recognize what they're doing. These events are part of a process shaped by the deep structuring of opportunity and a policing of Black bodies that is historically situated and

constantly re/created through myriad interactions in society. These processes are *especially* potent in the realm of special education, where students
of color often find themselves segregated and handed a third-class education on the basis of pseudo-medicalized labels, masquerading as scientific,
well-intentioned, and sophisticated. Special education has had the effect of
remaking centuries old categories that treat people of color as less able, less
deserving, and ultimately, less human.

Acknowledgments: This paper draws on data and analyses previously presented in Gillborn (2012) and Rollock et al. (2015).

CHAPTER 2

What a Good Boy

The Deployment and Distribution of "Goodness" as Ideological Property in Schools

Alicia A. Broderick
Zeus Leonardo

We respond here to Annamma, Connor, and Ferri's (2013) invitation to expand interdisciplinary thinking and dialogue around the intersections of race and dis/ability. Building upon our prior work on smartness as property (Leonardo & Broderick, 2011), we argue that like "smartness," "goodness" is so taken for granted as a central facet of the fabric of our cultural values that it is rarely remarked upon, let alone critically examined. Similarly, we argue that our identities as "smart" (or not) and "good" (or not) are actively constituted and contested from birth and that cultural institutions of schooling play central roles in shaping our identities within the boundaries of these ideological systems. The material-ideological system of "goodness" also plays a central role in the "interdependent ways that racism and ableism shape notions of normalcy" (Annamma et al., 2013, p. 11). Indeed, one of the foundational tenets of DisCrit "recognizes Whiteness and Ability as 'property,' conferring economic benefits to those who can claim Whiteness and/or normalcy (Harris, 1993) and disadvantages for those who cannot lay claim to these identity statuses" (Annamma et al., 2013, p. 16). Building on our previous theorizing about smartness as property (Leonardo & Broderick, 2011), we posit that "goodness" too operates as a form of property in schools. Moreover, the mechanisms of dis/ablement are crucial operatives in the constitution of student identities in relation to the construct of "goodness," which operate in schools wherein deeply inequitable relations of race, class, and gender take an institutional form. Further, we concur with Annamma et al. (2013) that "racism and ableism are normalizing processes that are interconnected and collusive. In other words, racism and ableism often work in ways that are unspoken, yet racism validates and reinforces ableism, and ableism validates and reinforces racism" (p. 6). Using DisCrit as a theoretical framework, we systematically explore these ideological systems that collectively work to constitute the normative center of schooling.

In the United States, education is racialized to reinforce the goodness of Whiteness. Thus, as Leonardo and Grubb (2014) contend, "from choosing school class presidents (therefore who is smart or popular), to homecoming queens (therefore who is beautiful), to targets of disciplinary policies (therefore who is the troublemaker), race is part of how schools perceive students" (p. 149). Gender, social class, and other domains of identity function in similar (albeit distinct) ways. Race, gender, and social class are part of not only how schools *perceive* students, but how they actively *construct* students' identities, self-perceptions, and subjectivities. In short, goodness is a central mechanism for creating normed subjects in schools. Through the powerful constitution of students' identities vis-à-vis "goodness" (as with "smartness"), material disparities manifest in students' experiences of schooling. Goodness is a central valuation of who deserves or does not deserve certain social and material goods that contribute to differential access to life chances. In other words, goodness is a mode through which dis/abling occurs, including the overvaluation of Whiteness and undervaluation of Blackness within educational practices.

THE DISCURSIVE WORK OF "GOODNESS": WHAT DOES IT ACCOMPLISH/DO?

As an ideological system, goodness is not expressed merely in a static set of beliefs. Rather, "goodness" (and smartness) are actively constituted through cultural discourse, or as Hatt (2011) says, "not just as an ideology or belief but as actual practice: more verb than noun . . . something *done* to others as social positioning" (p. 2, emphasis in original). In this sense, goodness is a set of material practices. It is recognized through gestures (raising your hand before you speak) and embodied performances (sitting quietly until told otherwise).

We want to distinguish what we are *not* talking about when we talk of "goodness." As with our analysis of smartness, we admit that some aspects of character and moral behavior are more culturally valued than others (for example, kindness, generosity, nonviolence, reciprocal assistance, and so forth). That is, share, take turns, don't hit, help one another, and so on are communitarian values that may be necessary in order to peacefully coexist in shared spaces like schools and homes. However, when we refer to the deployment of "goodness" as ideological property in schools, its referents are neither particular moral values nor specific behaviors (despite the fact that these dimensions may be recruited to do its ideological work). Indeed, goodness as ideological property is often differentially distributed quite ir-respective of the actions or behaviors associated with it. Thus, "goodness" in schools does not refer to an inherent feature of individuals' character or actions. It is neither the "stuff" nor the qualities that some people inherently possess, no more so than Whiteness is an inherent physical feature of White bodies (Leonardo, 2013).

The ideology of goodness is inextricably intertwined in the creation of good (and not-so-good) people, just as the ideology of Whiteness is inex-tricably intertwined in the creation of White people. Like Whiteness, the ideology of goodness recruits all students to abide by its regulations as a jus-tification of its very functioning. We understand goodness, therefore, to be a performative, cultural, and ideological system that operates in the service of constructing the normative center of schools. It is an ideological system that is materialist as Althusser (1971b) might suggest, as an outcome of social differentiation. Our contention is that students' identity as constructed as ei-ther "good" or "bad" produces material consequences vis-à-vis their access and sense of entitlement (or not) to opportunities, privileges, and myriad forms of cultural capital. In short, goodness is a form of property.

We base our thinking not only on our previous work on smartness as property, but also on the work of other educational theorists and ethnogra-phers who have documented the ways that being both "smart" and "good" in schools is discursively constituted by students and teachers alike as deep-ly intertwined forms of cultural practice (Annamma, 2014; Collins, 2013, 2013; Ferguson, 2001; Hatt, 2011; McDermott, Goldman, & Varenne, 2006). For example, Hatt (2011) found that "students were taught to un-derstand [that] smartness resulted from listening to authority" and that "listening to authority connected appropriate behavior and one's ability to become and maintain a docile body" (p. 15). Thus, Hatt's research illustrat-ed the complex ways that being "smart" was conflated with being "good" in kindergarten, and the ways that both were cast as being *compliant* with rules set forth by adults. To push this further, we suggest that goodness is a prerequisite of smartness such that a "smart" kid conceived as bad does not benefit maximally from this construction, whereas a "good" kid who does not perform smartly on assessments may be perceived as "smarter" than his or her academic performance warrants. The former's smartness is subject to scarcity whereas the second experiences a surplus, both instances irrespec-tive of accepted standards of evaluation. In other words, the label of smart-ness is not a taken for granted good-in-itself, but is judged by the contextual regulation of student subjects, such as "too smart for their own good" (that is, precocious) or girls who are too smart (emasculating of boys). We do not suggest that teachers are able to change a student's actual performance on tests and the like, but that the perception of goodness affects whether a par-ticular student is judged to be smart or not, which has material consequenc-es, not the least of which include teachers' recommendations for tracking purposes, academic awards, and leadership positions. Taking cues from their educational environment, these formal recognitions (or their absence) also affect students' self-concept. Our point is not that goodness trumps smartness, but that it validates and legitimizes it. Without the qualification of goodness (for example, willingness to listen, to demonstrate docility, compliance), smartness becomes something uncontrollable and potentially dangerous. In this instance, smartness is something external to the student, which is certainly manageable in one case (that is, to be regulated) or purged in another (too smart for one's good). By contrast, goodness is internal to the student, an intrinsic part of his or her makeup that is not teachable although certainly enforceable. It is in a student's assumed nature to be good or bad, which is something a trained educator knows when he or she sees it.

The belief that some students inherently *are* either "good" or "bad" by nature is problematic enough, but in the U.S. context such associations are also racialized. In Ferguson's (2001) appropriation of Foucault, she finds that Black boys are disciplined more harshly and assumed to be "bad boys" even when White boys participate in very similar behaviors. Thus, goodness is less about a set of behaviors and more a regulating system that justifies the differential treatment of students. It is a theoretical construct called upon to explain the intersection of social relations, such as race, class, and gender that are articulated into a formidable architecture of power. Even when "good" students benefit from this system, their horizon is also lowered because goodness requires their loyalty as docile bodies. They learn very early the rules of the game, and more important, the rewards that accrue once students are labeled as "good," and the punishments that ensue once students are labeled as "problems." Students understand what is at stake, but they may not know its logics, as it goes without explaining that goodness is the right path to choose; its criteria are observable but more often are simply assimilated. Yet, complications arise because social identities intersect, such as when middle-class boys' transgressions are forgiven and dismissed with a "boys will be boys" rationale (Sadker & Sadker, 1995). Goodness is then an assemblage of social forces that cohere under concrete and specific conditions, rather than an abstract system as such.

For the targets of goodness—those unruly bodies—the predicament is admittedly more difficult. They navigate a regulatory system that, once they have been labeled "bad" for reasons that are usually mysterious to them (because *they* are precisely the problem), is nearly impossible to undo. It follows them, like an albatross around their necks, throughout their educational careers because goodness comes with a bureaucracy that tracks students as they progress through the ideological state apparatus of education.

We explore briefly here two central facets of the discursive work of goodness. They are (1) the construction of student identities and subjectivities as "good" (or "bad"), and (2) the ways in which those identities are used and materially manifest as tools of both stratification and exclusion within schools. This work is accomplished in deeply raced, classed, and gendered ways; all of it strategically deploys the "mechanisms of dis/ablement" (Davis, 2003, p. 29; slash inserted) as both a means of accomplishment as well as a source of legitimation. Our usage of the term *dis/ablement* is meant to draw explicit attention to the fact that students are not only actively *dis*abled through these mechanisms, but others are actively and simultaneously *en*abled, or granted cultural privilege. Students who are discursively constituted as "good" are provided greater freedoms, more latitude, and more "free passes" when it comes to enforcement of behavioral rules and consequences in schools, whereas students who are discursively constituted as "bad" have their freedoms restricted, are heavily surveilled, are more harshly punished for infractions of behavioral rules in schools, and are particularly blameworthy when they infringe on the entitlements of good children.

Collins (2013) uses the term *ability profiling* to refer to "the process of responding to a student as though he is 'disabled,' that is, regarding all of his actions and interactions through the lens of deficiency" (p. xiii). Though we find the notion of ability profiling a useful construct, we believe that only half of its utility has yet been fully explored. Thus, while racial profiling may have been central in subjecting Trayvon Martin to increased surveillance, ultimately and tragically leading to his death at the hands of George Zimmerman, racial profiling is *also* what *en*ables young White men every day to walk through gated housing communities *without* being subject to high levels of surveillance. We therefore want to emphasize the *relationality* of dis/enablement (DisCrit's Tenet One). Just as the process of interpreting a student's interactions through the lens of deficiency is indeed a form of ability profiling, or *dis*ablement, regarding and interpreting another student's actions and interactions through the lens of capacity, privilege, pardon, and entitlement is also part and parcel of *ability profiling*, or ablement.

The events unfolding in Ferguson, Missouri, offer a cogent illustration of the symbiotic nature of this racialized profiling vis-à-vis "goodness" and its materialist practices. On August 15, 2014, the chief of police of Ferguson released the name of the White police officer who shot and killed unarmed Black teenager Mike Brown on August 9, 2014. The officer, Darren Wilson, was described by the White police chief as "a gentle, quiet man" (Vega, Williams, & Eckholm, 2014, para. 22), who had no formal disciplinary actions on his permanent record. Simultaneous with the release of this (White, and ostensibly "good") officer's name, the chief released convenience store surveillance footage that allegedly showed Mike Brown stealing a box of cigars, thus positioning Brown (a Black teenager) as a robbery suspect and therefore a "bad" kid. According to *The New York Times*, "The videotapes seemed to contradict the image portrayed by Mr. Brown's family of a gentle teenager opposed to violence [good] and on his way to college [smart]" (para. 8, bracketed text inserted).

Mere hours after the simultaneous release of this information by the Ferguson police department, a White resident interviewed by a reporter in an adjacent suburb asserted, "The kid wasn't really innocent. . . . He was struggling with the cop, and he's got a rap sheet already, so he's not that innocent" (Ioffe, 2014, para. 10). The reporter clarified that "While the first point is in dispute, the second isn't: The police have said that Michael Brown had no criminal record," and she reported further, "If anything, the people here were disdainful and, mostly, scared—of the protesters, and, implicitly, of Black people" (para. 11). Annamma (2014) reminds us that "Du Bois (1897) recognized that innocence was an intangible benefit of Whiteness" as property (p. 6). And if "good" kids are commonly afforded greater disciplinary latitude in schools, and "bad" kids disciplined more harshly for more minor infractions, how does this dynamic continue to play out, in amplified ways, in the criminal justice system?

Goodness and Identity: On Becoming a "Good" (or "Bad") Subject

Hatt (2011) documented the ways that being both "smart" and "good" in the kindergarten classroom were intimately connected to exhibiting prior knowledge of the curriculum and to anticipating or fulfilling teacher behavioral expectations. Hatt reported that she initially "interpreted being 'good' and therefore 'smart' simply as obeying classroom rules" (p. 12), until she discovered that "White males from middle-class families repeatedly avoided [the teacher's] surveillance," while "African American students, especially Black males, were repeatedly the first to get in trouble and received the harshest reprimands" (p. 12). As can be seen in the following vignette, being positioned as "good" or as "bad" has less to do with one's actual actions than with one's relationships to authority, power, and cultural capital in the classroom:

> When my (Broderick) son Nicky was in 2nd grade, a close friend, Jamal, kept getting "lunch detention." Nicky wanted to sit with Jamal at lunchtime, so every time he got a detention, Nicky would try to get one by doing exactly what Jamal had done, but he would only get a reprimand. At first he was mystified by this phenomenon, so for 2 weeks he kept data on a scrap of paper in his desk: *Jamal throws a paper airplane, he gets a detention; I throw a paper airplane, I am told to pick it up and put it in the trash and go back to my seat. Jamal doesn't turn in his homework, he gets a detention; I don't turn in my homework, I am reminded to do it tonight and bring it in tomorrow.* After 2 weeks of this, Nicky told me he had finally figured out how you get a detention in school. Apparently, he said, "You have to do one of the things on this list, and have brown skin. Mama, my skin's the wrong color," he cried. "I'll never get a detention!"

Nicky was the only White child in the class, with a White teacher. And unfortunately, he was correct. Having been constituted as a "good boy," Nicky reaped the material advantages of race, class, and ableist privilege, manifest in "goodness" as ideological property, even if he did not understand them as advantages at the time. Through the asymmetric and inequitable distribution of rewards and punishments for behaviors in the classroom, both Nicky and Jamal were actively interpolated into racialized identities as "good" and "bad" boys. Nicky was actively groomed to accept his expected role of White complicity with the racist practices of schooling, just as Jamal was materially constituted, over and over, to accept his designated and denigrated subjectivity as a "bad boy" (Ferguson, 2001).

As an ideological system, goodness, like smartness, is deployed via a meritocratic rationale that locates within individual children an explanatory narrative for the differential distribution of social and cultural capital that always is mediated by deeply unequal relations of race, class, and gender. Hayman (1998) argues "we make some people smarter than others, by rewarding the smartness of some people and ignoring the smartness of others" (p. 26). Likewise, we *make* some people "good" and other people "bad" by positioning them that way. We are not arguing that educators make children "good" and "bad" merely by labeling them as such, but more profoundly through the myriad discursive practices that circulate in the routines and practices of schooling: the public displays and artifacts of behavior management systems (star charts, stoplights, names written on the board to mark either "good" or "bad" behavior, and so on), the selection of children at teachers' discretion for privileges both large and small (line leader, messenger, "star" student of the week, and so forth), and daily decisions about what is rewarded, and as important, what is ignored. The sheer repetition of these rituals ossifies what is otherwise a social process into a naturalized one.

In the vignette above, *both* Nicky and Jamal were subjected to racialized ability profiling, not just Jamal. By avoiding publicly reprimanding or issuing detention to Nicky, the classroom teacher publicly constructed for him (and for all his peers to see) an identity as a "good" boy. This identity provided a protective buffer, just as the teacher's public reprimands and repeated punishments of Jamal (for the exact same infractions) placed him at constant risk of exclusionary measures. Positioning theory, thus, requires us to examine not only how some students come to be identified as disabled, but also how others come to be identified as normative: We must simultaneously examine *both* why and how Jamal is positioned as a "bad boy" *and* why and how Nicky is positioned as a "good boy."

There are myriad practices that take place in schools through which students' identities become "thickened" over time into particular "types" of students through raced, gendered, and classed mechanisms of dis/ablement. Most teachers daily employ these kinds of practices, and most parents actively encourage their children's participation in them without substantial critique: "Be a good boy today;" "Try to get a gold star":

> When Nicky was very young, he came home from school with a "star chart" at the end of the month with every single date on the calendar having a gold star affixed in its space (including a couple of dates I knew he had been absent from school).
> "What are these for?" I asked.
> "Those are because I'm a good listener," he said. "If you are a good listener, you get a star at goodbye circle."
> "Hmmmm . . ." I said. "You have a gold star every single day—does that mean that you listened really well, all day, every single day? Because I know that sometimes it's hard to listen well, especially all the time. Probably nobody can do that."
> "No, Mama," he replied, "you don't have to listen well; you have to be a good listener."

As an example, I reminded him of a minor altercation he'd had earlier in the week in which he'd refused to comply with a teacher's directive that he had judged to be unreasonable. "And look, you have a star on that day," I pointed out. "Do all the kids get a star, even if they might have had some trouble listening that day?"

> "If you're a good listener, you get a star, even if you had trouble, as long as you're trying to listen better," he said. "If you're a bad listener, I think you have to listen really well all day to get a star on your chart. Bad listeners don't get as many stars as good listeners. But that's because they're bad listeners."

Thus, we see that repeated instances of positioning result in a "thickening" process wherein students become recognized by peers and teachers as particular "types" of student: in this case, "good" and "bad" listeners. It is interesting to note that Nicky explicitly rejected the syntactic construction of the gold stars having anything to do with *listening well* (an actual, recognizable activity [verb] modified by an adverb denoting the quality of that activity), and reasserted that the stars had more to do with *being* (transitive verb) a *good listener* (a recognizable identity [noun—*listener*], modified by an adjective denoting the quality of that identity, and syntactically constructed through the verb "*to be*" as equivalent to the subject position). Thus, the whole point of the chart, from Nicky's perspective, had less to do with *what you did* than it had to do with *who you are*.

As a White parent, it was horrifying for me (Broderick) to hear my son offer up a learned rationalization for inequities that located both his own privilege (getting a gold star on a day he admittedly had not listened well, and therefore had not "earned" it) and other students' marginalization within individual student subjectivities, and not within inequitable mechanisms of distribution. Thus, he had internalized the meritocratic rationale that simultaneously reified his privilege and other students' marginalization. If children on both sides of the aisle can accept that it is *because of who they are*—because I am a good listener or because I am a bad listener—it is easier for them to later accept why one of them is granted a scholarship over the other. Likewise, imagine how much more easily both students might accept the reason why one of them is expelled from school for similar behavioral infractions. Every child in that classroom was harmed by the deployment of this ostensibly meritocratic rationale, even as my son was among those positioned to be materially advantaged by it. However, that material advantage comes at a cost, which is complicity with the deeply inequitable structures that reify one's privilege, and one's very identity.

For Foucault (1972), subjectivation is the process whereby people are filled with meaning through social, specifically discursive, processes. It is in this moment that discourse, or language in practice, defines, limits, and regulates how students become known by making them intelligible as specific human beings (see Youdell, 2010). Through subjectivation, students are recruited into particular self-understandings that structure (without determining) their educational experience. It is not the same as labeling; it goes further than that. As subjects of regimes of knowledge, students enter a world of statements wherein they find their identity and place of "belonging" (a contradictory desire, as it is also a site of exclusion), other subjects who occupy their same predicament, and the meanings that govern their possibilities for moving among social spaces.

Critical scholarship on subjectivity represents a general reaction to the humanist or liberal notion of a stable, knowing subject. Insofar as students and educators are interpolated by discourses that hail and compete for their subjectivity, they are not passive receptacles of discourses (Weedon, 1997). People do not assimilate concepts and notions of the self without making active decisions in the matter. However, this choice is made possible by virtue of discourses to which they have access. Material institutions, like schools, gain their power through discursive authority. Likewise, discourse lacks power without the institutional backing that makes the exercise of power more efficient and potent. In other words, the subject is created out of the dialectical tension between institutions and the discourses that regulate them.

With respect to goodness, Ferguson (2001) documents the racialized subject positions that are available for students. For Black boys, in particular, badness is the dominant expectation that awaits them and the discourse through which their subjecthood is understood. Ferguson's study shows how the regulatory functions of discipline are not completed when Black boys break classroom rules, but rather in the racialized anticipation that interprets their very being in the learning space. They are adultified with intentions beyond their level of sophistication as boys and surveilled more closely than their White counterparts, contributing to their criminalization and higher rates of incarceration. They are not afforded the mythical innocence of childhood and are forced to mature at a faster rate in order to navigate the social world's racial cues. Ferguson's data confirms the assumed guilt of the Black body, a subject created out of the depths of Whiteness and responsible for its existence. Many Black students succumb to its expectations; others perform acts of educational disobedience, pointing out the cruelties of such arrangements while finding ways to survive them.

For other minority children considered "good," there are ironies involved in accommodating White discipline. For "model minorities," such as Asian American students, goodness is not an unconditional valuation. A stereotype of another kind, this apparent compliment is also a disciplining mechanism that promotes docility even as it rewards Asian Americans for the very construction that is withheld from Black and Latino children. As a form of discipline in the Foucauldian (1977) sense, model minoritization exacts its price from Asian Americans through its expectations of normative obedience. It graduates from an externally imposed surveillance to an internally assimilated auto-surveillance. This norm is not without harms, not the least of which is its ability to recruit Asian American students to do the work of Whiteness as they accept their tenuous place in the racial hierarchy. Of course, the "goodness" of Asian American students is a rather recent phenomenon, owing itself to a specious timing when Black and Brown power movements proliferated during the civil rights era. The model minority myth also efficiently hides the real struggles that recent or poor Asian immigrants face. Previously considered heathens because they were not Christian, and unassimilable because of their culture and language, Asians in the United States experienced racial promotion during the height of racial unrest to exemplify the American opportunity structure that allows for a modicum of success even as it upholds the perpetual foreign status. Transgressing their assigned goodness brands them as ungrateful or, worse, un-American. Goodness, then, is not a sign of inclusion into Whiteness but an implicit agreement that those who are not White disappear into its expectations.

As arbiters of goodness in schools, White women comprise the vast majority of U.S. teachers, especially in the early grades. They enjoy a privileged subject position within the circuits of Whiteness (but not patriarchy), while simultaneously doing the "caring" work of racism (Coloma, 2011; Leonardo & Boas, 2013). In loco parentis, White women's "care" for students of color represents the mothering practices to which patriarchy has reduced them, thus bringing practices from the private sphere of the family into the public sphere of education. Within the limited sphere of the classroom, however, White women exercise considerable power to define goodness as well as the right to discipline and punish children who do not meet the expectations of goodness. White women's presumed racial innocence as targets of patriarchy makes their role in propagating goodness contradictory because they harbor racial interests even if they do not benefit maximally from them.

Goodness and Power: The Discursive Work of Stratification and Exclusion

Although the import of individual children's identity development cannot be overstated, we must also interrogate other kinds of discursive work that the ideological system of "goodness" accomplishes in schools. Perhaps most obviously, there are related tools of social stratification and in/exclusion as mechanisms of asymmetric access to material advantages. The discursive institution of special education is a key mechanism for constituting the normative center—and conversely, its margins (Baglieri et al., 2011) by, for instance, the persistent and pernicious overrepresentation of Black boys in the "soft" disability categories, such as intellectual disability and emotional disturbance (Harry & Klingner, 2014; Losen & Orfield, 2002). When we look specifically at the category of "emotional disturbance," we can see how the notion of "goodness" operates as an ideological system that asymmetrically distributes ideological and material property in schools. In addition to being overrepresented, in every state in the United States, "students from minority racial groups are [also] more likely than whites to be placed in restrictive educational settings" (Fierros & Conroy, 2002, p. 40).

Ferguson (2001) details the insidious impact that "disability" labels such as "oppositional defiant disorder" have had upon the schooling experiences of Black youth. She writes, "My conviction that children's school behavior was becoming widely explained and understood as a matter of *individual* children's pathology extracted from any social context deepened when, in 1994, children's disobedience was officially classified as a mental illness by the American Psychiatric Association (APA)" (p. 195). Since then, individual children's behavior has not only been pathologized as mental illness but also increasingly criminalized through the presence of metal detectors, surveillance cameras, zero-tolerance policies, and armed police and security officers in schools. Ferguson argues that this individualized perspective on student behavior necessarily "involves the diagnosis and treatment of an individual and his problem," such that the student is "characterized as emotionally disturbed" (p. 199)—a mechanism of dis/ablement. Seen through the lens of individual pathology rather than a racialized lens wherein racism is normative in schools and society, students' behavior is judged as deviant and students are deemed "unsalvageable" (p. 96), or described by teachers as "that kid [who] has a jail cell with his name on it" (p. 221).

Reporting on the first-ever federal level accounting of preschool suspension rates, Samuels (2014) documents that more than 8,000 children, "including a disproportionate number of boys and Black children—are suspended from school before reaching kindergarten." Additionally, "Black youngsters make up about a fifth of all preschool pupils but close to half the children suspended more than once. Boys of all races represent 54 percent of the preschoolers included in the report but more than 80 percent of those suspended more than once" (Samuels, para. 3). Tellingly, a state-level official quoted in the article stated, "I cannot think of any case—and I've seen some really extreme cases—where I thought [permanent removal] was warranted. In my mind, we might as well send them on over to the prison" (para. 11). Regardless of the precise mechanism for exclusion—be it formal disability identification and placement in a restrictive setting, or less formalized disciplinary suspension or expulsion (often an early stop on the school-to-prison pipeline)—it is clear that "disability has a distinct role in the pipeline" (Annamma, 2014, p. 2).

CONCLUSION: THE ABILITY LINE

During the early 1900s, Du Bois (1904/1989) ominously pronounced that the problem of the 20th century was the "color line." By this, he meant that the historical invention of race would not only become the structuring principle driving laws and policies, but for the social relations that guide everyday life. Du Bois was prophetic: Race has become the nation's common sense. To conclude, we appropriate Du Bois's insight by arguing that the problem of the 21st century is the *ability line*. By saying this, we do not argue for the displacement of race as a focus of social analysis but we highlight its articulation with the theoretical concept of ability. Rather, the ability line is a larger slice at the cross-cutting processes that always already include race, class, and gender. It represents the attempt to consolidate an analytics of power in education in order to illuminate the way schools segregate the "smart" and "good" from those cast as intellectually deficient and morally suspect in myriad ways that pass as common sense. The ability line connects with a DisCrit (Annamma et al., 2013) framework, as the ability line is a dehumanizing process. We extend this intervention to interrogate whether or not the educational goal is to advocate for the right to be on the privileged side of the relation.

We take our theoretical cue from Campbell (2009), whose articulated agenda is to "not only problematize but refuse the notion of able(ness)" (p. 3). We focus on what Campbell describes as "ableism's function in inaugurating the norm" (p. 5). Indeed, it is precisely "the notion of the normative (and normate individual) and the enforcement of a constitutional divide" (p. 6) between normative and nonnormative that may be regarded as the central problem of the 21st century. The "problem" is not the line itself, such as who is on which side of it, or what it "really" means to be on this or that side. Rather, it is through common sense ideological systems such as smartness and goodness that ideas about what is or is not normative are deployed; race, class, and gender are always central to these cultural processes and mechanisms of dis/ablement. According to Campbell (2009):

> The reality is that studies in ableism offer more than a contribution to rethinking disability. These studies provide a platform for reconsidering the way we think about *all* bodies and mentalities within the parameters of nature/culture. In that sense, studies in ableism have the capacity to reconfigure both race and gender studies. (p. 198)

Using the concept of the ability line allows educators and educational scholars to recognize the multiple, intersecting systems of power as they are articulated within a specific moment of time and space. This approach is sensitive to the differing configurations that power recruits to do its ideological work as well as the counterhegemonic attempts to disrupt it. The common sense constructs of goodness and smartness are routinely deployed in the creation and enforcement of this "constitutional divide"—the *ability line*. Raced, classed, gendered mechanisms of dis/ablement are central to the constitution of the normative center of schooling and society.

Part II

ACHIEVEMENT/ OPPORTUNITY GAP

CHAPTER 3

Understanding the Intersection of Race and Dis/ability

Common Sense Notions of Learning and Culture

Elizabeth Mendoza
Christina Paguyo
Kris Gutiérrez

In this chapter, we use cultural historical activity theory (CH/AT) to fore-ground how cultural mediation and artifacts shape how individuals view and make sense of race and ability. This approach deepens our understanding of the key tenets developed by DisCrit scholars who theorize and identify systemic inequities as "social constructions of race and ability" (Annamma, Connor, & Ferri, 2013, p. 11) that have consequences in everyday interactions. Although we are not scholars working in Disability Studies, our long-standing work examining issues of inequity with youth from nondominant communities shares many of the same goals and transformative agendas.

We bring a CH/AT lens to emphasize the role of learning and to explain how systemic issues of inequity are re-created in everyday contexts. Drawing on dynamic notions of culture and cultural mediation, we theorize the ways in which pervasive and false notions of racism and ableism are distributed across artifacts and human practices instead of being located at fixed points, such as traits attached to people (Cole, 2003; Engeström, 2001; Gutiérrez & Rogoff, 2003; Peck, forthcoming). The construct of cultural mediation allows us to comprehend more deeply the process of *how* inequities are mediated by ideologies and are indexed and perpetuated in routine inter-actions, including individual and collective actions and language practices.

Toward this end, we argue that inequities are mediated and perpetuat-ed by common sense beliefs about ability, race, and racialized communities, which facilitate human interactions and relationships within educational milieus. By understanding the process of how dominant ideologies manifest in commonplace interactions through mediation and artifacts, we can foster activism—Tenet Seven from DisCrit—and work toward praxis. CH/AT concepts of cultural mediation, artifacts, and tensions in activity help us understand race and ability as social constructs that have consequences and reify dominant ideologies in everyday interactions, an example of Tenet Three from DisCrit. To exemplify the power of these theoretical concepts, data from a social design experiment (K. Gutiérrez, 2008; Gutiérrez & Vossoughi, 2010) are presented that demonstrate how common sense notions around race and ability are mediated by artifacts and perpetuated in routine interactions. Through the use of intentional design, which leverages design principles from social design experiments and change laboratories (Engeström & Sannino, 2010), we can identify and examine tensions in the practices of activity systems, such as schools, classrooms, and teacher preparation. In this way, this chapter contributes to DisCrit's call to activism, and more specifically, to the purposeful organization for praxis in teacher education.

CULTURAL MEDIATION AND ARTIFACTS
AS TOOLS FOR UNDERSTANDING DOMINANT IDEOLOGIES

Cultural mediation fundamentally challenges the belief that individuals can be understood apart from social and historical contexts. Thus, cultural mediation brings to the fore the ways in which our daily practices and institutional contexts are socially created and mediated *in* and *through* history and culture (Wertsch & Toma, 1995). This articulation of mediation is often traced back to Vygotsky (1978), who, as Engeström notes, understood cultural mediation as a way to overcome the "split between the Cartesian individual and the untouchable societal structure" (Engeström, 2001, p. 134). Vygotsky used a close-ended triangle to visually represent the way human actions are mediated by artifacts, that is, anything that was created or interpreted by humans, such as language, contexts, and tools.

Cole and Levitin (2000) elaborated on this image of a closed triangle by opening the right corner of Vygotsky's triangle to emphasize that cultural mediation is a dynamic process. To demonstrate the process of cultural mediation, Cole and Levitin drew an analogy to saccadic eye movements, the back-and-forth eye movements that help humans create a stable image. In looking at a picture on a wall, our eyes constantly move back and forth, taking and combining smaller clips of the larger picture over a period of time. In reality, we do not see the whole picture at one time; however, we interpret a stable image. In the same way, we interpret our daily interactions through our back-and-forth movements between the natural line, which represents biological evolution, and the mediated line, which represents personal and social histories and human-laden ideologies. Any interpretation involves looking at both the natural line, for example, skin pigmentation, and the mediated line, such as personal and social histories that mediate interpretation of skin pigmentation as race. By understanding that each interpretation of a situation is always mediated by personal *and* social histories, no human interpretation can be truly objective.

Cultural mediation requires a careful examination of how history and educational practices, when plaited together, give rise to the ways in which People of Color are socially constructed, for instance, the interpretation of intelligence along racial lines. Therefore, cultural mediation has consequences for everyday interactions, for example, the tracking of students. Cultural mediation emphasizes that history is not something that simply happened in the past; instead, history still lives in the present as our "social inheritance" (Cole, 1998, p. 291), which shapes our dominant ideologies and normative practices. To illustrate this concept, we draw on the well-documented influence of eugenics and testing on schooling structures, practices, and perceptions of race and ability.

At the turn of the 20th century, an active eugenics movement was present and growing. Prominent leaders from multiple disciplines (including education) used pseudoscience and IQ testing to intentionally establish and rationalize an intellectual hierarchy based on race (Selden, 1999). During this same period, U.S. school systems were experiencing massive growth in enrollment that created a need for new organizational structures to maximize efficiency and use of resources (Tyack, 1974). Large-scale testing during World War I found that, despite a flawed methodology, high scores on IQ tests were positively correlated to higher ranking military status. Tests began to be used as predictors of performance and eventual career trajectories, which created a platform for organizing schools (Gould, 1996). Not surprisingly, and yet purposefully, intelligence test results "discovered" the need for a "special curriculum" for racialized youth. This conflation of race, culture, and ability was exemplified in the work of Terman (1916), a Stanford University education professor and eugenicist, who described the low educability of Children of Color as follows:

> And yet, as far as intelligence is concerned, the tests have told the truth. These boys are uneducable beyond the merest rudiments of training. . . . Their dullness seems to be racial, or at least in the family stocks from which they come. . . . Children of this group should be segregated in special classes and be given instruction which is concrete and practical. They cannot master abstractions, but they can often be made efficient workers, able to look out for themselves. (as cited in Valencia & Suzuki, 2001, p. 6)

In this excerpt, Terman drew explicit connections between test results and the educability of students based not on intelligence but on what could be discerned from both the natural line—pigmentation of skin color—and the mediated line—meanings assigned to dark skin color that signify Students of Color as "dull" and "uneducable."

The history of eugenics and testing reinforced an intimate relationship between race, intelligence, and ability in modern-day school structures. As mediated structures (Moll, 1998), schools were shaped by the intentional imposition of ideologies—an intellectual hierarchy based on race—that continues to influence school practices and structures through the overrepresentation of Students of Color in special education and tracking. The legacy of tests as cultural artifacts that allegedly measure intelligence is an example of the way history can shape dominant ideologies (Cole, n.d.), including our conceptions of what counts as smart and who is *allowed* to be smart (Leonardo & Broderick, 2011). Conceiving schools as mediated structures aligns with Tenet Five where DisCrit "considers legal and historical aspects of dis/ability and race and how both have been used separately and together to deny the rights of some citizens" (Annamma et al., 2013, p. 14). The legacy of the eugenics movement and the overrepresentation of Students of Color and English Language Learners, who often come from immigrant Communities of Color, continues today (Artiles, Harry, Reschly, & Chinn, 2002; Artiles, Rueda, Salazar, & Higardea, 2005).

Through cultural mediation, DisCrit scholars and Cultural Historical theorists foreground the way that history influences present-day structures as well as the understanding that notions of race and ability are socially constructed. The question becomes, then, how does this history become part of the present and *integrated* into routine interactions? In other words, through which processes do social constructions become consequential? We contend that the answer can be found, at least in part, in artifacts.

Artifacts

A key component of cultural mediation is the notion of artifacts. Artifacts, which gain their meaning and value through social and personal histories, shape the way society interprets ability and race. Artifacts are the "constituents of culture . . . and materialize in the form of objects, words, rituals, and other cultural practices that mediate human life" (Cole, 1998, p. 292). In other words, artifacts are both material and ideational (Cole, 1998) and can include physical tools that people can touch, practices in which people participate and enact, or intangible objects—such as language and ideas—that shape how people perceive their world. The affordance of artifacts is that we can draw on history to make sense of meanings and tools without having to re-create and rediscover the world every day. Constraints exist in that each artifact carries with it a set of histories and associated ideologies, values, and norms. Tests have simultaneous affordances and constraints. Although we have a loosely shared notion of what tests look like (affordance), tests can also perpetuate narrow notions of intelligence (constraint)

(Valencia & Suzuki, 2001). As described by Chapman (1988), one of the most important legacies of IQ tests is the ideology that "intelligence [can] be measured by tests and expressed in a single numerical ratio" (p. 92). In this way, tests have a material value, but also an ideological one; tests have come to represent who is and who is not smart.

Through the legacy of artifacts and the inscribed ideologies they carry, we can understand how dominant ideologies are carried out in common-place interactions, including classrooms. When Ladson-Billings (2006) suggests reframing discourse from the achievement gap to educational debt, she provides a powerful example of the way in which language is a mediational artifact (Vygotsky, 1978). This specific reframing of language shifts from deficit-oriented perspectives positioning Students of Color as problems who lag behind their White counterparts toward an expansive frame that foregrounds the historic and systemic nature of racism that shapes educational inequities. From this perspective, Ladson-Billings (2006) argues that notions of power and privilege are necessary to understanding learning, the development of learning, and the intentional organization of learning in classrooms. As described in DisCrit's Tenet Three, notions of race and ability are social constructions that have real material consequences. In this example, the achievement gap is a commonly accepted, socially constructed concept that "hold[s] profound significance in people's lives" (Annamma et al., 2013, p. 13). Here, the use of language (the term *achievement gap* or *educational debt*) largely influences the positioning of students. The term *achievement gap* blames students and their communities for poor academic performance, whereas the term *educational debt* recognizes the historical and systemic forms of oppression embedded in socially mediated school structures, policies, and practices. Understanding the role of artifacts—in this case, language—means understanding the way dominant ideologies are embedded in every interaction.

Shifts in language foreground the double-sided nature of learning, which is a key, but often forgotten, component of learning (Cole & Gajdamashko, 2009). The double-sided nature of learning reminds us that learning is not only the acquisition of new knowledge—new levels of awareness about educational debt, for example—but also the rupture of old knowledge, such as challenging the idea of the achievement gap and assumptions behind it in the face of new information. Ladson-Billings's (2006) reframing exemplifies the need to engage in reflective practices that make explicit values, norms, and ideologies embedded in our day-to-day practices, including language.

HIGHER PSYCHOLOGICAL FUNCTIONS, TENSIONS, AND COMMON SENSE

Learning is an ongoing process that leads to the co-construction of knowledge as first occurring on the social plane (Cole & Griffin, 1983; Vygotsky,

1978). Thus, learning necessarily needs to be defined as a socially mediated process in which knowledge and ideologies are not born out of the individual, but exist socially first and then are adopted and adapted by the individual over time. This social process of learning is central to understanding the role of artifacts that are carried into the present and assigned value through history (Cole, 2003; Vygotsky, 1978). Vygotsky (1978) determined that learning cannot simply be passed down from an adult to a child. Instead, through exposure to social interactions, a child is exposed to ideas and tools. Through a sequence of developmental events and repeated exposure to ideas, children start to refine concepts for themselves. Because learning starts on the social plane, we access dominant ideologies and begin to construct ideas of normalcy.

A child will learn, for instance, that her performance on a test may be judged as good or bad. As the child talks with family and friends about tests, she is rewarded with positive comments for a job well done. The child will continue to further internalize the idea that she must provide right answers for tests. By extension, she learns that only correct responses are seen as legitimate forms of intelligence. She may eventually learn that she is either marked as smart or not smart. Through repeated exposures to similar messages, the ideologies of tests become reified to the point where she no longer questions the idea that tests measure intelligence. The meaning attached to tests becomes embedded in her daily practices and is reinforced by societal norms. We call this assumed knowledge a form of common sense.

The notion of common sense was developed by Gramsci (1999), whose work was concerned with the maintenance of power relations and the role of dominant ideologies in cultural hegemony. He discussed "common sense" as an "uncritical and largely unconscious way of perceiving and understanding the world that has become 'common' in any given epoch" (p. 625). Gramsci argued the role of common sense in maintaining existing hierarchies contributed to allowing these ideologies to remain unexamined and unquestioned. Similarly, Haney-Lopez (2003) defines *common sense* as "standard responses that are consistently but thoughtlessly deployed quickly for routine functions, especially in highly organized settings" (p. 112). Taken together, these understandings underscore the unconscious actions employed by individual actors—actions that are grounded in social contexts and culturally mediated by dominant ideologies. In other words, people develop common sense notions through their participation in practices and tools (both ideational and material). Unexamined, these beliefs become part of the commonplace practices and normalized over time. Thus, in the example of eugenics and testing, the initial argument that intelligence could be measured by a single number is no longer questioned and, over time, it is simply assumed to be true.

To employ common sense as an analytical tool, we draw on activity theory to help understand how common sense gets (re)constructed and perpetuated across activity systems. Because within CH/AT tensions are perceived as a place of growth and learning as a process that occurs over a series of developmental events, we bring the notion of common sense into CH/AT and introduce common sense as the congruence, or non-tension, across activity systems or settings (Mendoza, 2014). Here, the term *non-tension* is not intended to convey that there were no tensions across any activity systems, but rather that the tensions did not create enough of a disturbance to become visible to the individual or alter their actions. Common sense notions are pervasive patterns that, although acquired through individual experiences, have a coherent narrative. Common sense is often communicated as an assumption made without systematic examination and acquired through participation in societal practices. Given that learning first happens on the social plane and is acquired over time through constant negotiation in social contexts (Vygotsky, 1978), common sense is central to understanding how dominant ideologies are perpetuated and provides insight into how we can work to create awareness, or start to rupture these routine, common sense assumptions around race and ability.

A congruence across activity systems, settings, and different individual trajectories is both subtle and powerful as it demonstrates the ways that dominant ideologies are perpetuated in a mundane manner. Non-tensions also provide support for Haney-Lopez's (2003) thinking about common sense in which (1) anyone who participates in practices shaped by dominant ideology is susceptible to perpetuating inequities through common sense; (2) common sense is so grounded in social practices and dominant ideologies that good intentions alone are not a guarantee that equity work will be done; and (3) common sense is not easy to overcome, but awareness of its development can allow for shifts in understanding. By defining common sense as non-tensions across settings, purposeful rupture of common sense notions can occur through intentionally organized learning environments—in particular, social design experiments that can rupture common sense (Gutiérrez & Vossoughi, 2010; Mendoza, 2014). Thus, we can intentionally organize for mediated praxis (K. Gutiérrez, 2008)—the intentional integration of theory (reflection) and action (practice) toward social change (Freire, 1970/2002). Intentional organization includes the deliberate use of artifacts—tools and language—in learning environments to provide a mirror to reflect common sense notions and create space for students to question and change practices. As called for by Freire (2005), mediated praxis unifies critical pedagogy with theories of human development.

COMMON SENSE NOTIONS OF RACE AND CULTURE AND LEARNING AND ABILITY

In this section, we draw on data from *El Pueblo Mágico*, a social design experiment organized around the notion of mediated praxis and a local adaptation of a prototype model of the Fifth Dimension (Cole & The Distributed Literacy Consortium, 2006). A social design experiment is the design and study of an intentionally organized learning ecology created to foster learning and movement toward praxis (K. Gutiérrez, 2008; Gutiérrez & Vossoughi, 2010). *El Pueblo Mágico* was designed as an innovative STEM after-school program paired with a university course, in which 25 preservice teachers had an opportunity to explore theories of learning. Through *El Pueblo Mágico* research project, we provide examples of how common sense notions are perpetuated in routine interactions and how we organized the learning ecology to help students shift toward new understandings of race, culture, learning, and ability. In this chapter, we separate out the common sense understandings between race and culture and common sense ideas of learning and ability for ease of reading; however, these concepts are intimately connected.

The racial makeup of the undergraduate course, mostly White women, and the after-school program, mostly Students of Color from low-income backgrounds, is reflective of the demographics in many public schools. We mention this to provide context for the racial demographics of the undergraduates and elementary school students, which is particularly relevant to this chapter. However, we want to make explicit that common sense notions and the unintentional reification of dominant ideologies can potentially occur among all teachers as we all participate in societal practices imbued with dominant ideologies on a daily basis. Although sensibilities will vary based on personal histories, it is important to remember that nobody is ever free of bias.

El Pueblo Mágico was organized through a broad spectrum of artifacts, including fieldnotes undergraduates wrote to document moment-to-moment learning at an after-school program and self-reflections regarding their own learning. To capture students' preconceived notions about their experiences, we draw primarily on student end-of-the-year self-reflection papers, a culminating assignment. We relied on self-reflections so we could document in students' own words the way they explained their notions of learning, culture, and teaching prior to the start of class; the shifts they articulated over the course; as well as any tools they believed aided in their new understandings. Findings from the self-reflections were also triangulated with analysis of the larger classroom video recordings and undergraduate fieldnotes (Gutiérrez & Vossoughi, 2010). In this way, we caught both student reflections in writing as well as the sense-making process on video. The examples highlighted in this chapter are a subset of a larger study (see Mendoza, 2014).

Common Sense Around Race and Culture

To illustrate the development of common sense notions regarding race and culture, we draw on the self-reflection of Daina, an undergraduate who proved to be a highly critical thinker engaged in ongoing personal self-reflections. In this first excerpt from Daina's self-reflection, she examined her preconceived notions about culture prior to the course when responding to a prompt to describe her ideas about culture:

> Throughout my childhood, I explored "other cultures." Each year in grade school we would have a mini-curriculum on Native American culture. In middle school, I learned about the "French culture" in my French class, and in high school, I learned about "Mexican culture" in my Spanish class. I dreamed about being an anthropologist and would spend hours leafing through *National Geographic* magazines, wondering what it would be like to live with people who had culture. In [our state] the natives always brag "we don't have an accent." Just as I had grown up believing I didn't have an accent, I also grew up believing that I didn't have a culture, because as an American, I was an individual. (Daina, self-reflection)

At first glance, this passage seems mundane. However, through a careful reading of the paragraph, how common sense understandings around culture were learned and mediated through school becomes apparent.

First, we draw attention to the ways that Daina learned about culture that were reified across both time and space. From early childhood through late adolescence, she learned about the Native American culture in a mini-curriculum, where culture belonged in a specific section of the regular school year and to a group of people. In middle and high school, her assumptions about culture continued and remained largely unchallenged, as her knowledge about the French and Mexican cultures was associated with her language classes. As Daina moved across settings (classrooms and schools), she (re)learned that culture belonged only in particular spaces, absent from the everyday curriculum. In all of these scenarios, Daina learned that culture was something that could be added to supplement class content. This supplement exemplifies the additive model of multicultural content, which further marginalizes notions of culture to secluded spaces leading to the normalization of White, middle-class values being privileged in schools (Penuel, 2010; Rogoff, Paradise, Arauz, Correa-Chavez, & Angelillo, 2003). Of significance, common sense understandings of culture create spaces where White norms are the center of educational systems and Students of Color become "other" or "marginal."

Second, the conflation of race and culture also went unchallenged in Daina's courses, which affirmed that culture belonged only to racially minoritized groups and foreigners. The conflation of race and culture is problematic because it assigns an unchanging and rigid understanding of culture as belonging solely to Communities of Color. Static and monolithic understandings can enable and perpetuate stereotypes of "other" people. Deloria

(1999) argues that White American identity is an incomplete, unfinished identity that is defined by what it is not; in other words, White American identity is defined by the "other." "Othering" is the practice Whites use to create distance between themselves and People of Color. When Daina articulated, "In [our state] the natives always brag 'we don't have an accent.' Just as I had grown up believing I didn't have an accent, I also grew up believing that I didn't have a culture, because as an American, I was an individual," she defined White American identity by what she perceived it lacked: culture. In this way, culture belongs to the racialized communities who engage in a static set of practices perceived as permanent traits of the group.

Additionally, the flexibility and privilege of White American identity simultaneously allows Whites to retain individualism, thereby avoiding group membership. Thus, grouping and "othering" across People of Color perpetuates monolithic views and fosters stereotypes, at the same time it allows for a White identity to remain individualized. Further, Daina redefined *native* as "American." In this subtle and common move involving using the term *American* as a surrogate for *native*, Whites are "perceived as native to the United States and all other groups [are perceived as] nonnative" (Pérez-Huber, 2009, p. 709). By distancing from the "other" and positioning American as "native," racist nativism serves as a tool to "justify racism, discrimination, and violence committed against various groups of people throughout history" (Pérez-Huber, 2009, p. 709).

The "other" is a label that exists to explain, rationalize, and distance the labels and realities of inhumanity and inequitable conditions (Deloria, 1999). Ideas about the "other" become cemented because as we move across multiple settings saturated with artifacts representative of dominant ideologies around racialized groups, including media and school practices, we often do not encounter counternarratives (Solorzano, 1998), interactions, or artifacts to rupture these ideas. This is particularly true despite demographic shifts toward increasingly heterogeneous populations given that racial and ethnic segregation continues to fragment social and educational settings (Anderson, 2010; Jayakumar, 2008; Kozol, 2005; Orfield & Lee, 2006). "Othering," then, is one vehicle through which common sense notions are perpetuated and remain uninterrupted. Organizing learning spaces in ways that work to create awareness of common sense notions around race and ability are imperative.

Understanding common sense as non-tensions across space, time, and experience (Mendoza, 2014) provides a framework to think intentionally about designing learning environments in which each activity is an opportunity to introduce new artifacts and critically interrogate old artifacts. Additionally, these pedagogical artifacts engage students in reflective practices that seek to disrupt common sense assumptions and foster equity-oriented practices. In this way, attention to mediation, specifically artifacts, can contribute to DisCrit's call to activism. By focusing on mediation and artifacts, we can intentionally organize classrooms to help teachers learn to engage in reflective practices that shift away from static notions of race, culture, and ability.

Shifting Common Sense Notions Around Race and Culture

One of the artifacts used in the course was the introduction of the notion of cultural practices as a way to rupture the conflation of race and culture. People participate in cultural practices, that is, activities grounded in historical contexts that highlight regularities and variances within groups (Gutiérrez & Rogoff, 2003). We underscore the idea that culture is not fixed, but instead is grounded in everyday practices. Thus, culture cannot belong to any one group

Over the course of the semester, Daina and three other undergraduates in the class explicitly recognized that race and culture were separate and distinct constructs. In the following excerpt, Daina explicitly discusses why "othering" is so dangerous:

> It is dangerous, though, once differences are attributed to a group, and these differences are seen as stagnant. It is then that the *"other" becomes alienated, and their personalities are frozen into a stagnant and foreign substance that leads to discrimination* [emphasis added]. This discrimination is often applied in the classroom sadly, because the teacher doesn't cater to the individual needs of the child but views the solution to be an overarching application for all the children of that specific background or race. (Daina, self-reflection)

Daina offered cautionary words after learning about the negative consequences of reductive notions of culture. She wrote that the other—in this case Students of Color—becomes "alienated" and this distancing can lead to discrimination. She further addressed the way that static views of race can lead to an "overarching application," or stereotyping, which often unintentionally foster deficit perspectives (Gildersleeve, 2010; Gutiérrez, Hunter, & Arzubiaga, 2009) and contribute to the overrepresentation of Students of Color in special education (Annamma et al., 2013; Artiles et al., 2002; Harry & Klingner, 2014).

We provide this example of Daina's deficit-based thinking to demonstrate how the classroom was organized to help students identify common sense assumptions about race and culture. We want to revisit how stereotypes stem from the conflation of race and culture that can perpetuate the belief that culture is static, is monolithic, and belongs to a person or group. However, when culture no longer functioned as the property of racialized groups but rather as lived experiences, students engaged in sense-making about their own assumptions about race and racialized practices. This is important because assumptions conflating race and culture can fuel cultural racism, which involves stereotypes used to "explain the standing of minorities in society" (Bonilla-Silva, 2006, p. 28).

Common Sense Notions of Learning and Ability

Learning is always happening through exposure to artifacts over time. Conceptualizations of learning, however, are often either associated with particular schooling practices or not explicitly defined (Mendoza, 2014). In our examination of how preservice teachers described learning, 17 out of 25 students described learning as something that they had not explicitly defined prior to the course, and further, said they often made sense of learning in relation to teaching. Below is an excerpt from Alice's self-reflection, which was representative of other undergraduates' understandings of teaching and learning prior to the course:

> The biggest thing that I am taking away from *El Pueblo* this semester is that learning is not a simple Black and White thing. . . . Coming into this semester, I had not really given any thought to what "engagement" in the educational system looks like. . . . I have always been under the impression that if you are not committing 100% of your focus on something (i.e., the teacher talking at the front of the room) that you are not focused enough to be learning from it. (Alice, end-of-semester self-reflection)

Alice described how she initially assumed learning was not a process, but an endpoint that was either reached or not reached. She initially conflated engagement with learning. For Alice, engagement had to look a certain way in order for the student to be able to learn. This conflation privileged physical positioning over intellectual growth. Further, understanding learning as being static and needing the student to look the part places the onus of learning on the student. An element of this responsibility requires students to communicate that they are paying attention through physical actions, such as looking at the teacher. In this way, the student "appears" to be learning and the teacher can continue the role of disseminating information, "from the front of the room," further creating a division of labor between the students and the teacher.

Allowing unexamined notions of teaching and learning to persist, like common sense understandings of what learning should look like, as described by Alice and other classmates, unintentionally reinforces the banking model of education (Freire, 1970/2002), whereby students are viewed as empty vessels to be filled with knowledge. This inherently undermines the rich experiences that students bring with them, disregards critical thinking, and perpetuates practices that closely align with White middle-class values and norms (Penuel, 2010; Rogoff et al., 2003).

We argue that reductive notions of learning can lead to increased reliance on social norms, such as looking at the teacher and sitting quietly, to designate learning. Too often, special education labels result from reductive notions of learning when educators make assumptions and interpretations about the abilities of their students, including privileging physical positioning to represent learning over actual sense-making. The overrepresentation of Students of Color in special education highlights how social constructions of race and ability become evident when special education labels are assigned, in part, when students behave outside constricted norms of how learning should look.

Shifting Notions of Common Sense About Learning and Ability

Given the historically and socially mediated perspectives about Students of Color, the pervasiveness of White middle-class norms found in school systems, and unexamined common sense notions around race, culture, and ability, we argue that robust notions of learning should be made central in educator training. By foregrounding learning as a mediated process in *El Pueblo Mágico*, undergraduates were able to comprehend learning as occurring in both informal and formal spaces and gained insight into the benefits of leveraging everyday knowledge in school settings. Further, many undergraduates shifted from understanding teaching as the dissemination of information to understanding teaching as the organization of the learning environment. By understanding teaching in this way, undergraduates understood learning as something co-constructed by the student, teacher, and the social organization of the learning environment. This reorganization, or re-mediation (Cole & Griffin, 1983; Gutiérrez et al., 2009), shifts the responsibility for learning, and the blame for not learning, from being centrally on the individual students to being a shared responsibility, thus decreasing the probability of engaging in deficit perspectives when a child is perceived to be off task (Valencia, 2010).

To triangulate self-reflections with classroom interactions, we highlight the following examples to demonstrate one of the ways students shifted toward more complex and robust understandings of learning during the course. In the example below, undergraduates were engaged in a class activity in which small groups of students summarized articles and then facilitated whole-class discussions.

The first group to facilitate a conversation provided an overview of a Hull and Rose (1990) article that discusses a student who "misinterprets" a poem, yet the misinterpretation was logical and based on the student's personal experiences with low socioeconomic status. As the group finished its summary, Jane, one of the undergraduate students, said:

One thing that we found that was problematic, or alarming maybe, was that if [the student in the article] was required to read this poem for a standardized test, he would not be able to explain his thinking, which was totally justified. . . . On a standardized test he might not be able to zone in on the mainstream standardized answer.

During this conversation, Jane pointed to the narrow room available for interpretation on standardized tests as "alarming," as they do not allow for students' lived experiences to be taken into account. Students in the class echoed Jane's concern and discussed the limitations of using primarily "right" answers as the dominant way to assess learning. They asserted that teachers can and should also seek to understand the origins of perceived "wrong" answers and mistakes as part of learning, as well as using ongoing assessments throughout the year to understand students' progress. We highlight this conversation because we want to underscore the way students were not only understanding learning in the context of standardized tests, but were also thinking about how to more robustly incorporate student knowledge into their classrooms. As the discussion continued, it shifted to a McDermott (1993) article, which argues for analyzing the role of context in understanding learning disabilities and challenges the label as a normative disposition. The focus on social organization of learning pushed on the notion that, like culture, ability is not static nor does it belong *in* individuals. After the group summarized the article, one member, Monica, stated the following:

The thing that stood out to me was that the environment was arranged around [the student's] disability and not around him. His learning was organized around the fact that he had a disability . . . where if any other student didn't understand they would find another way of explaining it. Rather than simply saying he is learning disabled, he doesn't get it.

Monica articulated the way that the learning environments described in the article were primarily reacting to the label of the disability—not the needs of the student—inadvertently undermining the student's ability and potential. As the conversation continued, students discussed the importance of challenging what is considered normal in learning.

The discussion of normal demonstrates an ongoing practice in *El Pueblo Mágico* of utilizing mediational tools—such as cognitive ethnographies, or low-inference fieldnotes (Gutierrez & Vossoughi, 2010), theoretical concepts, as well as readings—to help students recognize and rupture their own common sense assumptions about learning and ability, race and culture, and who possesses the ability to learn.

Common sense framing in the context of this study had several affordances for helping the course instructors understand how to mediate preservice teachers' beliefs and their related practices. Understanding that practices are grounded in common sense allows for a generous and developmental view of educators, rather than viewing teacher learning as static or an individual accomplishment (or deficit). With the understanding that we are all products of our histories (Vygotsky, 1978), common sense notions can be understood in the context of individuals' personal and social histories, which can be engaged through critical reflective analysis to examine and rupture assumptions carried about "other" groups. Common sense does not take away or minimize individual responsibility. Instead, developing an awareness of common sense and its related practices allows teachers to name the practice and to make informed decisions about how to reengage in the practices differently, in particular around race and ability.

CONCLUSION

Repeatedly, we all move through different settings and spaces—school, home, work—and interact with family, coworkers, friends, and media outlets from different communities. Embedded in each of these settings and interactions are historical and social ideologies that are carried forward through artifacts, both tangible and ideological. This makes evident the need to intentionally engage in reflective practices around artifacts, and by extension, dominant ideologies. Both CH/AT and DisCrit recognize that the social constructions of race and ability are mediated and grounded in larger historical, political, and social structures, which have consequences for the societal practices we participate in on a daily basis. Without critical reflection and strategic action, we allow dominant ideologies to persist. This is particularly relevant in relation to assumptions educators hold about race and ability that are pervasive in schools.

Introducing the notion of non-tensions in CH/AT and extending it into DisCrit as a point of entry, we show how we can begin to disentangle and interrogate the ways in which dominant ideologies get perpetuated in schools. Given that common sense is so embedded in everyday normative practices, disrupting common sense involves ongoing and deliberate reflective practices that provide the space for students to examine their own assumptions vis-à-vis the theory and the examination of practices. With a focus on non-tensions, we can organize intentional learning environments that, with theory and practice, help students engage in a deeper level of reflection to discover tensions. In essence, educators can create small areas of tension that allow learners to begin to interrogate their own previously unquestioned common sense notions of culture, race, and ability and start to challenge larger systems of power.

As the field of DisCrit continues to develop, we believe centralizing learning and the role of artifacts as a way to understand *how* notions of ability and race are constructed will facilitate a point of entry for bringing DisCrit into educational spaces, including teacher education. Challenging common sense notions to create tensions illustrates practices that respond to DisCrit's call to activism. Of significance, introducing a constellation of artifacts and pedagogical moves in research and teaching, and in particular in teacher education, that cultivates mediated reflection has the potential to create a foundation for future teachers to recognize common sense practices and shift how they perceive learning, ability, and race. In this way, future educators can work toward creating educational institutions founded upon equity-oriented ideals and practices.

CHAPTER 4

Expanding Analysis of Educational Debt

Considering Intersections of Race and Ability

Kathleen A. King Thorius
Paulo Tan

A RATIONALE FOR EDUCATIONAL DEBT ANALYSIS
AT THE INTERSECTION OF RACE AND ABILITY

As researcher/practitioners who have spent considerable time working, researching, and providing technical assistance (TA) in U.S. schools, we are continuously exposed to concerns about the "achievement gap" between students of color and White students. Indeed, as we work with state and local education agency educators and their community partners to address inequities in relation to race, language, and national origin, academic disparities are often referenced by stakeholders as their rationale for seeking our support. Moreover, our histories as nondisabled individuals who both belong simultaneously to majority and minority demographic groups and who are in professional and personal roles connected to issues of disability have also contributed to our perspective that the framing of the achievement gap is rife with problems.

Critiques of the achievement gap framing are not new. Scholars, educators, and community members have criticized the construct because it contributes to deficit thinking and discourses about marginalized students (Leonardo, 2007). Related critiques implicate narrow definitions of learning and equity (R. Gutiérrez, 2008) and assumptions that Whites are the "norm" group to which all other groups are compared (Foster, 1999). Irvine (2010) noted that many other gaps (including school funding and challenging curriculum) manifest as an achievement gap but are not part of the dominant discourse. We do not suggest that concerns with eliminating disparities in academic outcomes between student groups are without merit. Yet, as Ladson-Billings (2006) reminds us, achievement gap framings lead us to "short-term solutions . . . unlikely to address the long-term underlying problem" (p. 4).

Alternative conceptualizations of the achievement gap that have gained the most traction are the opportunity gap (Akiba, LeTendre, & Scribner, 2007) and educational debt (Ladson-Billings, 2006). The first emphasized inequities in opportunities to learn experienced by students throughout their education. It was grounded in the emergence of *opportunity to learn* as a research construct that developed into a set of education policy analysis standards (Elmore & Fuhrman, 1995; McDonnell, 1995). In the United States, inequities are embedded in structural racism and classism, which contribute to disparities in school funding, distribution of highly qualified and experienced teachers, and instructional resources (da Silva, Huguley, Kakli, & Rao, 2007; Ladson-Billings & Tate, 1995). The second alternative, coined by Ladson-Billings (2006), refers to the multiple forms of *educational debt* that have accumulated for students of color. These include historic, economic, sociopolitical, and moral forms of inequality that have accumulated into an unpayable amount. Taken together, these frameworks allow for more complex understandings of academic achievement inequities, as well as the development of solutions more likely to address complexities. Such a framework is also applicable for analyses of educational opportunities and outcomes for another group of students with a history of exclusion, marginalization, and discrimination in U.S. schools and society—those labeled with disabilities.

Ongoing concerns about the overrepresentation of students of color in special education and in segregated schools or classrooms, often referred to as "disproportionality," has been the subject of two National Research Council (NRC) reports (Donovan & Cross, 2002; Heller, Holtzman, & Messick, 1982). In brief, disproportionality illustrates the applicability of a DisCrit framework (Annamma, Connor, & Ferri, 2013). In the remainder of this chapter, we illustrate how the construct of educational debt may be developed to support intersectional analysis of race and ability in schools. Specifically, we expand Ladson-Billings's (2006) analysis of educational debt owed to poor students and students of color, by showing how these debts are compounded by those owed to students with disabilities. Finally, we present key features of equity-oriented technical assistance and "debt-paying" approaches.

Analysis of Educational Debt at the Intersection of Race and Ability

Analyses of historical, economic, sociopolitical, and moral debts outlined by Ladson-Billings (2006) may be applied to those accumulated throughout U.S. history involving individuals with disabilities. Expanded descriptions of the types of debt owed and to whom allow for explicit analysis of education debt at the intersection of race and ability, interlaced in complex ways through U.S. history.

Historical debt analysis. Ladson-Billings (2006) asserted that educational debt analyses must account for the history of exclusion from access to education for people of color, while also emphasizing that these groups have worked tirelessly to educate themselves. Analysis of historical debt in the context of laws that prohibited the education of enslaved African Americans and other racial minority groups on the basis of beliefs about their inferiority in comparison to Whites has particular relevance for analyses of the exclusion of people with disabilities as well.

Historically, constructions of disability as deviance (Artiles, 2013) have contributed to exclusion of disabled individuals from public education and from robust opportunities to learn. Although compulsory public education laws were in place for all states by the early 1900s, many states cited students with disabilities as "feeble-minded," "mentally deficient," and "nauseating to" teachers and other students as a rationale for enacting statutes specifically excluding children with disabilities (Yell, Rogers, & Lodge-Rodgers, 1998). The Education for All Handicapped Children Act in 1975, reauthorized as the Individuals with Disabilities Educational Act (IDEA), may be understood as an attempt to repay historic debt, yet concerns about access, participation, and outcomes for students with disabilities remain. Disability studies scholars critique deficit framings of disability as justifications for excluding students from general education (Reid & Knight, 2006) and special education practices (for example, segregated placement) as hegemonic (Reid & Valle, 2004) when they are emphasized over the goals of students and families (Brantlinger, 2006).

Analyses of educational inequities and civil rights responses to racial minority and disabled students throughout U.S. history are intertwined (Artiles, 2011). Apparent civil rights gains for individuals with disabilities (such as the IDEA) have been a "potential source of inequities" (Artiles, 2011, p. 431) for students of color. In 1973, Mercer questioned the legitimacy of labeling African American children as mentally retarded in light of their capability in home and community settings. Aspects of special education practice, including disproportionality and restrictive placements for students of color, continue to be "criticized as a means of reproducing societal discrimination and inequalities" (Thorius & Stephenson, 2012, p. 26).

Both of these forms of disproportionality are related to historical debt: ongoing exclusion of students with disabilities and, particularly for students of color with/labeled with disabilities, less access to general education settings, curriculum, and progress than White peers with the same disabilities. High-incidence special education eligibility categories (emotional disturbance, [mild] intellectual disability, specific learning disability, speech/language impairment, and other health impairment) are commonly referred to as subjective because of an overreliance on professional judgment in the decisionmaking process (Artiles, Bal, & Thorius, 2010; Losen & Orfield, 2002). African American students are most overrepresented in these categories. Native American and Black students are, however, overrepresented in almost all 13 federal special education disability categories (U.S. Department of Education [USDOE], 2010).

With regard to placement, the IDEA (2004) requires that students with disabilities be educated in the Least Restrictive Environment (LRE), "with children who are not disabled, and special classes, separate schooling, or other removal of children with disabilities from the regular educational environment occurs only when the nature or severity of the disability of a child is such that education in regular classes with the use of supplementary aids and services cannot be achieved satisfactorily" (Section 612 [a][5][A]). Yet, a disproportionate percentage of disabled students of color spend most of their day in segregated settings compared to White peers with the same disabilities. About 59% of White disabled students are educated in the general class most of the school day, compared to 44% of Black, 47% of Hispanic, 52% of Asian/Pacific Islander, and 53% of American Indian/Alaska Native students (USDOE, 2010).

Although race is not generally taken up by Disability Studies scholars (Artiles, 2011), some have expressed concerns that LRE creates a loophole (Taylor, 1988) that allows school systems to segregate students of color with disabilities in separate classrooms or educational facilities (Connor & Ferri, 2007; Ferri & Connor, 2005). Although the landmark case of *Larry P. v. Riles* in 1979 ruled that the use of IQ tests to label and segregate Black students was not supported, the LRE remains "a discursive tool for exercising White privilege and racism" (Blanchett, 2006, p. 24).

As we shift to consider why federal policies have not significantly mitigated historic inequities for students with disabilities, we reflect on Ladson-Billings's (2006) caution that framing the achievement gap and related short-term solutions narrowly at boosting the test scores of students of color is unlikely to remediate accumulated historical debts that contribute to such gaps. Heller, Holtzman, and Messick (1982) offered a similar warning, which appeared in the first of two National Research Council reports, stating, "Rather than suggest procedures that eliminate or reduce disproportion, we recommend practices that directly redress the inequitable conditions underlying it" (pp. x–xi). Their suggestion is germane in light of 2004 revisions to the IDEA that require states to enact policies and procedures designed to prevent inappropriate overidentification or disproportionate representation by race and ethnicity in special education (Thorius & Stephenson, 2012).

Good's (2011) analysis of macro-policies provides some insight into why regulations in the IDEA have not done enough to allay disproportionality. Much of federal policy work reflects an assumption that education is a technical process and, therefore, policies are focused on fixing problematic processes. Thus, although now required to measure and report inappropriate disproportionality, states and LEAs determine what counts as inappropriate.

Recently, scholars have emphasized balancing structural (that is, racist and class-based structures in schools and society) and practice-based (for example, procedures and policies for teaching, referring, and placing students in special education) explanations of disproportionality (Sullivan & Artiles, 2011; Waitoller, Artiles, & Cheney, 2010a, 2010b). These scholars critique explanations that point to student characteristics, noting, for example, that poverty is a weak predictor of disproportionality (Skiba, Poloni-Staudinger, Simmons, Feggins, & Chung, 2005). Instead, we argue that intersections between poverty, race, and disability intertwine in relation to economic debt.

Economic debt analysis. Economic debt is largely accumulated as deleterious effects of funding disparities that "map neatly and regularly onto the racial and ethnic realities of our schools" (Ladson-Billings, 2006, p. 6), as well as relationships between earnings and years of education. Factors contributing to school noncompletion, including "pushout" of racial minority students via harmful disciplinary practices and use of high school exit exams despite inadequate provision of educational opportunities (Tuck, 2012), are also relevant to economic debt. Likewise, many have argued that 21st-century economic access and full participation in the civic process depends heavily on technological skills and advanced knowledge of mathematics and science (see, for example, Moses & Cobb, 2001). Yet, students of color are less likely to attend schools offering advanced mathematics and science courses (U.S. Department of Education, 2014).

Charlton (2006) asserted that the world is not economically and politically formulated to need or accommodate people with disabilities in production, exchange, and reproduction of goods and services. Although activists have spurred considerable progress, economic oppression and disenfranchisement remain. Employment of people with intellectual disabilities, for instance, may be limited to sheltered workshops doing repetitive tasks where federal law allows pay substantially below the minimum wage (National Disability Rights Network, 2011). At the same time, scholars have critiqued special education for teaching isolated skills, for hyperfocusing on remediating skill deficits (Brantlinger, 2006), and for lowered expectations of students with disabilities (Shifrer, Callahan, & Muller, 2013), particularly those of color (Donovan & Cross, 2002; Harry & Klingner, 2014). These critiques raise questions about the purpose of education and its contribution to post-school and employment options and outcomes for students with disabilities.

Students with low-incidence disabilities (for example, intellectual disabilities, multiple disabilities) are less likely to graduate high school, graduate with a diploma, and go on to postsecondary education than their nondisabled counterparts. Students of color with disabilities experience compounded disparities compared to White students with these labels. In the latest reports, approximately 24% of White special education students did not complete high school, compared to 35% of Black and 42% of American Indian/Alaska Native special education students (USDOE, 2010). Furthermore, although the numbers of students with learning disabilities who enter postsecondary education has risen markedly since 1975, they are disproportionately White and middle-class (Henderson, 2001). Overall, students with disabilities from middle- to high-income households are more likely to enroll in postsecondary education compared to those from low-income households (U.S. Department of Education, 2011).

Given these statistics and the fact that years of schooling appear to predict one's economic earnings (Ladson-Billings, 2006), it is not surprising that in 2010, nearly 28% of people with disabilities aged 18–64 lived in poverty, as compared with 12.5% of the general population (DeNavas-Walt, Proctor, & Smith, 2012). Furthermore, although approximately 10% of those in poverty were non-Hispanic White, rates were much higher for Black and Hispanic individuals: about 28.5% and 26.6%, respectively (DeNavas-Walt, et al., 2012). Additionally, employment disparities between those with and without disabilities continues to be alarming, with 21% of working-age disabled people employed either full- or part-time compared to 59% of nondisabled people (Taylor, Krane, & Orkis, 2010). Together, these data suggest a compounded and obdurate impact of economic debt at the intersection of ability, race, and income.

Sociopolitical debt analysis. *Sociopolitical debt* refers to the "degree to which communities of color are excluded from the civic process" (Ladson-Billings, 2006, p. 7). Ladson-Billings noted that this disenfranchisement from the civic process has occurred throughout U.S. history and continues in schools today. She also asserted that although the 1965 Voting Rights Act has been interpreted as a debt repayment attempt, similar efforts in education have not occurred, as students' and families' voices continue to be marginalized in their quests for high-quality schools. We expand this definition of *sociopolitical debt* to include the extent to which individuals with disabilities and their families are excluded from decisions about their lives, civic engagement, and education.

The first civil rights law for people with disabilities, Section 504 of the Rehabilitation Act of 1973, included wording from the Civil Rights Act of 1964. Though the larger Rehabilitation Act was a spending bill, Section 504 was added to the end of the bill, making it illegal for any institution or activity receiving federal funding to discriminate on the basis of "handicap" (Shapiro, 1994). Subsequently, the 1990 Americans with Disabilities Act (ADA) prohibited discrimination against individuals with disabilities and required reasonable accommodations in and access to public spaces.

Together, these laws represent attempts to mitigate over 2 centuries of socio-political debt. Yet, scholars maintain that the ADA is grounded in a medical model of disability (Donoghue, 2003), and as a result, falls short in protecting the rights of individuals with disabilities to vote—for instance, because a majority of states still have troublesome language in legislation, which bars disabled individuals from voting:

> a total of forty-four states have either statutes or constitutional provisions that permit disenfranchisement for some people with disabilities. States use terms such as "idiot," "insane," "lunatic," "mental incompetent," "mentally incapacitated," "unsound mind," and "not quiet and peaceable" to characterize persons who will not be allowed to vote. (Schriner, Ochs, & Shields, 2000, p. 439)

Generally, states do not enforce such outdated legislation, yet a recent complaint filed with the U.S. Department of Justice alleges that judges in California used literacy tests to systematically deny thousands of individuals with disabilities the right to vote (Blood, 2014). This example illustrates the fact that unless such language is permanently removed, there is always the possibly that it will be enforced.

The exclusion of individuals with disabilities and their families in the civic process extends to education. Sociopolitical educational debt has continued to accrue, particularly in relation to the full participation of individuals with disabilities and their families in special education processes, all of which are regulated by the IDEA. The act requires states to provide students with disabilities a free, appropriate public education and to ensure certain rights and protections for students and families (Katsiyannis, Yell, & Bradley, 2001). The IDEA includes "procedural safeguards," guaranteeing parents' (and older students') *participation* in decisionmaking about services, evaluation, planning, and placement (IDEA, 2004). Parent or guardian participation has been tempered by the complex and highly technical nature of these safeguards and historically embedded power imbalances favoring school professionals (see, for example, Ferguson, 2008). Tomlinson (2012b) noted that families and students have limited influence in the special education process and are often pressured and coerced into making decisions aligned with the best interest of the schools and professionals. Again, imbalances are more pronounced in cases involving culturally and linguistically diverse families (Hess, Molina, & Kozleski, 2006; Trainor, 2010). Imbalances manifest in segregated placements for students positioned by intersecting marginalized disabled, raced, and classed identities in schools (Rogers, 2002). These students continue to be educated in segregated self-contained classrooms or schools where they are limited to a "life skills" curriculum that fails to prepare them for *real* life (Frattura & Topinka, 2006) or full civic engagement.

Expanding on Waitoller and Kozleski's (2013) definition of *inclusive education* and Fraser's (2007) social justice concepts of *recognition, redistribution*, and *representation*, our recommendations for repaying sociopolitical debt require that students with disabilities and their families be recognized as experts and regarded as such in making educational decisions. Moreover, schools must ensure dignified and valued representation of students with disabilities in *all* facets of schooling. Furthermore, power imbalances in the special education processes must be redistributed on the basis of historic disenfranchisement of disabled people that continues today and center the voices and goals of students with disabilities and their families. The parents-as-partners framework, implied in the IDEA, does not go far enough to remediate sociopolitical debt, as families with fewer social and economic resources are disadvantaged in the special education process (Trainor, 2010). The technical and legal nature of the IDEA means that families with adequate resources, most often White and middle-class (Ladson-Billings, 2006), have greater access to lawyers and educational experts, a distinct advantage in special education processes. Thus, the IDEA must be reframed and explicitly name students and their families as advocates and experts in designing students' educational programming.

Moral debt analysis. Ladson-Billings (2006) defined *moral debt* as what is owed to groups who "have been excluded from social benefits and opportunities" (p. 8). We expand on Ladson-Billings's analysis to include the extent to which individuals with disabilities are owed moral debt through forced institutionalization and sterilization in an attempt to exploit and socially eradicate disabled populations.

In the mid-19th century through the 1960s, legislation in many states required children with certain types of disabilities (for example, intellectual disabilities) to be placed in institutions for specialized treatment because they were assumed to be "feeble-minded" (Ferguson, 2008). Not only were individuals isolated from society, but they were also exploited as unpaid laborers for the financial benefit of institutions (Carlson, 2001). As we introduced in the discussion on economic debt, people with disabilities continue to be exploited as unpaid or low-paid laborers in sheltered workshops (Abbas, 2012). In a recent case, workers with intellectual disabilities at a meat-processing plant were for decades paid 41 cents an hour and were subjected to verbal and physical abuse and deplorable conditions (Foley, 2013).

Laws also targeted people with disabilities for forced sterilization. In 1907, Indiana became the first of 29 states to pass compulsory sterilization laws (Adams, Bell, & Griffin, 2007). In North Carolina, people with disabilities, including children who scored below 70 on an IQ test, were forcibly sterilized (Helms & Tomlinson, 2011). The 1927 *Buck v. Bell* Supreme Court decision upheld the practice of forced sterilization of individuals with disabilities, and by the 1970s, more than 60,000 individuals with disabilities had been sterilized (Adams et al., 2007), including disproportionally individuals of color and those with low socioeconomic status (Larson, 1996). Today, the U.S. medical community widely recommends and employs prenatal technologies to predict certain types of disabilities (such as Down syndrome), exerting influence on parents to terminate pregnancies they would not have terminated otherwise (Kuppermann et al., 1995). Technologies on the horizon promise to eliminate "hundreds of other conditions" (Saxton, 2013, p. 87).

In the case of forced sterilization, limited attempts to repay the moral debt in the forms of public apology and financial compensation have occurred. In 2002, the state government of North Carolina publicly apologized for its role in forced sterilization and more recently became the first state to compensate victims of sterilization (Helms, 2013). Payments to victims are set to start in 2015, more than 80 years after the North Carolina Eugenics Board first authorized forced sterilization. Although a few other states have issued public apologies, none of the other 31 states involved has plans to compensate victims (Lombardo & Hardin, 2013).

The National Longitudinal Transition Study-2 (NLTS2; Newman et al., 2011) reports that individuals with intellectual disabilities have the lowest hourly earning wage among all individuals ($7.60 compared to $13.20 for individuals without disabilities and $9.40 for individuals with disabilities as a whole). Students with intellectual disabilities have the lowest high school graduation rate among all students with disabilities (37% compared to 57%) (USDOE, 2011). Students with intellectual disabilities are twice less likely to enroll in postsecondary education than students without disabilities. Thus, the moral debt owed to individuals with intellectual disabilities continues to mount.

Repaying Educational Debt at the Intersection of Race and Ability: Features and Examples of Equity-Driven Technical Assistance

What follows is a discussion of some features of equity-driven technical assistance (TA) partnerships, which show promise for contributing to educational debt repayment to students with intersecting raced/disabled identities. We provide examples from partnerships to illustrate.

A key feature of equity-driven technical assistance is that it goes beyond proposing technical solutions toward demonstrating how to address historic, systemic, and structural contextual issues that contribute to a particular problem (Kozleski & Artiles, 2012). Relatedly, TA has potential to address debt at the intersection of race and ability, facilitating processes whereby stakeholders engage in historic, holistic analysis of systemic factors that contribute to local manifestations of disproportionality. Such TA also relies on the use of critical tools as drivers of such facilitation. This type of analysis is often overlooked in favor of implementing isolated technical fixes (Kozleski & Thorius, 2013). In terms of disproportionality, for instance, technical fixes include focusing on "getting the right students" identified for special education by replacing an assessment with one normed on a more racially diverse population. Initially, numbers of students from minority racial and linguistic groups identified may decrease, but this approach does not address the complex reasons why students are considered for special education eligibility in the first place (Harry & Klingner, 2014). These critical tools may be applied to any areas where gaps in access, participation, and outcomes exist between student groups. Next, we detail an example related to race and disability.

As EAC personnel, we are currently involved in a State Education Agency (SEA) partnership that builds from the first author's work as a professional learning coordinator with the National Center for Culturally Responsive Education Systems (NCCRESt), a federally funded technical assistance and dissemination center charged with eliminating special education disproportionality. In our current partnership, we are examining the role of policies, practices, and people across a set of systemic domains that contribute to or reduce the likelihood disproportionality exists. Local Education Authorities (LEAs)with disproportionate numbers of students of color identified as disabled, or placed in the least restrictive environment, are required to participate in TA. Moreover, any LEA statewide may voluntarily participate in an effort to prevent disproportionality. To start, LEAs came together with role- and demographically diverse teams to analyze evidence (such as policy documents and procedures for assigning teachers).

Although still in progress, we suggest that such efforts demonstrate the potential for remediating educational debt compounded at the intersection of race and ability. In particular, increasing students' access to robust general education curriculum and instruction, expanding opportunities for families and students to participate in governance and decisionmaking within schools, and planning systemic and strategic efforts to address shortfalls in these areas are promising starting places to begin to remediate educational debt owed to students of color with disabilities.

A key feature of equity-minded TA is that it facilitates educators' critical reflection on their own role in contributing to deficit framings of historically underserved students. With regard to remediating educational debt, TA must mediate educators' reframing of deficit-based understandings about students' capacities to learn and contribute to both school and out-of-school communities. At the center of these examinations is reflection about one's own identity, and issues of power, status, and domination in relation to one's students and their families (Thorius & Scribner, 2013).

CONCLUSION

In this chapter, we argued that the unique and overlapping oppression and accompanying educational opportunity and outcome disparities experienced by students with intersecting marginalized dis/abled, raced, and classed identities require that we expand existing theories of educational debt. Because of the relationship between economic oppression and educational debt, the impact of this debt compounds over time. In critiquing ways in which individuals with disabilities, particularly students of color with disability labels, have been excluded from the civic process and from decisions about their own educational programming and lives, we also made connections to the sociopolitical debt owed to these groups. Finally, in examining issues of moral debt, we documented decades of forced sterilization and institutionalization for individuals with disabilities who were disproportionately people of color, suggesting a need for serious consideration of financial and other forms of compensation. Finally, although briefly, we pointed to equity-driven TA that includes historical and systemic analysis of factors contributing to educational debt, as well as critical identity work, as meaningful suggestions for addressing the complexities of such compounded educational debt.

Note: The authors are grateful for the support of the Great Lakes Equity Center, under the Office of Elementary and Secondary Education's Grant S004D110021. The funding agency's endorsement of the ideas expressed in this article should not be inferred.

Part III

OVERREPRESENTATION

CHAPTER 5

Reifying Categories

Measurement in Search of Understanding

Elizabeth B. Kozleski

This chapter uses two data sources to examine prevailing assumptions about student characteristics and how these data sources focus the categorization of minoritized students within U.S. public education systems. The two sources, data from the Office of Civil Rights (OCR) and the National Center for Educational Statistics (NCES), offer a glimpse into parallel systems of counting and sorting students and have implications not only for reporting, but also for structuring how these data are interpreted and used to respond to persistent patterns of disproportionality in special education, in Section 504 plans (designed to support students in schools whose disabling condition falls outside of 13 federally designated disabilities), and in advanced placement courses in high schools across the United States. My aim is to expose the structure of the data and their underlying assumptions about categorizing and sorting. I argue that the OCR/NCES approach to counting and sorting students contributes to the persistent pattern of disproportionate representation of African American, Latino, and American Indian students in special education and in discipline referrals that has persisted for at least the past 30 years (Artiles, 2014a; Bal, Sullivan, & Harper, 2013; Skiba, Middelberg, & McClain, 2014).

Without a strong theoretical orientation undergirding the nature of data reporting itself, compromises in the design and structure of the data constrain the capacity of systems to account for the intersections of socially constructed multiple markers of difference (Artiles, 2014a). The ways systems such as education constitute difference create contexts that simultaneously exist and are resisted individually, collectively, and, culturally. This chapter draws on the notion of *infrastructural inversion* (Bowker, Baker, Millerand, & Ribes, 2010) to make the case that how systems develop and organize data about human beings frames how individual and collective schemas of practitioners, researchers, and policymakers understand, question, and connect markers that are proxies for the human condition (Zola, 1993). In this chapter, as Bowker et al. (2010) propose, I include the research tools of science such as taxonomies, peer-review systems, extant data, and their organizational structures in the notion of infrastructure. When in use, assumptions about infrastructure design and the decisions made during the construction of data systems are often invisible to users. Data users interpret and understand their own research questions in a dialectic with available tools, thus extending the power of infrastructure development through its use and influence on how users problematize and study research, practice, and policy. From this perspective, infrastructure becomes a relational construct that dynamically informs and is informed by thinking and action within a system.

Infrastructural inversion finds particular resonance in the ways in which data repositories, such as the one that the Office of Civil Rights makes available to benchmark how students identified by race, ethnicity, and ability, fare within schools and districts. The inversion comes from surfacing the underlying assumptions that determine the organization and interaction between elements within a data system. Bowker et al. (2010) refers to this process as a way of representing the "political, ethical, and social choices that have been made" (p. 99). Notions of how data are organized, what use might be made of them, and how they order human variance underlie the construction of any project that then incorporates or uses the data. Further, agreements made to structure data in particular ways may emerge from instrumental decisions to solve immediate and logistical concerns with little consideration for how personhood is represented in the long term.

Because data repositories are human inventions that represent socially constructed units of meaning, I bring a critical frame for understanding how data constructions frame and shape understanding and action. DisCrit (Annamma, Connor, & Ferri, 2013) offers a theoretical framework for troubling issues at the intersections of race and dis/ability, which are vital to understanding racial/ethnic disproportionality in special education. Data define much of the current conversation about disproportionality. At issue is the idea that current discourse about disproportionality ignores intersectionality and avoids more nuanced views of institutionalized minoritization. DisCrit offers a framework for exposing the underlying assumptions within the data:

> DisCrit theory in education is a framework that theorizes about the ways in which race, racism, dis/ability and ableism are built into the interactions, procedures, discourses, and institutions of education, which affect students of color with dis/abilities qualitatively differently than White students with disabilities. (Annamma et al., 2013, p. 7)

To extend the DisCrit analysis, I draw on cultural historical activity theory (Cole, 1996) to examine the ways in which four school districts that surround major, public universities report and perform within the categories that constitute OCR data collection. Reporting data according to pre-ordained categories narrows observers' field of vision. Through reporting structures, some characteristics are highlighted while others become invisible. As well, highlighting specific data is a way of prioritizing their value and, as a consequence, elevating the need to respond in some way to their valued status.

I examine results from data collected through OCR and NCES to understand how districts report and use these data and how they vary across four contexts. The data, structured in specific ways, mediate the work of practitioners and district leaders, sealing fractures and cracks in which errata might appear. In addition, I show how the ways in which meaning is made from these data in iterative discourses become a process of constituting difference. In doing so, practitioners reify relationships between categories foregrounding some factors (such as poverty) while downplaying others (such as race). In each instance, the use of categorical data constructs a "model" identity for the members created by the category, erasing possibilities of within group difference.

Infrastructural inversion requires two kinds of excavation. The first requires the researcher to uncover the interdependence between technical networks that seek to identify and address problems defined in discrete blocks and the work that occurs daily in producing knowledge to address the presumed problems. The second task, which requires a critical analysis of the epistemological choices made in creating data fragments, is fraught with political positioning and power for a number of explicit and covert agendas that I explore in the chapter.

INTERSECTIONALITY AND CONTRAPUNTAL UNDERSTANDINGS

I bring a layered, contrapuntal (Artiles, 2013; Chowdhry, 2007; Kozleski, Artiles, & Waitoller, 2011) understanding of culture to these data. I use the term *contrapuntal* to highlight the tensions, gaps, and assumptions in the ways that researchers organize, collect, interpret, and act on educational data. Contrapuntal analyses also afford opportunities to examine how multiple discourses collide, interrupt, and expose gaps as well as similarities in understanding (Baxter, 2011). They examine the dynamic intersections between individual and institutional histories and processes in schools. Exploring these intersections allows us to investigate the taxonomies that structure how students are counted in school and for what purpose. As Bowker and Star (1999) suggest, "each category valorizes some point of view and silences another" (p. 5). Here, I explore a contrapuntal discourse between the perspectives that inform taxonomies, the meaning-making that ensues from mining the data, and the daily work of informing practice through data. Culture continues to pervade my discussion here because culture is both what is brought to analysis and how that analysis unfolds in discourse with others, including research teams, participants, and the peers who will review and pass judgment on the value and credibility of any work that comes from the analysis. In the process, culture is constructed as well as reified.

I also recognize the identity politics that circumscribe students whose cultural histories, experiences, and practices are orthogonally positioned in relation to the normative culture instantiated in U.S. schools through curricula, practices, and school policies. Friction between the cultures of students and those of schools offers important contexts for the minimal progress that schools across the United States have made in terms of inclusivity and equity. Inclusiveness cannot stop at borders created by imposing data structures on the design and delivery of opportunities to learn. Nevertheless, for students who are marginalized for a variety of reasons, including language, race, ethnicity, and abilities, the question of inclusion is no small matter. What can be said about what matters in terms of becoming educated in the complex spaces of schools in the United States? It turns out that there is quite a bit to say, particularly because learning occurs at the crossroads of culture as (1) identity and toolkit, (2) institutional culture, and (3) the cultural dynamic of communities (such as classrooms) at work (Artiles, 2014a).

A CONTRAPUNTAL ANALYSIS OF DATA FROM OCR AND NCES

In this section, I examine the lack of intersectionality among historically constructed markers of difference embedded in the data infrastructure of OCR and NCES. This absence of intersectionality impacts the structural and human resources that are required for institutionally sanctioned learning to occur. I emphasize the notion of institutionally sanctioned learning because schools constrain what is *supposed* to be learned. I argue that data structures themselves reify the construction of difference.

District Selection

I began by identifying four school districts in the United States where, arguably, I might find relatively progressive school systems because major research universities are located within the city boundaries. Families who sent their children to these schools would include university employees, at least some of whom had not only undergraduate but graduate degrees. With community populations that included highly educated families working in universities, it might be anticipated that public schools would be well supported along with community support for a variety of cultural, immigrant, linguistic, and racial integration and inclusion in schools. Potentially, these school districts might have less disproportionate identification of students for specialized programs such as special education. I wanted to look at the demographics of districts to determine whether these assumptions might hold true. As well, I wanted to see how two ways of looking at school contexts and outcomes might help us better understand the dynamics underlying the data structures.

I chose the following districts: (1) Lawrence Public Schools in Lawrence, Kansas, where the University of Kansas is located; (2) Madison Metropolitan School District in Madison, Wisconsin, also home to the University of Wisconsin–Madison; (3) Seattle Public Schools, Seattle, Washington, where the main campus of the University of Washington is situated; and (4) Tempe Union School District, Tempe, Arizona, which is the site of Arizona State University. Once I selected the data artifacts from OCR and NCES, I examined what categories of data were available that provided information about the racial/ethnic composition of districts and schools, the poverty level of students, and the advanced placement of students into courses that prepared students for college.

Data Sources

The OCR data collection process, also known as the Civil Rights Data Collection (CRDC), was mandated in statute and regulation to gauge the degree to which U.S. public schools provide equal educational opportunity (CRDC, 2012). The CRDC is part of the OCR strategy for ensuring enactment of the civil rights statutes in the Civil Rights Act of 1964. The CRDC includes data that track progress under Title IX from the 1972 Amendments and Section 504 of the 1973 Rehabilitation Act. First conducted in 1968, the data are sampled from all public schools and districts. Data are included from juvenile justice facilities, preschools, charter schools, alternative schools, and schools that serve students with disabilities. The 2011–2012 data collection includes only data from that school year, even though some data used in the collection come from other data collection efforts of the Department of Education. Specifically, the OCR collection includes data reported by state education agencies to the Office of Special Education Programs on the numbers of students with disabilities by diagnostic category. In most cases, student data are disaggregated by race/ethnicity, gender, disability, and English proficiency, using Department of Education definitions.

CRDC Data

Through the CRDC database, users are able to gather information at the district level on the percentage of students by race and ethnicity attending the district. Additional information allows users to examine, through these same categories, the percentage of students receiving (1) special education services; (2) Section 504 accommodations; (3) early childhood education; (4) gifted and talented programs; (5) calculus, chemistry, or physics; (6) testing for college entrance (SAT and ACT); and (7) suspensions and expulsions. One example of data output is shared in Figure 5.1. Notice that the data are revealed in sections. The race/ethnicity figure shows the district enrollment by racial category and then shows the proportion of students with disabilities by racial category. Also in Figure 5.1, in a separate table, the proportion of students in the district by gender is juxtaposed with the proportion of students with disabilities by gender. For this analysis, I gathered these charts across all four districts. As well, I used charts of school-level data as part of an artifact analysis (see Figures 5.2 and 5.3). The data structures do not change across the districts, although the data themselves are specific to each school system. I selected the same data tables and figures for the four sampled districts from each data system: (1) CRDC graphs reporting students with disabilities served under the IDEA, (2) NCES school information from the CCD public school data for the 2011–2012 school year, (3) the CRDC district profiles, and (4) the advanced placement data by district organized by student ethnicity.

NCES Disability Data

NCES data on students with disabilities are available at the state level by number and percentage of children served by (1) disability, (2) educational environment, (3) age group, and (4) race/ethnicity (for example, Figure 5.3). The data tables from NCES present the percentage of children identified for a particular disability by race/ethnicity by state. These data are compiled from individual student records by local education agencies. Data are then reported to state education agencies and, in turn, submitted to the Office of Special Education programs annually. The data are now reported as part of the Common Core data, which are then collected and disseminated on the National Center for Educational Statistics website. In both the OCR and NCES data, it is possible to examine both district- and school-level data. NCES data report enrollment by grade, race/ethnicity, gender, and free and reduced-price lunch. NCES data identify schools that are part of Title I services from the Elementary and Secondary Act (see Figure 5.3). However, the percent of students identified for special education are not available at the school level. This is because, in some schools, the number of students with disabilities in any particular category is so small that naming

Figure 5.1. OCR Data on the Madison Public Schools

10/5/2014 Students with Disabilities Served Under IDEA

Madison Metropolitan School District, Madison, WI (Survey Year 2011)

PERCENTAGE OF STUDENTS WITH DISABILITIES SERVED UNDER IDEA

by Race and Ethnicity

Compared to the overall enrollment, what is the race/ethnicity, sex, and LEP status of students with disabilities served under IDEA?

	Enrollment (District)	Students in Category (District)
Total Number	26,816	3,814
American Indian/Alaskan Native	0.0%	0.0%
Native Hawaiian/ Pacific Islander	0.0%	0.0%
Asian	9.4%	3.9%
Black	20.0%	35.8%
Hispanic	17.9%	15.8%
White	45.3%	38.5%
Two or More	6.6%	6.0%

Of the total students enrolled in the district, what proportion are students with disabilities served under IDEA?

All Students	14.2%
American Indian/Alaskan Native	0.0%
Native Hawaiian/ Pacific Islander	0.0%
Asian	5.9%
Black	24.5%
Hispanic	12.6%
White	12.1%
Two or More	12.8%

by Sex

	Enrollment (District)	Students in Category (District)
Total Number	26,816	3,814
Female	48.7%	32.3%
Male	51.3%	67.7%

	Female	Male
American Indian/Alaskan Native	0.0%	0.0%
Native Hawaiian/Pacific Islander	0.0%	0.0%
Asian	4.0%	8.0%
Black	18.3%	32.2%
Hispanic	6.8%	17.9%
White	8.3%	15.6%
Two or More	6.8%	19.0%
All Students	9.4%	18.8%

NCES ID: 5508520, Survey Year: 2011; *Source:* Office of Civil Rights.

Note: These data have been reformatted for this text from its original source.

Figure 5.2. School-Level Data from OCR

Civil Rights Data Collection	**District Profile: 2011**

District Name: Tempe Union High School District
Address: 500 W. Guadeloupe Rd., Tempe, AZ 85283
NCES District ID: 0408340   **OCR Field Office:** Western–Denver

District Characteristics

Number of schools	7
Total grade span	9–12
Number of schools offering special education services only	0
Number of schools with magnet programs	0
Number of prekindergarten students in the district (total)	N/A
Number of children awaiting initial evaluation for special education programs and related services	5
Number of schools served in LEA schools (do not include students served in non-LEA facilities	12,971
Full Day Preschool	No
Part Day Preschool	No
No Preschool:	Yes
Are the LEA services available to IDEA students only?	N/A
Are the LEA services available to non-IDEA students aged 0–2?	N/A
Are the LEA services available to non-IDEA students aged 3?	N/A
Are the LEA services available to non-IDEA students aged 4?	N/A
Written policy on prohibiting harassment and bullying on the basis of disability:	Yes
Written policy on prohibiting harassment and bullying on the basis of disability:	Yes
Number of schools in which entire school population is in the magnet program:	0
Number of charter schools:	0
Number of alternative schools:	1
District offers a general educational development (GED) program for students ages 16–19	Yes
Number of children who have been identified as having a disability and are receiving related aids and services solely under Section 504 of the Rehabilitation Act of 1973.	204
Is this LEA covered by a desegregation order or plan?	No
Full Day Kindergarten:	No
Part day Kindergarten:	No
No Kindergarten:	Yes
LEA's Preschool services available to students with disabilities	N/A
LEA's Preschool services available to all students	N/A
LEA's Preschool services available to low income students	N/A
LEA's Preschool services available to students in Title 1 schools	N/A
LEA's Preschool services available to other	N/A
No written policy on prohibiting harassment and bullying	No
Written policy on prohibiting harassment and bullying on the basis of race, color or national origin	Yes

Figure 5.2. School-Level Data from OCR *(continued)*

Enrollment Characteristics

	Male	Female
American Indian or Alaskan Native	251	317
Asian	491	459
Hawaiian/Pacific Islander	14	12
Hispanic	2,111	2,061
Black	812	767
White	3,731	3,542
Two or More Races	107	101
Total	7,517	7,279
Students with Disabilities (IDEA eligible)	814	436
Students with Disabilities (504 Only)	126	78
Students with Limited English Proficiency	48	40

Due to rounding (both numbers and percents), individual and cell values may not add to the total shown. In 2011–2012, OCR implemented new rounding rules to protect individual student privacy. All data come from the U.S. Department of Education Civil Rights Data Collection.

Note: These data have been reformatted for this text from its original source.

Figure 5.3. School-Level Data from NCES

Broken Arrow Elementary Public School

Information

Institution Name: Broken Arrow Elementary **Institution Type:** Public School
Mailing Address: 2704 Louisiana St., Lawrence, KS 66046
District: Lawrence **NCES District ID:** 2008400
County: Douglas County **NCES School ID:** 2008400001363
Phone: (785) 832-5600

Characteristics

Locale: Rural: Fringe (41) **Type:** Regular school
Charter: no **Magnet:** no
Total Teachers (FTE): 20.08 Total Students: 305
Student/Teacher Ratio: 15.19 (National Student/Teacher Ratio): 15.96

Enrollment by Race/Ethnicity		Enrollment by Grade (Grade Levels: KG–05)	
American Indian/Alaskan Native	24	KG	59
Asian/Pacific Islander*	8	1st Grade	47
Hispanic	24	2nd Grade	44
Black, non-Hispanic	17	3rd Grade	42
White, non-Hispanic	211	4th Grade	58
Two or More	21	5th Grade	55

*combined Asian and Native Hawaiian/Pacific Islander categories
Source: CCD Public Schools data, 2011–2012 school year;
National Center for Education Statistics, Institute of Education Sciences.
Note: These data have been reformatted for this text from its original source.

the category may also reveal the student, which is a violation of the Family Educational Rights and Privacy Act of 1974 (FERPA, 20 U.S.C. 1232g). For this analysis, which examines the underlying structure of data used to assess disproportionality, I chose to look at figures and tables produced by the two agencies, which allow us to examine the data categories.

GUIDANCE ON COLLECTING RACE AND ETHNICITY DATA

Guidance provided by the U.S. Department of Education states that student-level information is gathered and compiled through student records maintained at the local education agency level. Race and ethnicity data are determined at the local level. A document published by the National Center for Educational Statistics (*Managing an Identity Crisis*, National Forum on Education Statistics, Race/Ethnicity Data Implementation Task Force, 2008) offers guidance on determining individual racial/ethnic identity. Parents or guardians are asked to identify their children's race and ethnicity, first selecting between what are called ethnic categories of Hispanic and non-Hispanic. Then, they choose from among six categories: (1) American Indian or Alaskan Native, (2) Asian, (3) Black or African American, (4) Native Hawaiian or Other Pacific Islander, (5) White, or (6) two or more races. Guidance for making selections includes hints for determining which of these categories best fits—for instance, students from Middle Eastern countries states White, not Asian. It also states that students from Spain should be identified as Hispanic and one or more of the racial categories. If individuals refuse to choose a racial/ethnicity, then school personnel are mandated to use what is termed *observer identification*. The guidance recognizes that in distance education cases, it may be difficult or impossible to collect race and ethnicity data, if individuals decline self-identification. The guidance includes 45 categories of self-identification that can help observers distinguish between Hispanic and non-Hispanic. This is followed by another table in the document, indicating how individuals from specific countries and nationalities could be identified. Another table lists a set of indigenous identities that may be classified as Alaskan Native or American Indian. This guidance applies to the data collected and disseminated through NCES and OCR. Great effort is made to ensure that the data are appropriately raced.

WHO IS BEING MEASURED AND WHAT GOOD IS DONE?

Our data from both sources suggest that disability, poverty, race/ethnicity, gender, and language are cataloged but not necessarily surfaced in interaction with one another. That is, a student's gender and race are noted as separate but not intersecting categories. This creates the opportunity for particular analyses to be used (as in Figure 5.1) such as who should be identified for special education assessment, without exploring the interactions between and among a number of identities simultaneously, such as race, gender, and language. Once characteristics are cataloged, they have a tendency to disappear, particularly once individuals enter special education (Artiles, 2014a). Disability categories seem to trump other characteristics in schools. This phenomenon means that schools focus on policy shifts about disability practices, services, and supports rather than examining the interaction among the multiplicity of descriptors that are available through the data sets. When disability trumps other characteristics, it masks the notion that race markers may have created likelihood that a student's academic performance, coupled with race, pushed decisionmakers toward disability labeling.

Using infrastructure inversion means looking carefully at patterns that, because of the narrow nature of professional expertise, may not be obvious. For instance, the concern with who is and is not disabled may shift attention from how gender, race, ethnicity, and language may be perceived and addressed within the pedagogies and curricular structures within classrooms. Teacher bias toward particular ways of knowing and behaving may also legitimize labeling processes. Yuval-Davis (2006) suggests:

> In this way the interlinking grids of differential positionings in terms of class, race and ethnicity, gender and sexuality, ability, stage in the life cycle and other social divisions, tend to create, in specific historical situations, hierarchies of differential access to a variety of resources—economic, political, and cultural. (p. 199)

Bowker et al. (2010) suggest that infrastructural inversion allows researchers to explore the interdependence of technical networks and standards, while attending to the exercise of politics and knowledge production. Both NCES and OCR databases and monitoring and reporting systems can be analyzed through infrastructural inversion—on the one hand, there are the data collected on placements by race; on the other hand, there is the work of database managers that refine these data collection systems, wherein politics, knowledge production, and power reside.

Troubling Trends and Comparisons

The use of contrapuntal analysis allows for examination of gaps and differences to determine how, in this case, various ways of categorizing and revealing data suggest differing types of analyses. This kind of analysis helps reveal potential silences around culture and identity (Chowdhry, 2007). My focus was on the infrastructure of the data, which, as I argue here, directs users' gaze to particular forms of analysis about categories or classes of students.

For instance, comparisons among data categories proceed as if the categories themselves are distinctive and free from within-category variability. Arzubiaga, Artiles, King, and Harris-Murri (2008) remind us of Bourdieu's use of the concept of *epistemic reflexivity* (Bourdieu & Wacquant, 1992), which requires examining the cumulative assumptions behind the analytic tools of a field. These tools represent a collective social and intellectual view through which analytic processes are inherited and honed over time. Of course, diagnostic and demographic categories constitute a tool that is rarely deconstructed to examine its underlying epistemological assumptions.

I began this analysis with the distinctions made about race and ethnicity in both the OCR and NCES data that I examined. Each school, school system, and state was required to report the numbers of students that fall into government-mandated racial and ethnic categories. The same categories were used in both data collections because the data came from the same source, student records. As explained above, parents or guardians select from among a predetermined set of categories to complete the race/ethnicity question on student records. If they decline to select among these categories, then school personnel are mandated to select a category using observer identification. The mandate to collect this information reifies the importance of race and ethnicity in the United States because it must be done, even when families decline to do so. And, more recently, such self-identification with the backup of observer identification is also mandated in school personnel records by state data collection protocols. On the one hand, demographers can argue that without these data the degree to which some populations are subordinated through disproportional placement in remedial versus advanced learning programs cannot be investigated. On the other hand, groups like the American Anthropological Association (1997) make the case for abandoning notions of race because they have been used historically to separate, select, and benefit some groups while minoritizing and withholding benefits from others. Further, because the categories exist, they become self-evident and are assumed to be biologically, rather than socially, produced (Roberts, 2011).

Moreover, the use of a single category, such as ethnicity, assumes that the category somehow defines something about a *class* of individuals that makes that specific distinction so useful as to predict something about how the entire class might experience, understand, or act in a particular way. Yet, in any social category such as ethnicity, the differences within groups are so vast as to make the category of little meaningful use. In a raced context like the United States, the categories used to build arguments about the treatment of individuals as a class create a double bind in which social injustice may both be exposed and reified. This stems in part from the act of categorizing itself, in which categories are thought to be distinct and stable. Thus, a young child identified by his or her parents as having a specific ethnicity, who later declines to self-identify in the same way, may still be categorized by the institution, which has a duty to the government to conduct an observer identification. However, individuals' identities are fluid and change according to the contexts in which they are situated (e.g., Bernal, Alemán, & Garavito, 2009). The act of categorization assumes that ethnicity and race are static properties that reside within an individual rather than an expression of the relationship between the individual and the social context in which he or she exists.

Annamma et al. (2013) point to policy changes made in 1973 to the cutoff scores on tests of intelligence scores to distinguish between intellectual disabilities and typical functioning as an example of the social conflation between race and ability. A single category for intellectual disability remains determined based on a score on an assessment (and concomitant limitations in social and adaptive functioning). Some of the push to make the change in cutoff score was based on the recognition that students who were categorized as African American were far more likely than White students to be placed in this category. Though qualifying for special education under the intellectual disability label was changed to allow fewer students in, the proportion of students by race changed very little (Annamma et al., 2013). Further, the geographic pattern of identification did not change. Southern states were more likely to identify disproportionately African American students as having intellectual disabilities while the northern tier of states (for example, Wisconsin, Minnesota, and Montana) were more likely to identify African American students in the category of emotional and behavioral disorders (Dyson & Kozleski, 2008).

My argument is that the infrastructure itself (the categories for establishing and maintaining a particular view of students) informs the conduct of practice and the kinds of research that can be done. In both examples of the categorization of race and ethnicity and the way that diagnostic categories within special education are formed (and reformed), the substance of this argument begins to take shape. Star and Ruhleder (1996) note the interconnectedness of infrastructure. Without categories, special educators cannot practice. Without the practice of special educators, researchers cannot pursue the development of evidence-based practice. Much of the work of special education that is visible on an everyday basis is technical. That is, the work of practitioners and researchers is to determine how things are to be done. But to ask how without understanding the social and institutional dimensions of how infrastructure has been developed to answer some questions but not others is to further some agendas without addressing critical social and organizational issues. This moves us back to the artifacts selected and shared in this article.

Within both the OCR and the NCES data collections, there is a focus on compiling data about individuals. The focus of analysis is to look at additive dimensions of the data. For instance, in Figure 5.1, the data are portrayed by the proportion of students within each of the ethnic and race categories, in education and then within special education. Illustrated by two stacked bars, the data indicate the disproportional percentages of students by race and ethnic categories who are included in special education. For instance, African American students comprise 20% of the typical school-age population, kindergarten through 12th grade, but they make up 35% of the special education population. A second set of charts depicts the same kind of analysis between general and special education, examining gender. Although I present one chart for the Madison Metropolitan School District, these data are not dissimilar to the differentials found in Lawrence, Seattle, and Tempe. The data show differences along a single dimension. Within both frames, race/ethnicity and gender, there are multiple indicators that *intersect* to produce these data, not a single variable. The point here is that the data array lends itself to examining a construct like disproportionality in an additive fashion. However, the contributors to a more complex picture for disproportionality lie in the ecology of the context in which technical, contextual, and institutional factors contribute to the nature of disproportionality and to responses to it. By ignoring how diagnostic and reporting practices emerge, the work of addressing disproportionality fixes on an array of possible dimensions that are designed to shift the data in the infrastructure without examining how those data became the indices of the history, trajectory, and outcomes.

Ervelles and Minear (2010) apply the discourse of intersectionality, initially introduced by Crenshaw (1989), to expose the multiple dimensions of life experiences that produce particular forms of oppression and subordination for individuals with disabilities. Intersectionality helps trouble how being Black, poor, homeless, and disabled conspire in particular ways in specific contexts to create a life experience that has unique topography. Further, an intersectional analysis belies the notion that lived experience can be separated so that individuals can be deconstructed and sorted into parts (Yuval-Davis, 2006). The current infrastructure in both the OCR and the NCES data does not lend itself to making the connections among these intersections visible.

A disability classification is not the same for all students. Disability categories, established to determine *educational* disability, are, for the most part, criterion-referenced categories that are determined by demonstrating deficits in specific human performance categories. For instance, in the category of learning disabilities, in many states, students must meet a standard in which all other possible explanations for a discrepancy between intellectual potential (as measured by IQ) and academic performance (as measured by individually administered assessments of academic achievement) are eliminated (Turnbull, Turnbull, Wehmeyer, & Shogren, 2012). Yet, students who are White are more likely to be served in general education settings than students with the same disabilities but who are culturally and/or linguistically minoritized (Harry & Klingner, 2014). This suggests that determining *what* category to place a student in is followed by another kind of decision in which constructions of race interact with disability to determine *where* a student will be educated.

Summary

My aim is to expose the structure of the data and the underlying assumptions about categorizing and sorting. Bowker and Star (1999) remind us that sorting and classifying is part of what humans do in their everyday lives. Order is created out of this process, order that points to particular kinds of behaviors that are produced automatically. The placement of doors, public restrooms that sort by gender, bus stops placed at the end rather than the middle of blocks—these are all ways that order and predictability are structured. These systems of sorting become part of our common sense way of living, a kind of normalized flow of life that narrows the number of decisions to be made because some have already been made. Data systems are like this. The decisions to catalog, separate, and sort in particular ways have been made. What scholars are most likely to do is develop methods to study the archives, the artifacts, the products of databases. They are unlikely to ask why this system, this sort, this collection. It is in the design of the catalog itself that social and political assumptions about what counts are instantiated. The pernicious result is that practitioners, researchers, and policymakers work to make meaning of the array without examining how the array was constructed. A glimpse at the ways in which the data are portrayed, and the discussion about how the sorting occurs, reminds us that the design itself normalizes certain views of the body, ability, and race.

Author's Note: Thank you to Alfredo J. Artiles and Beth A. Ferri for their excellent notes on this manuscript.

CHAPTER 6

Social Reproduction Ideologies

Teacher Beliefs About Race and Culture

Edward Fergus

INTRODUCTION

Since as early as the 1960s, documentation of disproportionality (Dunn, 1968) of racial/ethnic minority students (particularly African American and Native American students) in special education continues to raise various types of questions. These questions include whether disproportionate outcomes represent limited school structures and opportunities, such as poor instructional capacity and inadequate research-based interventions; an accumulation effect of social conditions, such as low income and mental health concerns: and/or discriminatory beliefs and ideologies that structure educational practices, for instance deficit thinking, color-blindness, racial discomfort, and racial microaggressions (everyday instances of derogatory reminders that intensify racial awareness).

There are at least three lines of research on disproportionality. The first involves documenting the intensity of the problem. Most recently, Zhang et al.'s (2014) analysis of a 5-year trend in special education enrollment data (2004–2008) demonstrates a decrease in the overrepresentation of Black students in ID (intellectual disability) classification. However, Zhang et al. found a continued pattern of disproportionality in the other high-incidence categories (learning disability [LD] and emotional disturbance [ED]). They also cite a growing pattern of Hispanic students labeled as LD. Zhang's research confirms 2 decades of studies that show a similar pattern (e.g., Coutinho & Oswald, 2000; Fierros & Conroy, 2002; Oswald, Coutinho, & Best, 2002; Parrish, 2002; Skiba et al., 2011).

A second and related line of inquiry focuses on student- and school-level factors that predict the presence and intensity of disproportionality in special education and suspensions. For instance, Beck and Muschkin (2012) identify student-level demographic factors (e.g., gender, race, free or reduced-price lunch eligibility) as variables that explain disciplinary infractions. Additionally, they cite achievement differences as a contributor to behavioral infractions. Sullivan (2013) identifies a similar pattern between student-level demographic factors and discipline infractions. In addition to students' race and gender, Bryan et al. (2012) found that teachers' general postsecondary expectations help predict behavioral referrals. Using multilevel modeling, Skiba et al. (2014) identify varying influences of infraction type and individual- and school-level characteristics in out-of-school suspensions (OSS). A higher proportion of Black students was a key factor in predicting OSS. Systemic school-level variables, in fact, were particularly important factors in determining Black overrepresentation in suspension.

Using an extensive multivariate regression analysis, a Council of State Government Justice Center report (Fabelo et al., 2012) highlights the effect of school- and student-level variables and identifies Black males with Individualized Education Plans (IEPs) as the most vulnerable population. Other research on the connection between school and juvenile justice supports this conclusion (Nicholson-Crotty, Birchmeier, & Valentine, 2009). Moreover, disproportionality for students of color has persisted despite various policy-level shifts over the past 2 decades (including Response to Intervention and Positive Behavior Intervention Supports). Clearly, disproportionality in special education and suspension is not occurring by chance.

A third line of inquiry focuses on the documentation of district- and/or school-level educational practices and policies that are "feeding the problem." Understanding disproportionality as an educational practice, this line of research examines how the adequacy and inadequacy of teacher practice can affect disproportionality rates. This research outlines the following practices as interacting with rates of disproportionality: inadequate or inappropriate interventions, procedures, and teams for implementing interventions (Gravois & Rosenfield, 2006); differential implementation of referrals (Harry & Klingner, 2014; Klingner & Harry, 2006); inappropriate approaches to behavior management (Milner, 2006; Skiba, Peterson, & Williams, 1997; Weinstein, Thomlinson-Clarke, & Curran, 2003); inadequate framing of zero-tolerance and other behavior management policies (Noguera, 2003; Skiba, Michael, Nardo, & Peterson, 2002); and problematic beliefs about poverty, race, and learning (Skiba et al., 2006).

In sum, these various lines of research demonstrate that school processes are flawed. Yet the question remains: If these system gaps exist, why do they disproportionately affect students of color? Are there interactional factors between teachers and students within disproportionate school settings? Do teacher beliefs and ideologies frame these interactions? The research work on disproportionality focuses mainly on the structural components of schools and less on the role of practitioner beliefs about race and cultural difference. Annamma, Connor, and Ferri (2013) offer a theoretical framework to examine gaps in our knowledge about disproportionality, including practitioner beliefs of race and disability that are laden with assumptions of cognitive and behavioral inferiority.

In this chapter, I examine the beliefs of practitioners in several school districts in a Northeastern state with a disproportionate number of Black and Latino students in special education and suspensions (see Tables 6.1 and 6.2).

Specifically, I analyze beliefs and constructs about race and culture, and how they intersect with teachers' expectations for students' achievement and their own self-efficacy as practitioners. To understand the continuous pattern of disproportionality in special education and behavioral referrals, we need to identify the beliefs and constructs about race and cultural difference that exist in schools.

This chapter juxtaposes Disabilities Studies and Critical Race Theory to examine educational practices that promulgate a deficit orientation for children from marginalized populations. As an empirical exploration, this chapter uses reproduction theories to explore the relevance of teacher ideology,

Table 6.1. School District Student Demographics

	Upper Falls	Schooner
Total Student Enrollment	6,376	9,606
Race/Ethnicity		
White	1%	33%
Black	51%	34%
Asian	1%	16%
Latino	47%	16%
Multiracial	< 1%	16%
Other	0%	
Special education status (%)	9%	17%
ELL status (%)	15%	4%
Free/Reduced-Price Lunch Program (FRLP)		
Free	44%	65%9%
Reduced	10%	9%
Disproportionality Rate (Risk Ratio) of Black Students		
Special education	2.8	2.1
Suspension	4.0	4.1

Table 6.2. Demographics of Survey Respondents

Survey respondents	713	Race/Ethnicity	
School Level		White	77.2%
Elementary	342	Black	8.2%
Middle school	150	Asian	0.5%
High school	214	Latino*	7.7%
Educational Position		Native American	0.5%
Teacher	66.5%	Multiracial	6%
Teacher aide/assistant	8.4%	Other	
Guidance/social work	6.6%	**Gender**	
School administrator	4.8%	Female	80%
District administrator	1.1%	Male	20%
Other	12.6%	**Years of Experience**	
		1 to 3 years	1.2%
		4 to 6 years	9.7%
		7 to 9 years	10.5%
		10 or more years	43.4%
		Missing information	35.3%

*Latino/Hispanic identification is not calculated into overall percentage because respondents were allowed to identify their own ethnicity and race.

not as an individually based phenomenon, but rather as dominant ideologies that are continually reproduced and nested within educational systems. By framing the study this way, I aim to avoid demonizing practitioners and to reify the notion that beliefs about race and cultural difference are part of the societal "water supply" that teachers are reproducing.

SOCIAL AND CULTURAL REPRODUCTION THEORY: CONNECTING TEACHER BELIEFS, RACIALIZED DIS/ABILITIES, AND SUSPENSIONS

Reproduction theorists argue that the main function of schools is to reproduce dominant ideologies, forms of knowledge, and the skills needed to maintain the social division of labor (e.g., Althusser, 1971a; Bourdieu, 1977a; Bowles & Gintis, 1976; Giroux, 1983). Thus, reproduction theory is involved in relationships among schools, the state, and the economy. In addition, a reproduction framework implies that in order to understand the underlying intent of schools, it is necessary to analyze the way schools operate as agents of social and cultural reproduction. This theoretical lens seeks to illustrate schools' role in reproducing class division, gender binaries, and racial/ethnic stratification.

In this study, I focus on economic and cultural reproduction to examine the significance of teachers' beliefs about culture, race, poverty, and difference. The economic-reproductive model offers several important contributions to DisCrit. The focus on the relationship between schools and the workplace illustrates the role schools play in reproducing the social division of labor. This framework has also illuminated the ideological convictions of class and power and how they shape educational experience, especially through the hidden curriculum (what is not explicitly taught, but is implicit in practices, such as the maintenance of social class). Schools can thus be seen as active agents in the reproduction of social inequality. As Bowles and Gintis (1976) contend, schools are "institutions which serve to perpetuate the social relationships of economic life through which these patterns are set, by facilitating a smooth integration of youth into the labor force" (p. 11).

Schools are designed to provide a reserve of labor that abides by and believes in a meritocratic system (that is, hard work equals high achievement). They reinforce the need to stratify people according to social groups and to instill social relationships based on dominance and subordinancy. For example, schools in working-class neighborhoods tend to stress rule-following, dependability, and learning to work without direct supervision. Such ideological orientations exist in both traditional public and charter schools that have developed over the past decade. Schools with this focus invoke strategies such as having students begin the school year sitting on the floor and making them demonstrate appropriate behaviors in order to "earn" their desks. These schools often have detention rooms with desks facing the wall and students being punished are required to write papers about how they need to "transform" their character. Schools in the suburbs and private schools, on the other hand, tend to have a more open atmosphere that emphasizes leadership norms and higher-order thinking.

Schools that maintain different class tracks and emphasize different values and expectations for students in various tracks also reflect these variations. For example, in New York City, different schools are co-located on different floors of buildings. School A may have a computer lab with new iMacs and on another floor School B may have a computer lab stocked with refurbished PCs from a decade ago. Teachers participate in this reproduction process by shifting their expectation levels for students from differing social classes. Thus, teacher expectations often interact with patterns of educational inequity (e.g., Oates, 2003; Shim, 2014).

Althusser (1971b) adds to Bowles and Gintis's (1976) structural analysis by stressing that reproduction in schools occurs through the legitimation of ideologies that include nationalism, educational opportunity, meritocracy, and achievement ideology. Educational practices based on these ideologies include special education classification, segregated classes, gifted program placement, and alternative schools for students with problem behaviors. Schools promote meritocracy by admonishing students to "do your best" and "put effort into your work," and by fostering an ideology of achievement based on individual effort and cognitive prowess. This absolves schools from any responsibility to promote access and opportunity for all students. Thus, as ideologies are absorbed and translated into educational practice, school practitioners receive a license to continuously frame issues such as overrepresentation of racial/ethnic minority students in special education and suspension, and underrepresentation in gifted and honors/AP programs, as a problem with individual students, not the system. These ideologies normalize tracking, special education seclusion, and so forth as rationalized structures.

Institutions are more than simply sterile and objective arenas, but rather environments latent with connected cultural understandings, beliefs, and expectations that mirror societal, social, and cultural reproduction. A noted absence in existing research is the need to attend to how racial and cultural differences frame educational ideologies and expectations, and subsequently reflect societal race-based stratification. Critical Race Theory (CRT) and Culturally Responsive Pedagogy (CRP) provide important theoretical terrain for outlining the significance of racial and cultural differences within schools. CRT scholarship helps us consider how race and racism are structured within systems (Bonilla-Silva, 2006; Ladson-Billings & Tate, 1995), how the reproduction of ideologies such as color-blindness and race neutrality minimize the social experiences of racialized groups (Bonilla-Silva, 2006), and how racist behavior exists and becomes operationalized in forms such as laissez-faire racism (Bobo & Smith, 1998) and microaggressions (Solorzano, Ceja, & Yosso, 2000; Sue, 2010). Culturally Responsive Pedagogy also establishes the relevance of cultural artifacts (e.g., home life artifacts, storytelling activities) as integral to engagement and learning (Brown-Jeffy & Cooper, 2011; Gay, 2010; Ladson-Billings, 1995). More specifically, CRP scholarship highlights the absence of the social experiences of marginalized populations in the framing of pedagogy and curriculum and identifies principles, such as identity development, cognitive engagement, relational engagement, and empowering curriculum and instruction.

CRT and CRP extend social and cultural reproduction theory by focusing on how the process of reproduction is also laden with deficit views of race. Overall, social and cultural reproduction and CRT provide an analytical framework for exploring how teachers' beliefs and ideologies interact with representations of societal ideologies that help reproduce social stratification.

Methods for Investigating Sociocultural Considerations of Disproportionality

Starting in 2011, the Disproportionality School Climate (DSC) survey was conducted annually as part of a statewide project, led by the researcher as principal investigator, with school districts cited for disproportionate representation of Black and Latino students in special education and suspension. The survey contains multiple scales and items that focus on teachers' perceptions of the following areas: (1) school-level pre-referral and intervention processes; (2) race and cultural difference; (3) teacher self-efficacy; (4) expectations of student educational achievement; (5) self-reports of monthly academic and behavioral referrals; and (6) cultural responsive instruction practices. Items are measured on a 6-point Likert scale where 1 = Strongly Disagree, 2 = Disagree, 3 = Somewhat Disagree, 4 = Somewhat Agree, 5 = Agree, and 6 = Strongly Agree.

Interestingly, all states are allowed to determine the formula and rate of classification and suspension that constitutes overrepresentation. This project works with school districts statewide that have a risk ratio rate of 2.5 and higher comparing White students and Students of Color in special education, and a risk ratio 4.0 or higher in comparing the suspension of nondisabled students to those with disability labels by race.

The survey data for this analysis comes from the 2012–2013 school year, when more than 1,600 practitioners from a Northeastern state voluntarily participated in the online survey. This chapter analyzes a subset of participants from two districts with similar rates of disproportionality during the same school year.

Findings

The survey's findings point to some important questions that have yet to be posed in current research on disproportionality (see Tables 6.3 and 6.4).

First, the teachers in the study maintained the highest average agreement with items on cultural responsibility, which measures the degree to which practitioners feel a sense of responsibility to learn about the experiences of students from racial/ethnic minorities and adapt their instruction/practices accordingly. On average, teachers in the study disagreed with notions of experiencing racial discomfort themselves. This suggests that the surveyed teachers report a degree of comfort in discussing notions of racial and cultural difference. However, among the other three subscales—color-blindness, deficit thinking, and cultural awareness—teachers report

Table 6.3. Descriptive of Perceptions of Culture and Race, Self-Efficacy, Expectations, and Confidence Variables

	Mean	SD
Perceptions of Culture and Race		
Responsibility	4.79	0.66
Discomfort	2.04	0.60
Color-blindness	3.74	0.80
Deficit thinking	2.86	0.84
Cultural awareness and knowledge	3.43	0.90
Educational Achievement Expectations		
Low-performing students	2.53	1.41
Moderate-performing students	4.09	1.37
High-performing students	5.54	1.27
Pedagogical and Instructional Capacity		
Confidence	3.15	0.90
Self-efficacy	3.71	0.39

ambivalence with color-blind perspectives. Similarly, teachers indicate uncertainty about having a responsibility to be culturally aware. Finally, teachers were on average situated between disagree and somewhat disagree on the deficit thinking subscale, which indicates they do not strongly disagree with items on deficit thinking.

Any patterns in the data must be situated within several contextual factors. Participants were all teachers who were practicing within (1) school districts with significant racial/ethnic disproportionality in special education placement and behavioral referrals, (2) school districts with a predominantly Black and Latino student population, and (3) schools where the staff was mostly White and female. Such contextual patterns pose some additional research questions and areas of inquiry. For instance, presuming that the beliefs these teachers expressed are typical across various school settings, how do these beliefs interact with teacher behaviors, particularly those related to academic and behavioral referrals of students?

The second important preliminary finding is a pattern of correlation between belief areas. Specifically, there was a negative moderate relationship between pedagogical confidence and deficit thinking ($r = -.359$; $p < .01$). In other words, the more pedagogical confidence participants had, the less likely they were to express a deficit orientation in relation to their students. Deficit thinking also had a negative moderate correlation with cultural responsibility ($r = -.360$; $p < .01$) and cultural awareness and knowledge ($r =$

Table 6.4. Correlations of Perceptions of Culture and Race, Teacher Self-Efficacy, and Student Achievement Expectations

Bivariate Correlations Between PCR, Self-Efficacy, Confidence, and Student Achievement Expectations

Scales	1	2	3	4	5	6	7	8	9
1. Low-performing student expectation	—								
2. Average-performing student expectation	.716**	—							
3. High-performing student expectation	.417**	.725**	—						
4. Pedagogical confidence	.235**	.239**	.206**	—					
5. Cultural responsibility	.182**	.213**	.203**	.262**	—				
6. Racial discomfort	-.096*	-.144**	-.149**	-.149**	-.267**	—			
7. Color-blindness	-.102*	-.129**	-.074**	-.097	-.173**	.208**	—		
8. Deficit thinking	-.337*	-.354**	-.232**	-.359**	-.360**	.413**	.508**	—	
9. Cultural awareness and knowledge	.097	.103*	.062	.013	.269**	-.125*	-.458**	-.309**	—

Note: Correlations marked with an asterisk (*) were significant at $p < .05$. Correlations marked with two asterisks (**) were significant at $p < .01$.

125

$-.309$; $p < .01$). That is, as deficit thinking increased, cultural responsibility, awareness, and knowledge decreased. In addition, deficit thinking had a positive moderate correlation with color-blindness ($r = .508$; $p < .01$) and racial discomfort ($r = .413$; $p < .01$). As deficit thinking increased, color-blindness and racial discomfort increased as well. These patterns raise questions, such as how these beliefs interact among teachers who write a high, moderate, and low level of academic and behavioral referrals. Given that most of the teachers in the study were White females, how do these belief correlations vary among White female teachers who write a high, moderate, and low level of academic and behavioral referrals? Also, could some of these belief correlations be mediated by exposure to, and experience with, racial/ethnic populations? Overall, these patterns indicate the need to explore the impact of deficit thinking, which affects various socially and academically marginalized groups in schools (such as students with disabilities, racial/ethnic minority groups, and English language learners).

CONCLUSION

The focus of this study was to use social reproduction theory to examine whether ideologies laden with racial constructs, such as deficit thinking, color-blindness, and others, interact with teachers' self-reports of their pedagogical and instructional capacities. Utilizing reproduction theory, and placing it in dialogue with DisCrit (Annamma et al., 2013) to examine disproportionality, allows for a macrolevel contemplation of the relationship among limitations ascribed by teacher beliefs, low expectations of student academic performance, disingenuous ideologies of color-blindness, deficit thinking, and low self-confidence in pedagogical skills. Specifically, DisCrit Tenet Three, which "emphasizes the social constructions of race and ability and yet recognizes the material and psychological impacts of being labeled as raced or dis/abled, which sets one outside of the western cultural norms" (Annamma et al., 2013, p. 11) provides an opportunity for this macrolevel theoretical approach that allows us to question how we approach the dialogue of race and cultural difference among adults in ways that result in changes to internalized behaviors and challenge social reproduction. Framing this examination of teacher beliefs and ideologies within these theories allows us to consider how macrolevel educational policies can consider the relevance of teacher beliefs and ideologies as a point of reference to develop new policies that can systematically address or tackle teacher beliefs.

This chapter outlines some terrain for exploring teacher beliefs and practices in disproportionate school settings and innovative ways in which to explore the relationship between the two. It also poses questions about why some relationships between teacher perceptions, beliefs, and pedagogy exist in relation to overrepresentation. This conversation is not new. We know from prior research that teachers' ideologies and beliefs about the student population they serve can have a positive or negative effect on student outcomes via the actions and behaviors teachers choose to employ in the classroom (e.g., Madon, Jussim, & Eccles, 1997; Madon et al., 1998, 2001; Proctor, 1984). The findings reported in these studies underscore the significance of teachers' beliefs, particularly the types of thinking that are laden with negative notions about race and cultural difference.

Part IV

SCHOOL-TO-PRISON PIPELINE

CHAPTER 7

Shadow Play

DisCrit, Dis/respectability, and Carceral Logics

D. L. Adams
Nirmala Erevelles

DIS-LOCATING PRACTICES: MATTER OUT OF (WHITE) PLACE

The shadows of Michael Brown, Renisha McBride, Jordan Davis, and Trayvon Martin cast a somber pall as we write this chapter—each of them unarmed young Black men and women shot down by White men simply because they were Black (and therefore *terrifying* to their killers). Following each murder were outraged protests from some in the community, horrified at what they perceived to be contemporary modes of lynching, while others have sought to explain away these murders on the grounds that every one of their killers faced a justifiable threat by the mere presence of young Black bodies "trespassing" in what are presumably White-only spaces. As we write this chapter, only Michael Dunn, who shot into a car of Black teenagers in a gas station when they refused to turn their music down, killing Jordan Davis, one of the car's occupants while injuring others, has been convicted. Ricocheting amid the whine of bullets shot in sharp succession, amid desperate pleas for life as victims' bodies fell, amid the poignant grief of parents having to assert their children's worth as human beings, and amid angry protests by people of color who followed with a simple plea of "Don't shoot!" was the even more somber lesson continuously reasserted as irrefutable fact—Black bodies are simply "matter out of place" (Douglas, 1966).

But there are other shadows that also cast a deathly pall on this chapter—other victims of police brutality—who make scarcely a ripple in our collective moral outrage at such violence. In early November 2014, Kaldrick Donald, a 24-year-old Black man with mental disabilities, was shot to death in his bathroom by a police officer who was responding to a call from his mother asking for help to get her son to take his medications (Inquisitr,

2014). In August 2014, 25-year-old Ezell Ford was shot to death on a city street in Los Angeles by two police officers who, neighbors insisted, knew that Ford was diagnosed with a mental illness (Vives, Mather, & Winton, 2014). Three years earlier, in College Park, Maryland, an autistic Black man, Isaac Yearby, acquired brain injuries after being Tasered by police officers when asked to remove his hands from his pockets (Chirico, 2014). These are just a few of the many names and stories of disabled Black men and women encountering police brutality that Black disabled activist and cultural worker Leroy Moore has generated in a CD compilation of Krip-Hop artists (disabled hip-hop artists) entitled *Police Brutality Profiling MixTape* (BillyJam, 2012). In this work, Moore collaborates with other Krip-Hop artists to point to how race, class, gender, and disability coalesce in often terrifying ways to justify the callous and often unremarked killings of Black disabled bodies. Why, Moore asks, is disability not foregrounded while protesting police brutality against Black citizens?

One can hear echoes of Moore's question in the arguments articulated by Annamma et al. (2013) who also foreground the intersectional practices of racism and ableism via their formulation of Disability Studies and Critical Race Theory (DisCrit). Like Moore, DisCrit scholarship also urges us to explore the violent material practices by which race and disability coalesce at the intersections of gender identity, sexuality, and class that enable the fatal dis-location of certain marked bodies as matter out of (White) (normative) place. But not all dis-locations are fatal. And not all dis-locating practices are readily recognizable by an outraged public, nor are all perpetrators and victims easily identified in these dis-locations. In fact, because some dis-locating practices are so obviously violent, they serve to obscure other normalized everyday practices enacted by seemingly well-intentioned individuals to dis-locate bodies from classrooms, families, and communities and into carceral settings such as alternative schools, prisons, and institutions (Ben-Moshe, 2013). Focusing particularly on educational contexts, in this chapter we describe how oppressive (rather than empowering) discourses of disability and race are deployed at the intersections of social difference to justify the casual dis-location of student bodies along the school-to-prison pipeline by conceiving these bodies as matter out of (White, normative) place.

To ground this argument, we provide examples from an empirical study conducted in an urban elementary school in the northeastern United States. Our objective is to map out the actual pedagogical and representational practices that track youth into the school-to-prison pipeline. We use the term *school-to-prison pipeline* to highlight a complex network of relations that naturalize the movement of youth of color (many with identified or unidentified disabilities) from our schools and communities into underemployment or unemployment, short-term detention, and ultimately long-term (or even lifelong) incarceration (Kim, Losen, & Hewitt, 2010;

Meiners, 2007; Wald & Losen, 2003). Such practices of pathologization, racialization, and criminalization deployed in educational contexts are social processes, not entities inherent in specific bodies. Further, these practices cannot be disentangled as they work in tandem to reduce the life chances of certain (disabled, gender-nonconforming) youth (of color) and not others. Additionally, an allegiance to dis/respectability politics (which we discuss in the next section) in schools casts the shadow of disability as dis/reputable so as to mute the violence in the everyday practices of schooling that justify the pathologization and criminalization of racialized bodies.

DisCrit and the Politics of Respectability

Moore's work on police brutality at the intersection of race, class, and disability also foregrounds the cruel irony that Black disabled people (as well as those from other racial and ethnic groups) also experience violence at the hands of members of their own community. Moore explains that discourses that frame disability as a dangerous burden are so pervasive that hateful language and imagery regarding disability is omnipresent in politics, in the media, and even in the work of hip-hop artists: "[F]rom Republican presidential candidate, Rick Santorum, who said that his disabled daughter cost a lot; to movies like *21 Jump Street* in which Ice Cube makes fun of people with autism; and, to musicians from hard rock to hip-hop who continue to sing lyrics like 'What a waste like a cripple . . .'" (Hills, 2012). So prevalent are these hateful representations that even in instances where parents have murdered their own disabled children, courts have been more sympathetic to the parents for the assumed hardships of raising a disabled child. Here, disability itself becomes the alibi.

In the online magazine *Bitch Media*, Tamara Winfrey Harris (2012) describes the troubling role that respectability plays in the intersectional politics of race, class, and gender. Harris writes:

> Respectability politics work[s] to counter negative views of Blackness by aggressively adopting the manners and morality that the dominant culture deems "respectable." The approach emerged in reaction to white racism that labeled Blackness as "other"—degenerate and substandard—with roots in an assimilationist narrative that prevailed in the late-19th-century United States. Black activists and allies believed that acceptance and respect for African-Americans would come by showing the majority culture "we are just like you."

The danger inherent in the assimilationist practices of respectability politics as described by Harris is that they unwittingly justify the dehumanization of Black bodies that fail to assimilate, and in doing so, also justify the violence meted out against them. For example, in the aftermath of each of the violent acts perpetrated against Black bodies described at the beginning of this chapter, violence was justified by their perpetrators and supported in the mass media by claims that these unarmed Black victims had histories and lifestyles that did not adhere strictly to some predetermined normative notions of respectability. By the same token, those who sought justice for those murdered by foregrounding their humanity could do so only through attempting to prove that the victims met the stringent demands of (White, bourgeois, heteronormative) respectability.

Notable in Harris's definition of respectability politics is the shadowy presence of disability that is unremarked upon. Almost intangible in its concrete form and yet insistent in its nebulous presence, the dis/respectable politics of disability hovers over these narratives, justifying the negation of Black life. Echoing Moore's assertion at the beginning of this chapter, Disability Studies scholars working at the intersections of race and disability (Baynton, 2001; Bell, 2006; Ben-Moshe, 2013; Blanchett, 2010; Chen, 2013; Erevelles, 2011b; Ferri & Connor, 2006; Samuels, 2014) have all described how oppressive discourses of disability have historically been used to justify the dehumanization of racialized bodies in ways that support oppressive practices such as slavery, settler colonialism, neocolonialism, educational and residential segregation, employment discrimination, as well as the institutionalization and incarceration of racialized bodies. As a result, Watts and Erevelles (2004) pointed out that even potential intellectual allies such as Critical Race Theorists have unwittingly sought to distance themselves from all associations with disability because disability has historically cast a long shadow on the humanity of racialized communities not just in the United States, but also in transnational contexts.

It is here, then, that we bring together the unsettling discourses of respectability politics in critical engagement with what Annamma, Connor, and Ferri (2013) have defined as DisCrit in order to account for what we are calling dis/respectability politics. According to Annamma et al. (2013), DisCrit rejects the habitual practice of simply adding disability to analyses of the intersectional politics of race, class, gender identity, and sexuality to argue that "racism and ableism are normalizing processes that are interconnected and collusive" (p. 7). Grounding their argument specifically in educational contexts (but not limited to these contexts), Annamma et al. (2013) describe how "dis/ability and race first became equated and molded through pseudo-sciences, but [were] later further cemented through seemingly 'objective' clinical assessment practices . . . [that were further] reified through laws, policies, and programs until these concepts became uncritically conflated and viewed as the natural order of things" (p. 15).

Nestled in the interplay of these discursive and material practices are the politics of citizenship that bring race and disability into play by "triggering stereotypic associations with weaknesses, including fears of individuals seen as unhealthy, unable to adequately compete in work and war, with their reproductive potential questioned, feared or even forcibly managed" (Annamma et al., 2013, p. 16). DisCrit foregrounds the problematic ways in which the (non)recognition of racialized bodies as citizens is materialized via the oppressive practices of, for example, educational segregation, immigration policies, and incarceration, by associating racialized bodies with discourses of disability that are the apparent embodiment of degeneracy and dis/respectability.

In this chapter, we locate DisCrit in critical engagement with the racial implications inherent in dis/respectability politics as it plays out in educational contexts. Although not identified as such until Annamma et al.'s (2013) article, there has been a significant body of research that has echoed several of the significant analytical tenets of DisCrit in its foregrounding of the overrepresentation of students from nondominant cultural groups in special education classes based on dubious labels such as *emotionally disturbed/behaviorally disordered* and *linguistically disabled* (Artiles, 2013; Blanchett, 2010; Erevelles, 2014; Harry & Klingner, 2014). Much of this research exhaustively highlights the complicated ways in which disability is attributed to racialized bodies to ensure their segregation in educational settings. In doing so, scholars argue for intersectional analyses that foreground the negative associations of disability for students in nondominant cultural groups in the United States and argue for culturally responsive interventions to reduce the detrimental effects of these associations with disability. And yet, in making what we believe are empowering moves for culturally responsive educational practices, we nevertheless continue to locate disability within the problematic purview of dis/respectability politics.

In making this observation, we have absolutely no intention of rehabilitating disability so as to meet the stringent demands of respectability. By refusing rehabilitation, we agree with Harris (2012) that respectability does not reside within individual bodies but within powerful institutions and systems that propagate normative ideologies that serve to control the oppressed rather than challenge the violent practices of the oppressor. What Harris (2012) fails to foreground is that these normative institutions and systems support ableist ideologies (Campbell, 2009) that cast wavering shadows on those subjectivities constituted at the intersections of race, class, gender identity, sexuality, and disability. Our interest in engaging both DisCrit and respectability politics is to show how both disability and race as socially constructed categories are mutually constitutive of each other. Our focus is primarily on the simultaneous process of "becoming Black" *and* "becoming disabled" that is usually uncritically defined as "natural" deviance or dis/respectability that also foregrounds a complex intersectional politics of race, class, and disability that is used to justify the pathologization and criminalization of racialized subjects in educational contexts (Ben-Moshe et al., 2014; Erevelles, 2014).

Background of the Study

Our argument is grounded in a study investigating current practices of discipline used in schools that initiate the dis-location of students along the school-to-prison pipeline. We argue that some students because of their race, class, and disability are marked as deviant through the everyday practices of school discipline by appealing to the seemingly innocuous logic of dis/respectability. Adams's (dissertation) research into school discipline and behavior management stems from various experiences as a special education teacher in segregated settings and as a graduate student and instructor in a teacher preparation program. Adams's teaching experiences in a limited secure residential facility (correctional facility) for boys in central New York, run by the New York State Office of Children and Family Services, foregrounded blatant inequities at the intersection of race and disability in the U.S. educational and penal system. The youth assigned to these services were from the boroughs of New York City, supporting a demographic of approximately 90% African American, 8% Latino, and 2% White. Most of the boys were enrolled in special education classrooms and arrived at the classrooms with school records contained in a three-ring binder filled with data on discipline that had been collected on the boys over their years in school.

Although some of the boys were "residents" (a label used by the staff) who were sent to the correctional facility for car theft or drug possession/sales, many others were placed there for violations as a result of school discipline issues and truancy (truancy can be related to suspension from school)—also known as Person in Need of Supervision (PINS) violations. According to New York State Unified Court System (n.d.), "A child under the age of 18 who does not attend school, or behaves in a way that is dangerous or out of control, or often disobeys his or her parents, guardians or other authorities, may be found to be a Person In Need of Supervision or PINS." Violation of PINS can place children as young as 8 years old in a juvenile residential facility. Thus, a child who does not attend school or has been disciplined by the school, leading to suspensions, can be taken to court through the use of PINS, creating another level of surveillance by local and state entities that can be used as a way to remove the child from school and possibly the family, now labeled as dysfunctional (dis/respectable), thereby providing an explanation for the attribution of delinquency to the child.

Although the number of youth being sent to residential placements over the past decade has decreased, there continues to be a statistical significance in the racial makeup of the population being placed in these segregated settings. The New York State Office of Children and Family Services (OCFS) 2012 Annual Report showed that 812 youth were placed in residential facilities, with 404 placed in voluntary agencies, such as foster care or private care centers that serve as alternative placements for youth in homes that are deemed unfit to support the needs of children living there. These voluntary agencies benefit from funding that comes from the state and federal government, which places them within the prison/disability industrial complex. The remaining 408 youth were placed in OCFS facilities. The demographics for the OCFS placements in 2012 were as follows: 84% male, 58% African American, 27% Latino, and 9% White. Of the 200 who were identified as needing special education services, 42% were classified as emotionally disturbed/autistic and 22% were labeled learning disabled. On an interesting note, placing emotional disturbance and autism under the same category revealed the problematic assumptions often made between aggressive /violent behavior and autism.

Schools, however, are not just conduits to the prison system, but also agents of the same carceral racist logic, even in the absence of imprisonment. Rodriguez (2010) states that

> the prison has become central to the (re)production and (re)invention of a robust and historically dynamic white supremacist state: at its farthest institutional reaches, the prison has developed a capacity to organize and disrupt the most taken-for-granted features of everyday social life, including "family," "community," "school," and individual social identities. (p. 7)

Thus, through the use of "zero-tolerance" policies, schools have created institutions that police students through the surveillance of behavior and a hyper-vigilance directed toward students marked as both raced *and* disabled, resulting in their overrepresentation in office discipline referrals, suspensions, segregated classrooms, alternative schools, and ultimately incarceration.

Although the statistics we include may reinforce what is already common knowledge in the research on overrepresentation of children of color in special education and in the prison system, we argue that these statistics also provide an empirical backdrop to understand the processes that are involved in positioning students located at the intersections of race, class, and disability in punitive segregated educational facilities. Research in Disability Studies in Education (DSE) demonstrates the ways in which students become "disabled" under specific social and educational processes that have the power to associate certain categories of students with specific labels and not others (Artiles, 2013). For instance, students of color and those from low socioeconomic status often receive labels such as emotionally disturbed/ behaviorally disordered while more affluent, White students receive labels such as a specific learning disability or autism (Mandell et al., 2009; Tincani, Travers, & Boutot, 2009). These differential labels lead to further inequalities in services rendered and treatment offered, resulting in the provision of medical treatment and educational interventions for some and criminalization (referrals, pushout, expulsions) for others (Erevelles, 2014). Similarly, Critical Race Theory (CRT) shows how these processes of criminalization

are also socially produced by labeling certain students, mostly boys of col-
or, as dangerous and in need of containment or expulsion (Artiles, 2013;
Watts & Erevelles, 2004). In this chapter, we combine the two theoretical
approaches of Disability Studies in Education and Critical Race Theory by
using the framework of DisCrit to discuss how the processes of labeling and
criminalization contribute to the school-to-prison pipeline for racialized students with special education labels by alluding to the oppressive discourse
of dis/respectability politics.

Notes on Methods: The Setting and Participants

The setting for this study is Morgan Elementary School (pseudonym), an
urban elementary school with 387 enrolled students. The demographics of
the student population at the time of the study was 83% Black, 11% White,
5% Hispanic, and 1% Native American. Of the total population, 84% of
the students were eligible for free lunch and 5% were eligible for lunch at
a reduced price, indicating that 89% of the student population came from
low-income families. Morgan Elementary had been under state review for 8
years for not meeting adequate yearly progress and for reporting the highest
incidence of discipline problems (such as office referrals and suspensions) of
all the elementary schools in the district, with an average number of discipline incidents of 25% over a 5-year period. In addition, Morgan had one
of the lowest student proficiency rates in the district, with approximately
only 20% of its students scoring at the proficient level on the state tests. The
community in which the school was located reported a child poverty rate of
62%, and 32% of the adults in the surrounding area had not earned a high
school diploma.

The data for the study were collected over 2 school years via open-ended
interviews conducted by the first author with six teachers who were White
women; one principal, who was a White woman; and two African American
women: the social worker and a school staff member. The participants were
all members of the Positive Behavior Supports (PBIS) Team in charge of
the implementation of their schoolwide behavior management system. In
addition to the interviews, Adams also attended the PBIS Team meetings
as a participant observer to the process of implementation. Although there
were rich data from multiple sources, for this study we only included the
interviews of three White teachers and the principal. Each of the classroom
teachers was struggling with managing the behaviors of students she worked
with while the principal made decisions about the way students were disciplined, and so their interviews highlighted the processes by which students
were framed as dis/respectable and therefore deviant.

Sixteen interviews were conducted in various locations throughout the
school building, along with 22 hours of participant observation. All interviews were transcribed and coded for themes that emerged from the data.

For this chapter, we draw on only a small portion of the data set that focused specifically on ways in which White school personnel pathologized the students, the families, and the community at large by appealing to the problematic discourses of dis/respectability. In the next section, we discuss the ways in which the shadows of race, class, and disability, both apparent and yet nebulous at the same time, served to pathologize students and justify their dis-location to segregated and ultimately carceral educational contexts.

Ideologies of Dis-Location

The interviews with the principal and faculty at Morgan Elementary address key concepts that point to the casual pathologization of students, their families, and their community. Listening carefully to the responses by the principal and the faculty, we found that although race, class, and disability are never explicitly mentioned in the interviews, their shadowy presence dominated the narratives by appealing to the oppressive deployment of respectability politics. We identified discourses of dis/respectability in the teachers' narratives by looking for coded language/catchphrases such as *gangs*, *drugs*, *rebellious*, and *the community*. In this section of the chapter, we identify the ideologies of dis-location as articulated by the principal and the teachers that locate dis/respectability as inherent in their students, families, and communities and explore the implications these ideologies have for students via the critical lens of DisCrit.

"Dangerous Minds in Criminal Space"

School personnel justified the transformation of educational institutions into prison-like settings by deploying the language of criminality—a more virulent marker of dis/respectability. For example, the new principal of Morgan Elementary, Wendy (a White principal who had been at the school for 1 year and an administrator with the district for 12 years) was hired to help with the school's discipline issues because of her prior training and experience implementing School-Wide Positive Behavior Supports (SWPBIS). SWPBIS was implemented in the school to address the outstanding number of discipline referrals and suspensions, as well as to improve academic performance. Wendy joked in an interview that she was referred to as "the closer" because wherever she went, the school would end up closing, although she claimed she was there to help. Unfortunately, Morgan Elementary closed after Wendy's second year there because the school had an increase in office referrals and suspension rates in addition to poor performance on state tests.

In the following quote, Wendy talked about a school (Wayne Middle School—a pseudonym) where she had formerly been an administrator. The school had a lot of behavioral referrals of students and was on the state's Persistently Dangerous Schools list. While describing the school, Wendy

referenced films that depicted teachers saving "bad" urban youth through
their talented pedagogies:

> And—but we [administers and teachers] . . . did a really good job
> with ending gang stuff, like the fights in school. The big thing that
> we saw is violence, like bringing weapons into school and you know,
> big gang kind of fights. So actually, we felt like from what we did
> from 2002 to 2003 were huge. We got the gangs and the drugs and
> the weapons out of the school, and the kind of referral[s]. . . . It was
> about disruptive behavior, like kids doing more like, "Fuck this, I'm
> not going to do it and storming out of the classroom." . . . So we felt
> like, what do you mean we're on a Persistently Dangerous list? This
> is a school that had actually kids dealing drugs in the hall, you know
> what I mean? It was like all those bad movies, you know, like *Stand
> and Deliver . . . Dangerous Minds*, that's—I mean, no kidding, that's
> what Wayne Middle School looked like between 2000 and 2003.

When the school decided to implement a schoolwide Positive Behavior
Supports discipline system to reduce the high rates of discipline referrals
and suspensions, a schoolwide token system was used as a motivator to
provide Positive Behavioral Supports. Here, the implicit assumption was
that bad behavior is an individual choice and has no social history. Wendy
discussed the use of "Wayne Dollars"—tokens given to students as rewards for making good choices. Unfortunately, the value placed on Wayne
Dollars by the students in Wendy's former school did not manifest itself in
a positive way. Students who were unable to earn the Wayne Dollars because of discipline problems resorted to alternative methods of acquiring
them. Wendy noted that the Wayne Dollars thus began to circulate within
a counter-economy:

> Yeah, that was within the first 3 months of implementation. We had
> Wayne Dollars and then—(laughs) and then it was funny because . . .
> the [public] library that was down the hill from the school, it was
> having a problem because kids were trying to counterfeit them using
> the [copy machine]. . . . And then the police were about to arrest some
> kids for playing craps and they thought it was real money and it was
> fake, you know, it's the Wayne Dollars. And then another funny story
> about that first, like, 6 months of implementation at Wayne. . . . There
> was a kid who was able to sell a Wayne Dollar for a real dollar and,
> like, we were trying to explain to [the] kids, "Wait a minute. . . . Don't
> give away real money for Wayne [Dollars]!" But, it showed you . . .
> to the point of how much they valued those dollars (laughs) that they
> would give up real money. And, then, we're talking about the poorest
> kids in the city, you know. . . .

From the above quote, it is apparent that the students at Wayne valued the token dollars, because they wanted to participate in the school activities and needed the dollars to do so. But rather than serving as a reward system, which was the original intention, the token system served as a punishment system, excluding students with behavioral referrals. Students who did not meet behavioral expectations were supposed to see the other students being rewarded for their "respectable" behavior and then want to behave similarly in order to be included in the token economy. Students, however, apparently resisted this exclusion by creating their own counter-economy that was, of course, disruptive to the school's punitive token economy. However, rather than reading the student actions as a critique of a token economy, student actions were described in criminalizing language, such as *counterfeit* and *gambling*, and students were described as "naturally" dis/respectable. Additionally, they were also seen as "naturally" unable to make correct choices even though a system was put in place to rehabilitate them. Wendy, and the staff at Wayne, worked hard to end gang-associated behavior in the school. They had no control over the behavior outside of the school. However, the behavior that Wendy described in the above quote, though it happened outside the school, was still associated with the school through the Wayne Dollars. Although Wendy laughed while telling the story, indicating that in her perception these behaviors were amusing rather than dangerous, these same behaviors resulted in office discipline referrals that labeled the students as "offenders" in the discipline data for the school. Here, though race and disability are never mentioned, the shadows linger in the pauses, the laughter, the words, and ultimately, the disciplinary actions.

Moreover, the repeated exclusion of "dis/respectable" students from school community celebrations further alienated these students from their peers. These students were pathologized and labeled as *disruptive, dysfunctional, naughty, in crisis, frequent fliers, on the edge, ED*, and *offenders*—all terms teachers used in the school to describe dis/respectable students. Much of these practices and the language deployed at Wayne mirrors language used in prisons, an argument supported by scholars of prison abolition.

Pathologizing Student Behavior

Teachers used different terminologies to construct the dis/respectable student. For example, Robin, the White physical education teacher who has been at the school for 19 years, distinguished between students who made good decisions and the "naughties," who made bad choices. The language of choice placed responsibility squarely on the student to face the outcomes of engaging in "disruptive" behaviors. Noticing that the same students did the "right" thing, and realizing that she was unable to help the students who acted up and made bad choices, Robin turned to the language of pathology to explain her dilemma:

Right. I mean, it's so frustrating, I can imagine for a good kid who
always makes good choices and, you know, just sits there while there's
chaos raining around them. And, like, "Okay . . . what the hell is
going on here, you know?" . . . [S]o I try to reward them for following
directions, because you're doing what you should do, you know? And
if I see a child who always makes bad choices making a good choice,
yeah, I'm going to reward him, too. But I'm not going to go out of my
way to get him [the kid making bad choices] on track. I'm sorry; you
have 20 kids here making good choices and you have five not. And it's
always the same ones, so I don't know of any interventions in place
for them.

She went on to suggest that rather than try to intervene or support these
students whom she described as "naughty ones," she was simply waiting
them out until they moved on to the next grade—which she realized was a
Sisyphean task:

Well, a lot of the naughty ones are 5th-graders and they're leaving.
However, there's always going to be kids to take their place. You
know, there's 4th-grade naughty children that are going to move up to
5th grade, and there's 3rd grade that are going to become naughty
4th-graders. Yeah. So, I don't know of anything [behavioral inter-
ventions] that's been done for them.

Thus, rather than recognizing her own inadequacies as a teacher in finding creative ways to encourage students to cooperate with her in class or the
lack of positive interventions, Robin pathologized these students, attribut-
ing their failures to meet the codes of dis/respectability in her classroom as
an inherent deficit within the student. Once again, discourses of race and
disability have a shadowy presence in her assertions of inadequacy.

The pathologization of students and their families by the school staff
was foregrounded in many different contexts to explain away the failure of
the school to meet the needs of the students and their community. Thus, for
example, Sally, a White 2nd-grade elementary teacher who had been at the
school for 26 years, when asked about how previous principals had handled
discipline in the school, had difficulty relating structural problems in the
school to discipline issues. Instead, Sally resorted to the pathologization of
students and their families:

So, I mean, at that point, yes, she [the principal] was supportive and
we could make a change. There may have been one or two children
that I would consider to be in crisis, and then a few who were on the
fringe, but you could get them to move toward the [middle] but the
culture and the society of where I worked also looked and sounded

different at that time. So it was still easier to get parent involvement and contact and those kinds of things. The administrator that I have now, I believe is very supportive and working hard. But again, there's more that we're up against. There's just more out there. I mean, for example, there's a gun for hire in our neighborhood right now where you can literally hire the gun for a couple of hours, do whatever you need to do. . . . Yeah, and the kids know about it. And I mean, that's going on. And that's just one small example. They're walking to school literally crossing dead bodies because there's shootings in the morning or whatever. So those things have always kind of been here. I don't think to the severity that it's here now. And so even though . . . this administrator's only been here for this year, and although I believe she's supportive in putting things in place, it's sort of like comparing apples and oranges, if that makes any sense.

Sally created an elaborate scene of violence in the community that could be taken from a crime drama. Although the neighborhood has one of the higher crime rates in the city, the degree that Sally described was certainly an exaggeration. Although the city, for its size and population, has a higher crime rate than New York City, the majority of the crimes committed include aggravated assault, burglary, and larceny. Further, although the city had 11 murders that year, none occurred in the surrounding area of the school. By describing the community as a war zone, Sally was able to pathologize the entire community and the students as deviant, thereby locating the problem as endemic to the community, rather than recognizing structural issues within the school or community. Although Sally recognized that Morgan has had a high turnover rate for administrators, which can create instability at the school, a point she began with in the interview, she had difficulty separating the changes that took place within the school that affected the dynamics of the school climate from the changes in the community, families, and students that she gave as a factor in the discipline and academic achievement issues in her classroom and the school in general.

This trend continued in the interview with Sally. Like Robin, Sally's inability to manage her students' behavior in class was attributed to her students' "crisis" rather than to her own methods of engaging her students in her classroom:

This particular school year for me, I have a lot of children that I would consider to be in crisis and I'm really struggling with maneuvering their behaviors, I guess is a good word for it. And I know it's because of the quantity of the children who are in crisis. . . . And I think . . . as much as they are rebelling and stuff with their behavior, I still believe that when they walk into the classroom, that that's their safe place to fall. They know that there's certain parameters. For example, they know that legally, I'm not going to put my hands on them where at home, culturally the form of discipline may be whoopings or beatings or whatever. You know, I don't put any personal bias on that, but that is the culture. But they know that that definitely is not a choice, so that's already one thing off the plate.

In the above quote, "You know, I don't put any personal bias on that, but that is the culture," Sally distanced herself from any perceivable racial bias. And yet her arguments place the failure to connect with students solely on the pathologized families and communities her students come from. Here again, disability as dis/respectability is deployed as a justification for the pathologization of racialized bodies.

CONCLUSION: SHADOW PLAY

This chapter investigates the way students in an urban elementary school were "simultaneously raced and dis/abled" through the discourse of "dis/respectable politics" as the participants describe the students, families, and community they work with, justifying the negation of Black life. DisCrit allows us to examine how the discourse of race, although not explicitly discussed, is coded throughout the participants' dialogue and brings to the foreground the ways in which racialized bodies are pathologized and dis/abled. As the educators construct the students as dysfunctional, naughty, criminal, and dis/abled, the students move from the classroom, through the office, past the professionals with the diagnosis and treatment, into the segregated spaces, and out the door. In this way, oppressive (rather than empowering) discourses of disability and race are deployed at the intersections of social difference to justify the casual dis-location of student bodies along the school-to-prison pipeline by conceiving these bodies as dis/respectable and therefore as matter out of (White, normative) place.

Our argument, while insisting on analyses that engage the simultaneity of race and disability as articulated in DisCrit, also insists that discourses of disability as dis/respectability are not pathological attributes but rather are social processes constituted within oppressive historical conditions that also associate disability with dis/respectable deviance (Erevelles, 2012). Our argument disrupts the historical seamless association of disability with dis/respectable deviance by rejecting the pathological in favor of a political economic analysis. In this way, our argument, situated in the more generative tradition of DisCrit, seeks to build critical alliances that could potentially improve the lives of many students living at the intersections of difference.

CHAPTER 8

The Overrepresentation of Students of Color with Learning Disabilities

How "Working Identity" Plays a Role in the School-to-Prison Pipeline

Claustina Mahon-Reynolds
Laurence Parker

INTRODUCTION

For nearly 4 decades, the pervasive issue of overrepresentation of students of color in special education programs in the United States has become a policy issue of increasing concern (Blanchett, Klingner, & Harry, 2009; Blanchett, Mumford, & Beachum, 2005). As the disproportionate placement of students of color in special education continues, there is a paramount need to examine alternate ways to increase student achievement and educate all students (Artiles, 2009; Blanchett, 2006, 2009; Blanchett, Brantlinger, & Shealey, 2005; Patton, 1998; Sleeter, 1998). The Office of Civil Rights (OCR) and the Office of Special Education Programs (OSEP) have consistently documented the overrepresentation of students of color (Ferri & Connor, 2005; Losen & Orfield, 2002), and the risk ratio has remained steady over the years (see Table 8.1).

In addition, schools are being increasingly seen as the lynchpin connector institution that contributes to the school-to-prison pipeline, moving students of color from classrooms to prison cells (Sussman, 2012). Uneven distribution of school resources and broad discretionary discipline policies have led to a greater reliance by school administrators on police officers to conduct searches and to control minor rule violations, which has created a school climate of fear in many schools that are comprised of majority

Table 8.1. Risk Ratio Table for 26th–31st Annual Reports to Congress

Risk Ratios disaggregated by ethnicity for students ages 6–21 served under IDEA in the Specific Learning Disability Category, Part B, as reported by states for the 26th–31st Annual Reports to Congress

Ethnicity	26th Annual Report	27th Annual Report	28th Annual Report	29th Annual Report	30th Annual Report	31st Annual Report
American Indian	1.53	1.79	1.8	1.8	1.81	1.84
Black	1.34	1.42	1.4	1.43	1.46	1.47
Hispanic	1.1	1.15	1.1	1.17	1.19	1.22
White	0.86	0.8	0.8	0.78	0.77	0.75

Source: the 26th to the 31st Annual Reports to Congress found at www.ed.gov
Note: These data have been reformatted for this text from their original source.

students of color (Bahena, Cooc, Currie-Rubin, Kuttner, & Ng, 2012; Kim, Losen, & Hewitt, 2010).

The purpose of our chapter is to connect the overrepresentation of youth of color in special education to the school-to-prison pipeline, drawing on Critical Race Theory and DisCrit (Annamma, Connor, & Ferri, 2013). We believe that ideally, special education law should be used to help dismantle the pipeline so that punishment through incarceration is not the norm for students of color who may have undiagnosed or unmet special needs. The law could be used to secure, for example, special education services that address the kinds of behaviors (such as "unruliness in school") that could serve this population of youth better than being suspended or expelled for minor offenses because these punishments often lead to increased confrontations with school police officers and even criminal charges. However, in reality, some teachers' and administrators' enforcement of discretionary discipline policies creates a school climate that solidifies a "racial working identity" (Carbado & Gulati, 2000), which punishes any acts done by African American or Latino students, especially those with special needs, that may appear to violate school culture and normative expectations around how students should behave and learn (Rivkin, 2009/2010; Tulman & Weck, 2009/2010). Therefore, DisCrit allows us to interrogate both the punitive response of schools to the behaviors of students of color and the concept that special education services can address their education without a whole-school commitment to valuing what children of color bring to schools.

DISABILITY CRITICAL RACE THEORY

According to Annamma et al. (2013), Disability Studies and Critical Race Theory (Dis/Crit) is a theoretical framework that examines the constructs of disability and race that are intertwined within the educational system. DisCrit also acknowledges that disabilities are impacted via individual and societal beliefs about race, positioned within social and institutional contexts. Within education institutions, a clear divide exists between general education and special education classrooms and teachers. Special education teachers are thought to be imbued with "special knowledge" to educate students with disabilities. This divide determines which students get access to inclusionary practices, and therefore, which students have access to general education experiences, peers, and content. Students and teachers are given labels (for example, general versus special) and these labels determine how students are served and where and with whom they are taught. If a student is categorized as a general education student, then a general educator can teach the student. If the student is categorized as a "special education student," the label becomes reified. In other words, the label becomes the students' defining feature and they are deemed to need special education services, including teachers, curriculum, and resources, to meet their academic needs (Harry & Klingner, 2014). To acknowledge this division between special education and general education is not to argue that the differences do not exist, but rather to shift the focus to how those differences are perceived and the ramifications this has for all students (Baglieri & Knopf, 2004). A DisCrit analysis would also consider what happens when a layer of race is added to the complexity of having a disability and how disability also adds complexity to the experience of race. For example, it has been shown that students of color with a disability label are more likely to be placed in restrictive settings than their White peers, limiting their access to the general education curriculum, resources, and teachers (Fierros & Conroy, 2002).

Like CRT, DisCrit embodies several tenets or systems of beliefs. DisCrit incorporates the following tenets:

1. Disability discrimination or ableism and racism are mutually dependent, and are used to espouse beliefs of normalcy. In other words, DisCrit acknowledges the operation of ableism and racism as they work in tandem to perpetuate the marginalization of people of color—namely, students of color (Ladson-Billings & Tate, 1995).
2. Multidimensional identities are valued and are not seen as singular identifiers. Singular identifiers would include defining a person solely by race, ability/disability, gender, class, and so on. DisCrit argues that each individual has a multidimensional identity that should be valued and taken into account.

3. DisCrit reaches outside of the cultural norms of Western civilization by highlighting the social constructions of ability and race, while conjointly identifying psychological and material influences that are incurred when labeled as "raced" or "dis/abled."

4. DisCrit values and makes central the voices of people of color/ marginalized populations.

5. DisCrit focuses on how race and dis/ability have been used historically and legally to deny citizens' their rights.

6. DisCrit views Whiteness and ability as forms of property wherein marginalized groups experience gains as a result of interest convergence. Interest convergence is a theory that revolves around the premise that those in power will be advocates of racial justice to the degree that there is something to gain for themselves. In other words, there has to be a convergence among the interests of those in power and oppressed populations.

7. DisCrit views activism as essential to the framework. Researchers who are steeped in DisCrit postulate that the inquiry should connect to communities (Annamma et al., 2013). Connecting to communities includes being active participants within those communities to combat injustice and act on inequity in order to promote equitable outcomes for all.

For the purposes of this chapter, Tenets One and Three are the most important for our analysis. If racism and ableism circulate interdependently, then we can, indeed, view how individuals who are raced are more likely to be seen as different and therefore deficit in ability and behavior. Though both are social constructions, the psychological and material consequences of students constructed as *both* raced and dis/abled in relation to the norm are more likely to experience education focused on surveillance, containment, and punishment. It must be duly noted that DisCrit is a theoretical framework that seeks to address the intersectionality of race and dis/ability with regard to society's repeated and perpetuated system of oppression that has justified limited access to marginalized populations and the overrepresentation of students of color in high-incidence disability categories. In the remainder of this chapter, we explore how teacher attitudes and personal beliefs impact the way students of color are perceived through the deficit lens of disability.

TEACHER ATTITUDES AND HOW A "WORKING IDENTITY" WORKS AGAINST STUDENTS OF COLOR WITH DISABILITY

In thinking about the overrepresentation of students of color identified for special education services, Ahram, Fergus, and Noguera (2011) posit that deficit thinking and personal judgments on the part of teachers influence the referral process for students and how they are deemed eligible for special education. Teachers' perceptions have a deep influence on how teachers view students from racially, ethnically, and linguistically diverse backgrounds (Ahram et al., 2011; Ladson-Billings, 1999). Ahram et al. (2011) conducted a mixed-methods study in two multiracial suburban, New York State school districts where overrepresentation existed. The purpose of their study was to identify the root cause of overrepresentation of students of color within these districts, the strategies the districts employed to combat overrepresentation, and the implications the strategies had on the discourse for Disability Studies. According to Ahram et al., when these districts were asked to look at overrepresentation and give reasons why they felt overrepresentation existed within their district, district personnel employed cultural deficit thinking to arrive at their answers. The reported causes of overrepresentation included (1) low-income status, (2) lack of books at home, (3) lack of belief in education among the students and parents, (4) a "ghetto" culture that students bring into the school, and (5) students' linguistic diversity, to name a few. It was clear that students' families, cultures, ethnicity, and socioeconomic status were seen as the root causes of students' lack of ability or their disability status, according to the responses of school personnel (Ahram et al., 2011). Looking at teachers' responses in these two districts, it was clear that the relationship between teachers' beliefs, attitudes, or biases and their practices influenced their perceptions of the academic ability of students and likely contributed to the overrepresentation of students of color (Ahram et al., 2011). Furthermore, the biases entrenched in the teachers' perceptions of their students were not addressed or seen as problematic until the number of African American and Latino students referred and placed in special education increased dramatically.

Skiba et al. (2006) conducted a study involving 66 educators. The researchers interviewed educators about their attitudes regarding urban education, special education, diversity, disproportionality, and the availability of needed resources. In considering why overrepresentation was a problem in the racially, ethnically, and linguistically diverse district involved, one teacher said, "They don't know their letters. They don't know what the alphabet song is. They are very street savvy. . . . But they don't have those educational tools" (p. 1432). A different teacher noted "High transience . . . so the kids kind of come in having gone to six schools already by second grade," while another stated "People who are very transient don't tend to get involved. . . . They are just not really interested in their child's education anyway" (p. 1432). A fourth teacher reported, "A lot of times I see students where education is not a priority and it starts at home. If mom or dad is just not into it and they're not helping with homework and they don't view that as special—a lot of times, it's just right there" (p. 1433). Their research clearly validated that teacher attitudes, perceptions, and biases about their students and students' families can influence judgments about students' academic ability. This type of attitude transforms a student who is struggling into a student who has special education needs, thus resulting in overrepresentation of these students of color (Ahram et al., 2011). In both of these studies, when teachers' beliefs were examined in relation to over-representation, teachers' perceptions about a student's ability or disability status was rooted in deficit thinking and infused with cultural and racial factors (Ahram et al., 2011; Skiba et al., 2006). This reinforced previous research that has found that teacher perceptions or biases often operate in less overt and even unconscious ways that perpetuate overrepresentation (Artiles, Harry, Reschly, & Chin, 2002; Collins, 2003, 2013; Harry & Anderson, 1994; Harry & Klingner, 2014; Hart et al., 2009). These studies show how the beliefs of teachers about race, cultural and linguistic diversity, and class impact the referral process for students of color to special education.

The literature on subjective judgments of teachers and administrators contributing to overrepresentation leads us to posit that one of the connectors between special education and the school-to-prison pipeline is the maintenance of a *racial working identity* through implicit bias. Though systemic issues of institutionalized racism and ableism also contribute to the overrepresentation of children of color in special education, we highlight the individual problematic attitudes of teachers and administrators, as we see these views as an accessible entry point for intervention. Carbado and Gulati (2000, 2013) discussed racial working identity in terms of employment, noting that although businesses want to appear to be fair and value diversity in the workplace, employers have an implicit basis regarding which types of racial minorities they want to see in their companies. Therefore, employees who are racial minorities feel a degree of pressure to conform to expected racial norms, so that majority-White employees and supervisors can feel they are in a relatively comfortable racial zone with others. Those racial minorities who do not conform to implicit and biased expectations will face isolation, may not be promoted, or may be asked to leave the company, despite being capable and competent at their jobs.

We argue that the majority of students of color in particular face a similar racial working identity situation when they come to school. Because the concept of "Blackness" has been associated with crime and deviant behavior, students of color are perceived through this lens. The prevailing attitudes and institutional and organizational culture based on White norms and White notions of appropriate expressions of multiculturalism determine how students should act and behave. This means that students of color who misbehave are often disciplined and punished with greater severity, leading to higher rates of suspensions and expulsions, disproportionate labeling of emotional or behavioral disabilities, and earlier and more frequent engagement with the criminal justice system (Meiners, 2007). In other words, the school-to-prison pipeline track often runs through special education via a racial working identity (Wald & Losen, 2003). Students of color, thus, have a working identity imposed that requires them to conform to the school norms of multicultural diversity. If students challenge those norms, it is often interpreted as willful defiance, rather than how students perceive themselves in their own reality and use this as a frame of reference (Ferguson, 2001; Vaught, 2011). We can see parts of this phenomenon at work as Annamma (2014) documents that teacher dispositions, based on unquestioned assumptions of the criminal intent of young women with disabilities in a juvenile justice facility, persisted despite the teachers' well-intended efforts to create relational approaches to daily interactions.

In general, the concept of implicit bias has received new attention with the development of Implicit Association Test (IAT) research. This test measures implicit attitudes or unconscious racial bias of different groups of people (Lawrence, 2008). Those who are administered the IAT are required to link words and images to see what comes to mind when testers practice distinguishing different groups of people (for example, African Americans versus European Americans). Testers are required to associate certain words with images of African American or European Americans as the faces flash across the computer screen. Testers are also given positive meaning words and words that are associated with a negative meaning. Then testers are exposed to all four testing items, including African American images, European American images, pleasant meaning words, and negative meaning words. The test is taken under time pressure. To date, the test has been taken by more than 2 million people and the results have revealed that the majority of the testers do exhibit implicit and unconscious racial biases. According to Lawrence (2008), implicit bias can be a pivotal part of the policy choices of legislators, as well as the behaviors of employers, teachers, and police. With that said, implicit racial biases are thoughts and acts that we carry without conscious direction or awareness (Kang & Lane, 2010). When enacted in schools, they have major consequences for students of color in terms of special education placement, school discipline, and the school-to-prison pipeline.

These implicit biases have direct implications for a racial working identity, as when students are put under constant pressure to conform to norms, the minute they act in a way that is in contradiction with those norms; teachers' implicit biases are confirmed and students of color are punished more severely. The racial working identity imposed on students of color puts them under additional strain without additional protection. School personnel's implicit biases are triggered in moment-to-moment interactions and impacted by a racial working identity wherein students of color are judged through a lens of White supremacy and consistently found to be lacking. This racial working identity provides another opportunity to punish instead of educate and route children out of schools and into prisons.

CONCLUSION

Despite these measures designed to address the overrepresentation of racial minority students in special education, the problem still persists in most U.S. schools (Sussman, 2012). Furthermore, the problem has become even more of an issue when coupled with the increased police presence in many public schools as a result of perceived violence in the schools. Conceptually, police officers are assigned to keep order in the public schools, but in reality they have come to be (over)relied on by school personnel to respond to minor infractions (APA, 2006). This has resulted in disproportionate rates of African American, Latino, and American Indian students (among other students of color) being removed from school because of their racial working identity (Sussman, 2012). Furthermore, school administrators in some large school districts have been allowed to use discretionary powers to immediately suspend a student without cause because the student is believed to pose a threat to school safety (APA, 2006).

As schools apply increasing resources to school safety and punishment and correcting youth behavior, more students of color with special needs are caught in the web of public school racism. Each year, almost 400,000 youth spend time in juvenile detention centers because juvenile courts are prosecuting many of these youth for school misconduct that used to be handled informally (Sussman, 2012). Many of these youth are students of color with special needs; special education law could help them if it were used to truly provide equitable education services by schools and if defense attorneys worked to help parents of color obtain appropriate special education services to address the child's needs (Tulman & Weck, 2009/2010). However, even when provided with special education services, the outcomes for students of color with disabilities are significantly worse than for White peers with disabilities (Parrish, 2002; Reid & Knight, 2006). Specifically, suspension is used aggressively for children of color with disabilities: One in four boys of color with disabilities and nearly one in five girls of color with disabilities receives an out-of-school suspension (U.S. Department of Education, Office of Civil Rights, 2014). We see an increasing number of students with disabilities prosecuted in juvenile court for school misconduct (Rivkin, 2009/2010). This in turn leads to what Alexander (2010) discussed as the massive lockup of Black and Brown in the era of color-blind law. Therefore, we cannot offer special education services as the sole answer to the punitive response of general education to children of color. Instead, a whole-school commitment must be made to value what children of color bring to schools instead of investing in a racial working identity. We believe that there is a connection between what schools do when creating and enacting discipline policies and procedures and the realities of present-day effects of historic racism on how students of color are perceived as threats in school. Furthermore, this phenomenon of segregation is evident in the overrepresentation of students of color in special education and in the greater likelihood of these students being profiled for school discipline violations instead of having their educational needs fully met. Both of these outcomes further inhibit these students' chances for higher education.

The notion of the school-to-prison pipeline became popularized in 2000 when a report from the Justice Policy Institute titled *Cellblocks or Classrooms?* (Schiraldi & Ziedenberg, 2002) found that there were more Black men in the U.S. prison system than in postsecondary education. That said, we note a recent *Chronicle of Higher Education* article (Patton, 2012) that reported that, starting in 2002, the number of Black males attending college started to outnumber those in the prison system. By 2010, approximately 1.34 million Black males were enrolled in some type of postsecondary education, as compared to 844,600 in the prison system. This shift provides us with hope, but we are also realistic about the fact that there are many children of color with disabilities being deeply impacted by the pipeline via a racial working identity.

In conclusion, the persistence of the school-to-prison pipeline is dependent on the assumed beliefs and underlying racial association of Blackness with crime. This association is linked with the implicit biases of school personnel that are triggered when a child of color acts in ways that contrast with racialized normative expectations. Racial working identity limits education opportunities for children of color and routes them out of schools. Muhammad (2010) argues that since the United States started to collect crime statistics at the turn of the 20th century, there has been an explicit racialized link between the public perceptions of who commits crime and the documentation of this through prison descriptive statistics. Muhammad also posits that the school-to-prison pipeline is a pretext for a firm belief in the public policy discourse that most of these Black males would not be destined for college anyway. We believe that it is this type of racial working identity of Black and Brown youth that is etched in the mindset and everyday practice of discipline in schools that needs to be interrogated regarding the connection between race, special education status, and the school-to-prison connection.

Part V

SCHOOL REFORM

CHAPTER 9

Race, Class, Ability, and School Reform

Sally Tomlinson

The rise of a neoliberal ideology linking economic competitiveness to reforms in education has been dominant for over 30 years in developed economies and increasingly influences developing countries. Governments around the world believe that all citizens in nation-states are subject to the forces of globalization and that higher levels of educational attainment are necessary for successful competition in knowledge-driven economies. Young people are urged to invest in their own human capital and compete with one another in stratified education systems and uncertain job markets. Schools are expected and often coerced by legislative and funding reforms to credential all young people to higher levels. Governments are increasingly reforming their school systems on the basis of school tests such as Programme for International Student Assessment (PISA), whose test results of students rank countries in international league tables (see Meyer & Benavot, 2013). This leads to a "blaming" of teachers, students, families, and communities for lower rankings. Inevitably, given the historical and structural development of Western education systems, those designated as lower achievers are primarily working-class, racial minorities, and those with assigned disabilities. There is a pressing need, as DisCrit points out, for new ways of articulating and theorizing about ways in which race, class, gender, and dis/ability intersect, and a continuing need to question ways the major social institution of education functions to advantage and disadvantage some groups of students (Annamma et al., 2013). DisCrit may be "a theoretical framework that is very much a work in progress" (Annamma et al., 2013, p. 24), but it holds the promise of engaging those concerned with education in understanding more deeply problems that are often considered intractable.

INTRODUCTION: BACKGROUND UNDERSTANDINGS

This chapter examines some of the history and policy responses to those groups likely to be regarded as lower achievers, disruptive in schools, and/ or requiring some form of special education. It primarily refers to England but includes information from a research study into lower attainment carried out in five countries in 2010–2012, including the United States, where market ideologies and high-stakes testing have driven school reforms (Tomlinson, 2013). The theoretical intention of the research study was to present a critical account of current political ideologies whereby young people are expected to contribute to wealth creation, but those with lower attainments or disabilities were not prepared in schools to "compete" on equal terms. A theoretical background was derived from Rawls's *A Theory of Justice* (1971), a text that has had much influence on affirmative action and redistributive theories of justice. The study noted that in countries embracing competitive neoliberal market beliefs, there is a particular contradiction between the rhetoric of social, educational, and economic inclusion and the realities of injustice, divisiveness, and inequality. A conclusion to this chapter is that DisCrit and social justice are inseparable.

Education systems in developed countries from the mid-20th century experienced a rapid expansion as groups previously excluded were drawn into longer formal systems, usually at lower levels of schooling. Those having difficulty performing in formal testing, failing to attain constantly raised qualification levels, or acquiring labels of special educational needs, were now to be offered or coerced if necessary into education that would ensure that their labor was profitable and they were not a drain on national economies. But schooling was still to take place in stratified systems, and within schools, students were still to be placed according to perceived levels of "ability" or "disability." Moreover, social class, race, minority status, and gender continued to play an important role in the segregation of particular students via lower tracks, sets, streams, units, classes, or segregated schools.

England: Lower Attainers and School Reform

In England, historical definitions of lower attainers were based on beliefs in the biological and cultural inferiority of lower social classes and racial groups, and assumed inabilities among the groups were conflated. In common with eugenicists in the United States and Europe, links were made between feeblemindedness, low school attainments, unemployment, and criminality, all of which were assumed to produce a degenerate social class. Supposedly feebleminded women, especially if unmarried, threatened what in early-20th-century England was described as "the racial stock," by producing degenerate children (RCCCFM, 1908). Beliefs in the genetic inheritance of mental defects, a longstanding theme in the writings of eugenic believers in Europe and the United States, strengthened popular notions about the links between intellectual deficit, unemployment, criminality, and other assumed social evils. The political ruling classes in both countries certainly had interests in suppressing what were seen as lower-class "vices." Victorian thinking on race, despite the abolition of slavery in British colonies in the 1830s, incorporated a powerful racial hostility based on economic exploitation and beliefs in "the Empire's Black and brown subjects as natural inferiors" (Lloyd, 1984, p. 184). The expansion of schooling for the working classes in England from the 1870s and the development of special schools for the increasing variety of those assessed as defective or disabled has been variously presented as enlightened progress (DES, 1978) or as contributing to the social, educational, and economic control of subordinate social groups (Richardson & Powell, 2011; Tomlinson, 1982), but in the hierarchies of schools that have developed over the 20th and into the 21st century in England, the place of lower-class students judged to have lower abilities, both White and minority, either in segregated or inclusive settings, has remained remarkably constant.

Race, Class, and Ability in England

Black children from the Caribbean and those from the Indian subcontinent, arriving in England from the 1950s, were incorporated into an English education system imbued with negative beliefs about them and their families. As the parents largely took jobs that the White working class did not want, schools and teachers made doubly negative assumptions about children who were from both working-class and racial minority backgrounds. The way in which learning disability and race had, from the beginnings of the eugenics movement, intersected in the United States (Beratan, 2008) applied equally in England. Negative assumptions about the potential ability of minorities has underlaid the schooling of several generations of young people. Schools developed strategies to deny overt racism, which resulted in a discourse of low ability rather than racial characteristics (Ferri & Connor, 2006). Although in the United States this may have encouraged a "resegregation" of schooling, in England it has persisted in negative beliefs about Black, especially Caribbean descended, students and their potentiality for learning and their social behavior.

The presence of children from former colonial countries coincided with an expansion of categories of special education. In particular, from 1946 "educable defective" and "dull" children (terms that were utilized in educational discourse at the time) were merged into a category of "educationally subnormal" (ESN), and children displaying emotional and behavioral problems were labeled "maladjusted," and later "emotionally disturbed," then "behaviorally emotionally and socially disturbed" (BESD). Black children were quickly overrepresented in ESN schools. Bernard Coard (1971/2005) produced his book *How the West Indian Child Is Made Educationally Subnormal in the British School System*, and the relegation of their children to these schools became a "very bitter area for Black parents" (House of Commons, 1976). The ESN issue became symbolic of the failure of the whole school system to educate Black children successfully. A study of children referred into schools for the educationally subnormal during the 1970s indicated that head teachers identified Black children, especially boys, as educationally slow and behaviorally troublesome. They located the cause of their difficulties in disorganized families and poor socioeconomic backgrounds (Tomlinson, 1981, 2012a), and these "explanations" for lower school performance persisted. In retrospect, this original 1981 study was an early attempt at understanding the intersection of class, race, ability, and gender. Eventually, schools, mindful of parental concerns about ESN schools, began to refer Black students into segregated units and schools for the emotionally and behaviorally disturbed. A major report during the 1980s, which was produced by Lord Swan's committee on the education of ethnic minority children, examined the lower achievement of various minority groups and also commissioned a study of race and IQ, which discussed Black–White differences on IQ tests (Jensen, 1969). This study was widely regarded as a concession to claims of genetically influenced lower intelligence of Black students, although it concluded that environment had more influence on school performance than genetic inheritance (see DES, 1985).

Competition and Ability in English Schools

By the 1990s, a competitive market for schooling had been established in the United Kingdom, with tests results being published in league tables, and a semiprivatized inspectorate deciding that failing schools should go into special measures or close. The "failing schools" were largely those attended by the working class and minorities. Rates of referral for some kinds of special education and for school exclusions rose, and the special units, now known as Pupil Referral Units, expanded. Students with learning or behavior problems—rejected by some schools—were accepted by others, which were then penalized for low test results. An example of this was Hackney Downs School in London, demonized in the media as "the worst school in Britain" and closed in December 1995, when the school included 80% minority students, 70% of them second-language speakers, 50% from households with no employment, and a majority having some kind of special educational need (O'Connor, Hales, Davies, & Tomlinson, 1999).

The teaching and test results of students from all groups improved slowly but unequally as governments took on the consequences of the expansion of mass education and more young people were now taught and entered for public examinations. By the 1990s, children from minority groups extended to refugees and asylum seekers from conflicts around the world. Governments from all parties were notionally committed to closing achievement gaps between social and ethnic groups, but a review of research evidence to the year 2000 suggested that social class, ethnicity, and gender were associated with differences in attainment, with African Caribbean, Pakistani, and Bangladeshi students less likely to achieve the benchmarks at the General Certificate of Secondary Education (GCSE) level (Gillborn & Mirza, 2000). These authors warned against the dangers of setting some ethnic groups above others based on their performance levels—holding up "model minorities" as more successful than others and thereby ignoring differences in the histories, backgrounds, and school experiences.

Using a government-funded Longitudinal Study of Young Persons in England (LSYPE), Strand and his researchers (2011) asked, "Why do these differences persist?" (p. 76). Discounting socioeconomic and family background explanations, the authors concluded that within-school factors were the most likely to account for White–Black Caribbean differences in attainment. Strand and Lindsay (2009) conducted what they claimed was "the first large-scale quantitative study in England that investigated disproportionality (in special education) with respect to ethnicity, taking account also of socio-economic disadvantage, gender and age" (p. 174) and came to the same conclusions that smaller-scale and qualitative studies had found from the 1980s. Black Caribbean students more likely to be referred for emotionally and behaviorally disturbed schooling rather than schools for mild learning difficulty. Strand (2011) also raised the issue of students of Black African origin being less likely to have learning difficulties and to achieve rather better than Black Caribbeans, with some disregard for the historical differences between the groups and the way schools respond to them, and to the developed education systems that most Black African students come from. The small numbers of Black Caribbean middle-class families were not immune to negative views of their children, with a recent study noting that the families have to make strategic decisions in supporting their children against seemingly entrenched low expectations (Vincent, Tobin, Hawken, & Frank, 2012).

Political Concerns

The New Labour government of Tony Blair, coming into power in 1997, asserted a commitment to education as a means to create a more socially just society. Government was also becoming concerned about the increasing number of parental claims for resources for special needs. Although historically all social classes had produced children with physical or sensory needs, middle-class parents had avoided the more stigmatized categories of learning and behavioral problems. Now, middle-class and aspirant parents were increasingly claiming funding and resources for all their children who were unlikely to achieve in competitive schooling, especially claiming the labels of dyslexia and other specific learning difficulties and autistic spectrum disorder. As teachers and administrators in the research carried out in 2010–2012 noted, there had been a medicalization of behavior, with parents wanting a pseudo-medical label such as autism, Asperger's syndrome, or attention deficit hyperactive disorder (Tomlinson, 2013). The costs of funding these extra claims, plus anxiety over young people leaving education at 16 but not being in any further education, employment, or training—the so-called NEETS (Not in Education, Employment, or Training)—worried the outgoing Labour government, who had noted again the "strong connection between having SEN and being from a low income family" (Department for Children, Schools and Families, 2010). The incoming Conservative government in 2010 quickly confirmed that 916,000 students were in "school action" and a million over-16's were NEETS, many with special educational needs. This label quickly became yet another derogatory one. The new government promised to simplify the system and reduce what was termed *perverse incentives* to overidentify students as "having SEN." From 2014, there was to be one school-based category and an Education, Health and Care Plan, replacing the Formal Statement of Special Education Needs, with parents promised more control over the funding for these plans. The goal age of leaving education or training was changed to 18 in 2015. But reforms to the GCSE from 2016 were now intended to measure the progress of all students in eight subjects, with higher standards expected in each subject and end-of-year exams replacing any continuous assessment. The advanced-level exams at 18 were to be similarly "reformed," and only selected vocational courses counted as "equivalent" to academic courses. It is likely that the schools mainly attended by working-class and minority children will be affected by these raised expectations.

The government devoted a whole chapter on "Behavior" in a white paper in 2010 focusing on disruptive Black and White working-class boys (Department for Education, 2010). Political concerns about the social control of predominantly the lower class and minorities were highlighted in August 2011 when riots broke out in English cities, triggered by the police shooting of a young Black man and leading to media designations of young rioters as a "feral underclass" (Compass, 2011). Suggestions for a unified curriculum for all 14- to 19-year-olds, or for well-resourced technical and vocational education, have been largely ignored by all political parties in England, resulting in most low-attaining students' taking low-wage jobs or lower-level post-16 college courses or joining the NEET groups. Although even students credentialed to higher levels now join an uncertain job market, the 20% youth unemployment in 2011 was largely made up of working-class lower attainers, with some 31% of Asian young people and 48% of Black Caribbean young people age 16–24 unemployed. Those not destined for university—around 60% of all young people—attend courses at some 250 largely vocational colleges of further education, take up apprenticeships in a recently expanded apprenticeship scheme, or enter low-level employment.

A Resurgence of Genetic Explanations

The reluctance of school systems set up for White majorities to include minorities fairly has a long history in the United States, echoed in the English school system. This reluctance is further reinforced by a continuing debate on the contribution of genetic inheritance to low intelligence (as measured by IQ tests) and low school attainments. This debate has continued throughout the 20th and into the 21st century, despite the consensus that eugenics has no scientific base. Lewis Terman (1917), in the early 20th century, considered that feebleminded children contributed to a "spawn of degeneracy" in the population. In England, Cyril Burt (1937) claimed that his twin studies demonstrated heritability of ability, although his research was later shown to be fraudulent. Jensen (1969), a student of Burt, made similar claims, and Hans Eysenck (1971), who, surprisingly for one who had escaped persecution in Nazi Germany and had become a professor in London, suggested some dubious explanations for what he considered the lower intelligence of Black and Irish children. He even suggested "the abolition of the proletariat, both Black and white" (p. 150), which at least he suggested was a political rather than an academic problem! Herrnstein and Murray (1994) in the United States claimed in their controversial book that cognitive ability was predominantly heritable and constituted a great dividing line in society, with dull (Black) women giving birth to an underclass community. Fifty-two professors signed a public statement published in the *Wall Street Journal* supporting Herrnstein and Murray's book. The statement was signed by Roy Plomin, who continued to work in the psychometric tradition carrying out twin studies both in the United States and at Kings College, London University (Asbury & Plomin, 2014; Plomin, de Vries, Knopik, & Neiderhier, 2013). He has claimed the overwhelming importance of specific genes in reading disabilities, aggression, ADHD, and other conditions. Although politicians are presumably not so dull as to openly claim that potential lower-class and Black voters are inherently deficient, it was surprising to learn in 2013 that an advisor to Michael Gove, then the United Kingdom education secretary of state, had introduced Plomin to his minister and presented the minister with a 237-page paper that quoted Plomin as asserting that scores in national curriculum tests were 60–70% dependent on genetic heritability. Cummings (2013) also asserted, echoing Jensen's 1969 claim that money spent on compensatory programs was wasted, that "political pressure to spend money on such things as Sure Start" (a program for disadvantaged children 0–3) had resulted in "billions spent with no real gain" (p. 69).

Cummings also quoted a study by Lewis Terman, presumably unaware of Terman's questionable eugenic views. As Steven Rose (2014), professor of neuroscience at the Open University in England, has noted, "Plomin . . . is the current standard-bearer in the long quest by geneticists and psychologists to discover the relative role of genes and environment in determining, or at least shaping, intelligence" (p. 26). As Rose pointed out, genome-wide association studies (GWAS) carried out by more than 200 epigeneticists have concluded that only 2% of differences in genetic variants can account for differences in educational achievement.

Race, Low Ability, and School Reform in the United States

The decentralized structure of education in the United States means that the federal government sets a framework within which the 50 states must function, but largely delegates educational control to states, local districts, and school boards. This provides a contrast to England, where local authorities have progressively lost decisionmaking and funding powers. Although other chapters in this book focus much more on what happens to students designated as lower attainers and/or having special educational needs in the United States, the history and treatment of these groups is similar in both countries. Compulsory school attendance laws in the United States brought a variety of largely unwelcome children into the public school systems—those from poor homes as well as those who were immigrant and foreign-born. As one social historian noted, "Truants, incorrigibles, cripples, the deaf. Those with visual or speech defects, the feeble-minded and moral delinquents" (Lazerson, 1983, p. 23) were all candidates for exclusion from schools and regular classes and were destined to be the lower attainers. As in England, teachers were expected to teach children to required levels, which were constantly raised, and race and class were, and continue to be, markers in deciding who should receive an inferior rather than a high-quality education. Literature continues to demonstrate that Black, Hispanic, and Native American students are more likely to be considered lower attainers or in need of special education. As Blanchett (2008) has noted, "It is no secret that African-American and other students of color, a disproportionate percentage of whom live in poverty and are educated in urban schools, have experienced educational inequality for decades, while their white peers have received a higher quality education" (p. xi).

A major difference between the English and U.S. education systems is that in England the education system is heavily centralized, with legislative requirements and funding flowing from central government departments, while the United States has a decentralized system whereby the Federal government sets a framework within which the 50 states function. A major similarity is that both countries subscribe to neoliberal market ideologies, with market reforms instigated during the Thatcher government in England

and the Reagan government in the United States from the early 1980s, and beliefs that "raised standards" in education will improve the nation's position in a competitive global economy. In both countries, this has led to a blaming of schools and teachers if current requirements are not met. The history and treatment of lower attainers, racial minorities, and those falling within categories of disability and special education in the two countries are remarkably similar, with beliefs that racial minorities are more likely to be of lower ability and more likely to be candidates for lower-skilled jobs. Both countries subscribe to a belief in the effort of individuals to improve their own human capital, and a minimum of social benefits for the unemployed and untrained.

EDUCATION AND SOCIAL JUSTICE

School reforms in England and the United States continue to be driven by a competitive agenda that demands higher levels of academic credentials, which it is assumed will bring standards up to those of competitor countries. The assumption is made that, in particular, China, Japan, Singapore, and South Korea have superior education systems. There continues to be rhetoric emphasizing the importance of improving education at all levels for "the disadvantaged," alongside a continued belief in the deficiencies of the working class and racial minorities. Government-sponsored research has focused on the numbers of these students who fail to achieve well or are disruptive in schools, with explanations for this situation now moving back to outdated theories of class- and race-based genetic inheritance. There appears to be little political will to examine causes or solutions other than blaming families, schools, and teachers. Though governments endorse the notion of a "global skills race," there continues to be minimal interest in and a reduction of funding for vocational education (Keep, 2014). There is also a growing contempt for young people who take lower-level courses and are likely to take lower-level jobs, which actually are of increasing importance in economies dividing more sharply into rich and poor. The market created by competition between schools, and the increased diversity of secondary schooling with hierarchies of desirability of the schools dependent on their student population, has led to more unequal outcomes in schooling than in other richer countries globally (Wilkinson & Pickett, 2009). Boudon (1974) pointed out over 40 years ago that in societies structured by class and other inequalities, the more routes through the education system, the greater the possibility that there will be class, race, and gender inequalities, and this is increasingly happening. A pointless cruelty of the system is that those schools that take in those students considered problematic are penalized if attainments are not raised to the levels demanded of schools that serve more privileged students.

A social justice analysis of what is happening could consider Rawls's view of what is just and unjust in societies. For Rawls, the primary subject of justice is the way in which major social institutions—political, economic, educational, and social—distribute resources, rights, and duties. If prevailing social structures are built on deep current and historical injustices, as class and race are in England and the United States, inequalities cannot be justified by any appeal to birth, merit, or desert. The justice of any social arrangement depends on how educational and economic opportunities are distributed, and a first principle of justice is fairness (Rawls, 1971). In societies where education is a source of intense competition, driven by parental fears that "their child" will not get ahead in a competition for credentials that are assumed to lead to material success and well-being at the expense of others, fairness is not a consideration, and social justice is not served. Neither is justice and fairness served if there is an unequal distribution of resources, a value system that denigrates some groups, and vested interests that resist change. DisCrit, though a work in progress, is inevitably a part of a theory of justice; it is rooted in the notion that ability and disability are currently based on an oppressive value system that sustains beliefs in class and racial hierarchies (Annamma et al., 2013). DisCrit recognizes "ways that the forces of racism and ableism circulate interdependently, often in neutralized and invisible ways, to uphold notions of normalcy" (p. 24). The distribution of educational resources and access to particular kinds of schooling is unjust if it is based on this derogatory value system, which normalizes ways in which racism and ableism circulate. The belief that some individuals or groups are of less worth than others and can be treated in damaging, unfair, and unequal ways contradicts the first principle of social justice in a democratic society.

CHAPTER 10

Toward Unity in School Reform

What DisCrit Contributes to Multicultural and Inclusive Education

Susan Baglieri

According to the official discourse on public schooling in America, education should provide experiences through which children attain college and
career readiness. Arguably, this rhetoric positions education as a means to
cultivate adults who will secure America's status within the global knowledge economy and who will serve domestic interests as a skilled labor force.
The ensuing homily of opportunity and advancement emphasizes the spoils
to be gained from academic merit. The infamous achievement gaps between
poor and affluent children, students of color and White students, students
with disabilities and nonidentified peers, and English language learners and
English dominant students are a call to action to ensure that all students
are enabled to achieve. Liberal school reform initiatives emphasize funding,
staffing, curriculum, and accountability improvements intended to equalize
the opportunities provided to all children in schools. There are, however,
winners and losers in American schools, whose statuses are shaped by an
economy, politics, and ideology. The concept of the meritocracy offers a narrative in which privileges and goods are distributed by a sensibility of worth.

Schooling is property. Achievement in schooling is earned, owned, and
deployed to access privilege. Hierarchies of merit justify an unequal distribution of goods and status. Derived from one of the primary tenets of
Critical Race Theory (CRT), the notion of schooling as property is a useful conceptual tool to explicate the machineries of class, race, and ability
at work in school discourses. CRT argued, "the main basis for civil society in the United States was property rights, not human rights" (Ladson-
Billings, 2009, p. 116). Cheryl Harris (1993) asserted that Whiteness is a
form of property, which functions to allow White people a set of privileges
that are inaccessible to people of color. Applying this notion to education,

Ladson-Billings and Tate (1995) argued that diminished access to high-quality curriculum and instruction, unequal impact of assessment-based accountability measures, segregation, and funding inequities combine to limit the educational opportunities of students of color. The ability of students of color to attain the property of school is mitigated by the naturalization of poverty and race-based inequity, which subsequently naturalizes poor quality in the material property of education. In short, the entanglement of race, poverty, and ghettoization of particular neighborhoods and schools reinforces and reifies enduring discourses in which racism is normalized. If property rights trump human rights, then action related to racial inequity is more achievable when centered on a material analysis of inequity, rather than on a diffuse conceptualization of human equality.

CRT affords an analysis of the proprietary function of Whiteness, drawing attention to economic relationships inscribed within and through racism. Materialist theories of disability, described by Oliver (1999), add another layer in thinking about those dispossessed by the political economy of schools and society. Normalization theories of disability propose a social interactionist model to interpret the construction of disability as a comparative activity of categorization reproduced through cultural interactions (Oliver, 1999). The theory posits that a possibility for a less stigmatized experience of disability could be achieved through disabled people's access to and engagement in a range of life activities. Better economic positioning for disabled people could be sought in civil rights/disability rights. In material terms, anti-ableist action can enable disabled people to participate in the political economy, at which point they would be granted access to the property heretofore denied them on the basis of disability. The desire to negate the naturalized condition of ableism through seeking access to the privileges afforded to those deemed "able" parallels the argument of Whiteness as property. The production of disability may be understood as a "set of activities specifically geared towards producing a good—the category disability—supported by a range of political actions" (Oliver, 1999, p. 164). As a good, disability is exploited as a serviceable condition, giving rise to a service economy. Residential facilities that house the disabled, private special education schools, professional training, diagnostic batteries, and the publishers of remedial programs comprise an economy built on identifying adults and children as disabled. In capitalism there is substantial reason to maintain disablement as an exploitable and serviceable commodity (Oliver, 1999).

Material analyses of disability and race have been drawn together in educational literature. Leonardo and Broderick (2011) offered "smartness as property" as an analogous construct to Whiteness as property, wherein the privilege of agency is afforded to those presumed intelligent and denied those who are not, particularly those deemed intellectually disabled. They highlight the conceptual interdependence of smartness and Whiteness and bluntly state that to be smart is to occupy Whiteness. School reifies a racialized practice of intelligence and is the obstacle course through which one may assert the property rights contained therein. Erevelles (2000) contextualized disability in a robust material analysis to theorize disability as "*the* organizing grounding principle in the construction of categories of gender, race, and class within the context of schooling" (p. 47). She argued that "othering" is a process of disablement in which notions of unsuitability are conflated with gender, race, and class. When "others" are deemed unable or unworthy to participate in the knowledge economy—in the case of poor school achievement, for example—their dispossession in the capitalist ideology is justified. Harris (1993) argued that the property of Whiteness encompasses the right to exclude others, which facilitates the ease with which dispossession can be performed. Analysts working from material perspectives call for attention to the broader capitalist economy within which labor must be produced and to the liberal ideology within which unequal distribution finds moral justification.

The discourse of school reform centers on inequalities and opportunity gaps to acquire schooling, as a form of property through meritocracy. Working through what we would now recognize as DisCrit perspectives, Erevelles (2000) and Leonardo and Broderick (2011) articulated the use of disability as a conceptual tool that naturalizes, justifies, and/or insists upon the denial of schooling as property to children who are minoritized by race, class, and ability. To challenge the entrenched nature of racism and ableism is to challenge, perhaps, the base ideology of schooling itself, a task compounded in Oliver's (1999) proposition that disability is a commodity around which an economy flows. Drawn together, the political-economic conceptualizations of race and ability in CRT and materialist theories of disability comprise a framework to examine the material impact of raced and disabled positions on those so "othered," as well as on those who benefit from such dispossession.

The communion of Disability Studies and CRT as Dis/ability Critical Race Studies (DisCrit) invites conversations that elucidate how, as Annamma et al. (2013) assert, racism and ableism interconnect and collude to construct an idea of "otherness" within which Whiteness and ability are constituted as privileged positions. It is a theoretical framework that centers a desire to examine the ways in which "racism validates and reinforces ableism, and ableism validates and reinforces racism" (p. 6). Drawing these frameworks together in a materialist analysis enables a discussion that challenges a notion of incremental school reform. More important, DisCrit calls for a strategic alliance among the dispossessed in schools. Through outlining initiatives in urban and special education reform, in this chapter I demonstrate how strikingly similar perspectives on diversity have shaped curriculum reform narratives. I conclude with a general proposition for tenets that may inform a unified DisCrit reform agenda.

TO BE "URBAN" AND/OR "SPECIAL NEEDS":
RACE AND ABILITY IN SCHOOL REFORM

The discourse surrounding American school reform offers two primary narratives. One narrative is the nation "at risk" of losing its place in the global economy. Another reform narrative points out persisting inequalities between the opportunities of children of color and White children, which become magnified in and through special education (Blanchett, 2006; Ladson-Billings, 2006). The notion of the "at-risk" child is one of the primary conceptual tools deployed by each narrative to illustrate the problem. The "achievement gap" is constructed in order to define children as "at risk," which signals the need for school reform. Whether construing the problem of poor school achievement as a danger to the economy or as an indication of injustice, both narratives objectify the "at-risk" child to make an argument.

School reform discourses reify co-constructions of race, class, and ability that naturalize inequity in education and society as well. The wide reporting of comparative measures on education assessments among groups serves to affirm ableist and racist ideologies. Thus, the tools that are proffered to illustrate *inequity* in opportunity simultaneously perpetuate determinist narratives about difference and diversity that underscore *inequality* between children. The interlocution of race and disability is pronounced in the "medical *language of pathology*" to characterize individuals as being "at risk" of school failure (Swadener & Lubeck, 1995, p. 2, emphasis in original). In other words, to be poor and Brown *is* construed as pathology. The discourses of race and class, as Erevelles (2000) and Leonardo and Broderick (2011) have argued, rely upon the concept of disablement. The result of a pathological characterization of difference is that even when school reform discussions explicitly locate ableism, socioeconomic inequity, racism, Eurocentrism, patriarchy, and/or White privilege as root problems, the most easily discernible measures of failure and success emphasize the individual, community, or group who is "at risk."

The comparatively poorer achievement of students of color is on the national agenda, as is the same pattern of achievement of learners identified with disabilities. Agendas for Black, Brown, and poor children become signified as "urban" and children with identified disabilities are those with "special needs," and both readily become the banners for the movements, within which the complexities of the identities, histories, and positions ascribed to race and disability are obscured. In a full circle, the narrative of school reform refers back to the intractability of urban plight and the outright assertion that education for students with disabilities is, well, special. The moniker, *school reform*, suggests systemic change, yet the discourses that comprise narratives about such change almost immediately collapse to a focus on the individual "at risk," which, in turn, invites a response that seeks to remedy a particular pathology. Subsequently, a pathological approach to what is suggested by the "achievement gap" routes discussion away from systemic school reform and toward a focus on specific practices for specific persons or groups of people. School reform becomes a divided enterprise, with "urban school reform" being taken up on different turf than "special education reform."

MULTICULTURAL AND INCLUSIVE CURRICULUM REFORM

Arguing for equal access to facilities, materials, and resources is a fairly forthright enterprise when compared to the struggle, to use Kliebard's (1995) characterization, for the knowledge and practices that structure curriculum. *Multicultural education* and *inclusive education* are two fields of study that seek to reform the White, Eurocentric, and ableist discourses that constitute the explicit and hidden curriculum. Both disciplines are varied and have come to signify interest in (1) the access and achievement of students with disabilities and students of color, respectively, in schools, and (2) the role of school curriculum and pedagogy in social reconstruction. A brief conceptual outline of various approaches to inclusivity and multiculturalism yields insight into the strikingly similar ways in which difference is positioned within ideas of curriculum and pedagogy reform.

In 1987, Sleeter and Grant provided a taxonomy of research that claimed multicultural education as its subject. The structure they provided more than 25 years ago continues to organize the book *Making Choices for Multicultural Education*, now in its sixth edition (Sleeter & Grant, 2007). The classification scheme organizes types of approaches to multicultural education in terms of goals, topics, curriculum and instruction, and policy, leading to several categories: Teaching the Culturally Different, Human Relations Approach, Single Group Studies, Multicultural Education, and Multicultural Social Justice Education. The literature in special education and inclusive education offers a similar array of approaches regarding whether and how to instruct students with disabilities in general education environments. Literature in Disability Studies comments on the production of knowledge about disability and disabled experiences. I unite the approaches in four themes that make up the next sections of this chapter: (1) An Individual(ized) Approach to Difference, (2) Pluralism as a Social Practice, (3) Diversity as a Curricular Practice, and (4) Social Justice as a Curriculum Project.

An Individual(ized) Approach to Difference

One way to account for differences among students is to address the aspects of particular individuals that appear to place them "at risk" of failure within the curriculum. The individualized approach to difference is not conceived as change to a general curriculum, but rather inserts supplemental and remedial practices in response to the needs of particular individuals and groups. Special education practice, for example, is premised on documenting the ways in which an educational program may be individualized for a student with a disability, which is written in the Individualized Education Plan. Examples of individualized approaches include strategy instruction or the provision of accommodations designed to help a student gain access to and find achievement within the general curriculum. In multicultural education, the framework of "Treating the Culturally Different" (Sleeter & Grant, 2007) focuses on individual or cultural group approaches that may include, for example, teaching Standard English to those who speak Black English. An individualized approach aims to provide specialized treatment to the individual student or group of students and is not extended to students who are not positioned as "at risk." Ostensibly, the individualized approach to difference positions diversity as student-centered and strives to supplement instruction as needed.

Pluralism as a Social Practice

Another approach present in literature on multicultural and inclusive education conceives of inclusion and pluralism toward the development of positive intergroup social human relations (Sleeter & Grant, 2007). This family of practices extends the educative benefit of inclusion and pluralism to include students who are not "at risk," and positions knowing about the "other" as beneficial to peace, recognition, and appreciation of diversity. Including materials that depict notable accomplishments and contributions of people of color, those with disabilities, women, people with lesbian and gay identities, and so on allows all students to broaden their knowledge and appreciation of diversity. Diversity-related content is adding to the educational environment for the express purpose of increasing pluralism. Desegregation, in terms of race and disability, is argued from a stance that asserts togetherness as a mechanism to enable young people to resist stereotypes. Adding information about diversity and making efforts to create classrooms comprised of different-looking children enriches and enhances the curriculum and school experience for all.

Diversity as a Curricular Practice

Both the individualized approach and social practice approaches to inclusivity and plurality account for difference and diversity in supplemental curriculum practices. Neither treating "different" individuals differently so they may achieve in the standard curriculum nor incorporating diversity as part of an accumulated knowledge and experience attempts to unpack the power underlying the subjectivities and positionality of minoritized experiences. In contrast, a framework of "Multicultural Education" (Sleeter & Grant, 2007) is an integrative practice that strives to articulate knowledge production as a diversity-rich endeavor. Knowledge construction (Banks, 1993) attends to the power relationships expressed in curriculum, which affect how students experience identities and positionalities vis-à-vis official knowledge that reflects White and ableist perspectives. Changing the knowledge construction compels us to examine the ways in which the school curriculum depicts diverse people in, for example, historical events: To what extent are African American experiences characterized almost exclusively by enslavement and the Civil Rights Act? Attention to knowledge construction also demands thoughtfulness about varying perspectives on events imbued with conflicting accounts, such as European exploration and colonization. Changing the cultural narratives within curriculum has been addressed in multicultural education, notably articulated in the oeuvre of Banks (1993) and Asante (1991), respectively. The basis of an analogous approach can be found in Connor and Baglieri (2009) and Baglieri and Shapiro (2012), who cite disability-critical approaches to history and literature, as guided by works including Longmore and Umansky's (2001) *The New Disability History* and Mitchell and Snyder's (2000) *Narrative Prosthesis*. The collective arguments of multicultural and inclusive education draw from the desire to write difference into the knowledge tapestry taught in schools in ways that (1) render difference visible and (2) pose "othered" experiences as empowered or resistant, rather than incidental or perpetually subjugated, as in colonial discourses.

Although most multiculturalists and disability-critical curricularists desire to practice diversity in ways that inform social reconstruction, most curriculum reform conforms to what Banks (1993) describes as Contributions and Additive approaches and that Steinberg and Kincheloe (2009) might regard as liberal and pluralist practices in multicultural education. Contributions and Additive approaches add diversity content to the curriculum without changing the knowledge-power construction. These efforts to change curriculum practices tend toward supplemental lessons, which is more closely related to Pluralism as Social Practice. Disability awareness events and the ubiquitous simulation "games" in which children learn what it is like to be blindfolded or how to take a ride in a wheelchair simply underscore disability as an experience of loss and disadvantage (Brew-Parrish, 1997). Reading Langston Hughes only during February or eating "Tex-Mex" food on Cinco de Mayo tends to characterize racially minoritized experiences and works as supplemental and/or to reinforce cultural essentialism and stereotypes (Cochran-Smith, 1995; Nieto, 1995). Nonetheless, scholars, such as Banks (2002) and Connor and Baglieri (2009), optimistically imagine that Contributions or Additive approaches, or curricular infusion, respectively, may incrementally lead to more antiracist/anti-ableist practices.

Social Justice as a Curriculum Project

A fourth way that curriculum reform in multicultural and inclusive education has been proposed involves approaching curriculum and pedagogy as
a project in progress, characterized by the class or school community's engagement in social action. Sleeter and Grant (2007) describe Multicultural
Social Justice Education as practices that include the perspective and ideals
in multicultural education and extend to emphasize the study of power relations that assert the domination of particular perspectives and subvert
others. Thus, disability inclusivity and multiculturalism may be active processes constructed by class members as they seek and identify sites of inequity and then work against them. Disability has increasingly been included
in the pantheon of topics described by multicultural literature. A critical
Disability Studies perspective that construes disability as an experience
informed by minoritization and subjugation is also increasingly included
in social justice in education literature (Connor, 2012). Education that is
disability-critical, is multicultural, and works toward social justice depicts
knowledge construction as an agentive process, which actively affirms or
produces ideologies that reflect the culture of power. Curriculum reform
might aim for a version of multicultural education described as Critical
Diversity and Multiculturalism (Steinberg & Kincheloe, 2009), also related
to Banks's (1993) Transformation and Social Action approaches to curriculum reform. Herein, knowledge is treated as information within which
power relationships are embedded that, when rendered visible, may guide
agentive work, rather than something that can be "banked," to use Freire's
term. Challenging the knowledge-power construction through curriculum
reform by engaging students' critical thought and social action is decidedly
antiracist and anti-ableist.

Positioning Race and Disability in Curriculum Reform

There are various typologies used to describe the many facets and approaches to multicultural and inclusive education currently in use. As race and
ability are co-constructed through ableist and racist ideologies in cultural
practice and school histories, movements in curriculum reform are born
within the same constructions. It should not be surprising, then, that multicultural and inclusive frameworks for curriculum reform occupy similar
positions in relation to schooling. As two projects that fundamentally seek
to unravel the fabric from which schooling is sewn, multiculturalism and
inclusive frameworks have been resisted or kept separate. Multicultural
education is resisted by, for example, those concerned about (non-White)
cultural infringement on the school's role in national unification (Feinberg,
1998). Inclusive education is resisted out of concern for equal resource al-
location, with particular attention to how staff can provide appropriate

teaching and curriculum for all students in a heterogeneous environment (Cole, 1998). The separation of multicultural and inclusive reform agendas from the broader enterprise of public schooling is emphasized in the designations *urban* and *special education* reform.

Of the multicultural practices that have been taken up, Steinberg and Kincheloe (2009) argue that the current mainstream articulation—that is, pluralist diversity practices—merely "exoticizes difference and positions it as necessary knowledge for those who would compete in the globalized economy" (p. 4). In this view, the traction that multicultural curriculum reform has gained may be attributed to what Bell (1980) calls *interest convergence*. What may have been characterized as knowledge practices designed to empower Black and Brown learners is actually taken up in the mainstream because it is presumed to contribute to White privilege. The idea of the Individualized Education Plan for students with disabilities has pervaded educational practice to such an extent that many recommendations can be described as essentially "acurricular" (Pugach & Warger, 1996) and they have not yielded attainment of schooling as property for learners. The practice of differentiating instruction, once associated only with special education, however, is now widely recommended, along with the assertion of Universal Design for Learning (UDL) as a framework to seek equity for students with disabilities and others who may be excluded within regimented curriculum and instruction. It may not be a coincidence that differentiation and UDL have gained wider support as the audit culture of high-stakes testing is once again ratcheting up, perhaps threatening otherwise privileged children with being identified as "at risk." That multicultural education and universal design are increasingly present in education discourse may not be an indication that schooling has become more embracive of raced and/or disabled experiences. My critical concern is that the reforms toward multicultural and inclusive curriculum practices that have been taken up are done in ways that protect or forward White and abled privilege.

Others point out that the implementation of multicultural and inclusive curriculum and practices in schools has already been co-opted by ableist and racist discourses in play. Graham and Slee (2007) point out that the idea of inclusivity in education, which was once offered as a protest calling for a radical change to the classificatory function of schooling, has become a means to uphold the status quo. Placement and training practices "intended to promote the inclusion of students with disabilities [has become] understood as the achievement of an inclusive education system" (pp. 2–3). Rather than change how schools contribute to the disablement of children, schools continue to engage special education practices in which one must first be labeled and classified as disabled, and thus presumed excluded, in order to become "included." This predicament points to the ableism embedded within inclusive education reform. On multicultural education, Schoorman and Bogotch (2010) observe that teachers tend to think about multicultural education in terms of "demographic diversity rather than with social justice, strategies for instruction rather than with theory" (p. 79). In both examples, the desire for an active and critical approach to inclusivity and multiculturalism is co-opted to serve dominating narratives about the pathology of difference. Whether inclusive and multicultural education is unable to escape racist and ableist discourses or whether the spread of critical multiculturalism or universal design is to progress as an exercise of colonialism, a liberatory experience, or stasis for students of color and students with disabilities remains in question.

ABILITY AND RACE IN NEOLIBERAL REFORM

It is impossible to talk about school reform without noting the embattled discourse of neoliberalism. Neoliberalism in education is a many-armed concept, with privatization of the management of schools at its center. In short, the idea is that private sector entities may develop, fund, and/or manage schools, replacing the public provision of such services. Saltman (2007) invokes the concept of disaster capitalism to point out the inordinate impact neoliberal reforms have had in urban areas. The production of the achievement gap and the ongoing designation of urban children as "at risk" construe schools that primarily serve children of color as disaster zones. In turn, the need for "development" provides opportunities for profit.

The deployment of disaster capitalism to drive arguments for the privatization of urban schooling is a clear echo of disability capitalism, noted by Oliver (1999). A publicly funded, tuition-driven privatized system of schooling has long existed for students with disabilities. There are private schools devoted to all manners of disability types that range in form and cost and vast diversity in the quality of schools. For example, The Darrow School, a private boarding school in New York, advertises teachers who are "exceptionally attuned to each student's learning styles and proficiencies" (Darrow School, n.d.), while the practices of shock treatment and restraint at the Judge Rotenberg Center in Massachusetts have been accused of violating the United Nations convention against torture (Ahern & Rosenthal, 2010). Privatization in special education has not automatically led to positive innovations and has perhaps allowed for egregious practices in some cases. The privatization of special education has, perhaps, fueled other independent competitors because of its profitability but has not generated reform in public schools. Quite to the contrary, the existence of private alternatives has further dispossessed children with disabilities within public schooling by making the decision to send a child "out of district" possible. From a broader perspective of reform, aspects of neoliberalism such as more prevalent charter schools and "school choice" may offer a redistribution of privilege for some but are not a promising plan for broader school reform toward equity for all if special education privatization is an exemplar of the possible systemic impact.

DIVIDED AND CONQUERED

Multicultural education and inclusive education have been divided, and as a result of these divisions, supporters of each movement have also been conquered. Segregated special education operates as a practice of White and classed privilege, allowing White students with social capital access to the property of schooling and dispossessing students of color (Blanchett, 2006; Brantlinger, 2003). As historical distance from race-based biological deter-minism and discourses of cultural deprivation has been sought, disablement of students of color has become a reinscription of these legacies (Irvine, 2012; Sleeter, 1987). As special education has flourished on a foundation of scientific neutrality, the production of disability and a body politic of disability remains unexamined in schools (Baker, 2002). It may be argued that both fields of multicultural and inclusive education's claims have led to a pile-up of curriculum and instruction reforms that have become sanitized at best, or white noise at worst, overwhelming educators who are then accused of being "bad teachers" from all fronts (Kumashiro, 2012). Multicultural education projects can become stronger through engagement with disablement as a conceptual tool that renders dispossession more visible (Erevelles, 2000). Inclusive education projects are made stronger by engaging with a notion of curriculum as property. DisCrit offers a way to unravel the experiential and conceptual histories that have distanced disability studies from critical race studies and inclusive education from multicultural education. It provides a theoretical framework that instructs us in what we must learn about ourselves from one another.

A UNIFIED MOVEMENT: THREE PROPOSALS

What could be the tenets and logic informing a unified DisCrit voice on school reform?

1. Resist the meritocratic practice of schooling and normative assessment structure. Normative approaches to assessment will always characterize half of all children as below average, within which many will become disabled and identified as "at risk" (Ball & Harry, 2010; Gallagher, 2010). When more than half of children achieve on a measure, assessment measures are revised in a process of "norming" to increase the level of challenge (Kohn, 2004). The impossibility of equality in this context is clear. Merit sought through school achievement is a moving target. Erevelles (2000) argues:

Despite the ways in which proponents of inclusive education have worked toward radically redefining the field of education, these redefinitions still exist within a social and economic context that nevertheless demands "productivity" and "efficiency" as the hallmarks of success within capitalism—concepts that have historically required the category of "disability" to enable schools to perform such sorting practices effectively. (p. 45)

As long as schools rely on normative assessment and disability identification practices, they comply with a system that presumes inequity as a foregone conclusion. Because DisCrit forwards a worldview in which we are embedded in networks of racism and ableism that tend to transmute rather than subside, we should assume that norming practices will seldom be in service to people of color and students with disabilities.

2. Reconceptualize curriculum as being in service to communities, rather than in service to individuals or the economy. If the curriculum were to become more pluralistic, universally designed, or taught in culturally relevant ways, it is possible that "other" children's funds of knowledge, skills, and experiences may gain prominence, which could equalize curricular advantages. An argued benefit of a reconstructed curriculum through multicultural and inclusive education is the enfranchisement of groups that are currently dispossessed, leading to increased individual school successes. The aim, however, is to enable targeted individuals to gain traction in the meritocracy. Thus, many foci in curriculum reform enable individual achievement but do not aim for a reconstruction of the system in which many children will always be dispossessed.

Instead of seeking a revised curriculum that operates to sanction particular forms of knowledge, plural or culturally relevant as they may be, we might instead agitate for a curriculum comprised of community-focused critical pedagogies. A materialist analysis of DisCrit asserts that racism and ableism are active processes with material implications. On the notion of inclusion, Graham and Slee (2007) point out "an implicit centred-ness to the term inclusion, for it discursively privileges notions of the pre-existing by seeking to include the Other into a prefabricated, naturalised space" (p. 2). In seeking education that is inclusive and multicultural through the creation of critical Disability Studies and multiculturalism, we must be wary of simply asserting a new center that is equally fixed and prefabricated. Critical pedagogies insist on learning practices that are alive and ever-imbued with attention to the stakes held by their immediate participants. I acknowledge Gabel's (2002) critique of the abled notion of voice in critical pedagogy, however, in which she points out the potential for disabled students to remain marginalized in group contexts. Attention to accessibility in critical pedagogy, noted by Johnson (2004), may offer promising directions.

3. Support community-based control of the economies built up around disability and disaster capitalism. Activists in the independent living movement of people with disabilities have argued for self-directed support and services, in which clients select and direct providers and the course of services. This type of resistance in relation to schooling is, at minimum, an argument for the preservation or reinstatement of local school boards. It is certainly a movement against privatized, market-based reforms seeking to attract investors. The challenge to securing leadership in, of, and for dispossessed communities will only be greater if public education funds are diverted to private or charter schools through tuition or vouchers.

None of these ideas for a platform of unified DisCrit school reform is new to the discussion on democratic education. But an alliance among voices in school reform and a reclamation of all that is done in the name of urban and special education reform would be a new and large constituent. In solidarity.

Part VI

RACE, DISABILITY, AND THE LAW

CHAPTER 11

A DisCrit Perspective on *The State of Florida v. George Zimmerman*

Racism, Ableism, and Youth Out of Place in Community and School

Kathleen M. Collins

> If we in America have reached that point in our desperate culture when we must murder children, no matter for what reason or what color, we don't deserve to survive, and probably won't.
>
> —William Faulkner, 1955, on the murder of Emmett Till

INTRODUCTION

As I am drafting this manuscript, my 7-year-old son is reclining on the daybed next to my desk in my home office and playing his Nintendo DS. It is winter in Pennsylvania, a season of snow, school closures, and illness that often finds us juggling our responsibilities from home. We are used to this collaborative writing routine, and usually it works well and makes us both happy.

But today he is not quietly playing his computer game. Today he is humming, and occasionally, he bursts into actually singing. It's a song he's been singing constantly for weeks, one that he learned in music class in 2nd grade. The first and third verses are sung in a manner that echoes the traditional spiritual from which they are drawn, while the middle verse is a fast-paced rap, embellished by my son with a bit of improvised beat-boxing. It's a very, very catchy song . . . and it's distracting.

Free at last
Free at last
Thank God Almighty I'm free at last
* * * *
Martin had a dream that he could see
Once upon a time there was kid like me
* * * *
Free at last
Free at last
Thank God Almighty I'm free at last

I stop typing, and look at my beautiful, Brown-skinned child. "So," I ask him, "what do you think that song means?"

"I think it means Martin's Luther King's *I have a dream* speech. He had a dream about Black kids and White kids going to school together. And holding hands." He looks up from his game, his face drawn into a serious and pained expression. "And I don't understand why someone shot him, Mom. Why *did* someone shoot him?"

Why did someone shoot him? My son has asked a lot of similar questions in recent months and I have struggled to answer them.

Why won't they let the kids with disabilities go to school in New Orleans?
Why did they arrest him (Reginald Latson) for going to the library?
Why did George Zimmerman shoot Trayvon Martin?
Why didn't Zimmerman go to jail?
Why did the policeman shoot Michael Brown?
Why didn't the policeman go to jail?
Why did the policeman choke Eric Garner?
Why didn't *that* policeman go to jail?
Why did the policeman shoot that little boy (Tamir Rice) in the park?
Why didn't *that* policeman go to jail?
What would you do if that was me, Mom?
Why are you crying, Mom?

Writing as a scholar, a teacher, and the single, White mother of a biracial son who is most often read as Black, I offer this chapter as an exploratory response to these questions. In it, I present an analysis of *The State of Florida v. George Zimmerman* framed by Disability Critical Race Theory (DisCrit) (Annamma, Connor, & Ferri, 2013). This intersectional analysis of the case sheds light on how ableism and racism work to shape identifications of youth *out of place* and to justify exclusion of, incarceration of, and violence toward youth so identified, a dynamic present in all of the cases mentioned above (and so many more).

The State of Florida v. George Zimmerman is more than one legal case; it is emblematic of our country's history of state-sanctioned physical, discursive, psychological, and symbolic violence against Black, Brown, and disabled youth. A DisCrit lens reveals George Zimmerman's trial and subsequent acquittal for killing 17-year-old, unarmed Trayvon Martin as a case example of the synergistic nature of racism and ableism in fueling state-sanctioned physical, psychological, and symbolic violence against Black, Brown, and disabled youth marked as out of place. I use the term *out of place* here to (1) illustrate being considered geographically and culturally out of place, as in contexts where one's very presence is treated as transgressive, and (2) describe being considered socially and discursively "out of line," as in interactions with authority figures where one's responses are interpreted as challenging the power of that authority or as "not knowing one's place."

In the following section, I present a brief summary of the events leading up to George Zimmerman's trial for the killing of Trayvon Martin, *The State of Florida v. George Zimmerman*. I then describe DisCrit and the questions this theoretical lens positions us to ask. I follow this section with a DisCrit analysis of one important aspect of the trial, the profiling and presentation of Trayvon Martin as a "dangerous Black boy." I conclude with a personal story that illustrates the implications of this analysis for understanding the daily exclusions and deficit positionings experienced by youth pushed *out of place* in school. This juxtaposition of my analysis of the processes that turned Trayvon Martin into a "dangerous Black boy" with my experiences as a White mother raising a biracial son is designed to make visible the connections between the physical violence inflicted on Black youth racially profiled as out of place in communities and the discursive and psychological violence of racist, ableist, and segregationist educational practices that push some children out of place in school. DisCrit theory makes apparent that these forms of violence are part of the same continuum of exclusion; one begets the other as Black, Brown, and dis/abled bodies are marked out of place in school and in community.

Data for my narrative and discursive DisCrit analysis of *The State of Florida v. George Zimmerman* are drawn from the 183 pages of case discovery documents released by the court, video recordings of the 5-week-long trial, and newspaper and television reports as noted. Data for my personal story are drawn from my own journals and email communications with my son's teachers.

THE STATE OF FLORIDA V. GEORGE ZIMMERMAN

On the evening of February 26, 2012, 28-year-old White Hispanic Neighborhood Watch captain George Zimmerman profiled, shot, and killed Trayvon Martin, an unarmed, 17-year-old Black male high school student walking outside the condominium home of his father's fiancée in the Retreat at Twin

Lakes Community. At 6:34 P.M. Trayvon left a 7-Eleven convenience store near the community to walk home with his purchases (a bag of Skittles and a can of AriZona brand watermelon drink). At 7:11 P.M., George Zimmerman called the nonemergency police line to report Trayvon's presence. Portions of the official transcript of that call released by the City of Sanford, Florida, Police Department are reproduced here:

> *Dispatcher:* Sanford Police Department. . . .
> *Zimmerman:* Hey, we've had some break-ins in my neighborhood, and there's a real suspicious guy [gives street name]. This guy looks like he's up to no good, or he's on drugs or something. It's raining and he's just walking around, looking about.
> *Dispatcher:* Okay, and this guy is he White, Black, or Hispanic?
> *Zimmerman:* He looks Black.
> *Dispatcher:* Did you see what he was wearing?
> *Zimmerman:* Yeah. A dark hoodie, like a gray hoodie, and either jeans or sweatpants and white tennis shoes. He's [unintelligible], he was just staring.
> [exchange describing the area]
> *Zimmerman:* Yeah, now he's coming towards me.
> *Dispatcher:* Okay.
> *Zimmerman:* He's got his hand in his waistband. And he's a Black male.
> *Dispatcher:* How old would you say he looks?
> *Zimmerman:* He's got button on his shirt, late teens.
> *Dispatcher:* Late teens okay.
> *Zimmerman:* Something's wrong with him. Yup, he's coming to check me out, he's got something in his hands, I don't know what his deal is.
> *Dispatcher:* Just let me know if he does anything, okay?
> *Zimmerman:* How long until you get an officer over here?
> *Dispatcher:* Yeah, we've got someone on the way; just let me know if this guy does anything else.
> *Zimmerman:* Okay. These assholes, they always get away. [exchange regarding directions to community] Shit, he's running.
> *Dispatcher:* He's running? Which way is he running?
> *Zimmerman:* Down towards the other entrance to the neighborhood.
> *Dispatcher:* Which entrance is that that he's heading towards?
> *Zimmerman:* The back entrance. Fucking [unintelligible word; disputed in media as possibly the racial slur *coons* or *punks*]
> *Dispatcher:* Are you following him?
> *Zimmerman:* Yeah.
> *Dispatcher:* Okay, we don't need you to do that.
> *Zimmerman:* Okay.
> [exchange regarding name and phone number and more directions; there are a lot of wind and air noises at this point in the call]

The entire phone call took 4 minutes and 9 seconds, ending shortly after 7:15 P.M. Despite being told by the dispatcher *not* to follow Trayvon, after hanging up the phone Zimmerman confronted him as *out of place*.

During much of his attempted walk home, Trayvon was on the phone with Rachel Jeantel, an 18-year-old Black female high school student who later became a key witness for the prosecution. Rachel reported hearing Trayvon say, "What are you following me for?" and Zimmerman saying, "What are you doing here?" before her call with Trayvon was cut off at 7:16 P.M. The first officer to arrive on the scene testified that Trayvon was dead when he arrived at 7:17 P.M., approximately 2 minutes after Zimmerman ended his call with the police dispatcher. When the police arrived, George Zimmerman admitted that he had shot Trayvon Martin in the chest, and claimed the killing was a matter of self-defense. Zimmerman was questioned by the police but not arrested.

On March 22, 2012, Florida governor Rick Scott appointed attorney Angela Corey as special prosecutor on the case. Shortly after her appointment, on March 26, 2012, Corey made a public statement to the press emphasizing that the lack of charges against Zimmerman was because of the complexities of Florida's self-defense laws. Corey stated, "The Stand-your-Ground law is one portion of justifiable use of deadly force. And what that means is that the state must go forward and be able to prove its case beyond a reasonable doubt. . . . So it makes the case in general more difficult than a normal criminal case" (Gutman & Tienabeso, 2012, p. 1).

Public outcry mounted as weeks went by and George Zimmerman remained free of imprisonment and criminal charges. Martin's parents started an online petition addressed to the U.S. attorney general, Florida's attorney general, the prosecuting attorney, and the Sanford police chief, calling for the "prosecution of George Zimmerman for the shooting and killing of Trayvon Martin" and garnered 2,278,945 signatures (Martin & Fulton, 2012). On March 23, 2012, President Obama commented on the case, noting in part, "My main message is to the parents of Trayvon Martin. You know, if I had a son he'd look like Trayvon. And I think they are right to expect that all of us as Americans are going to take this with the seriousness it deserves, and we are going to get to the bottom of exactly what happened" (CNS News, 2012).

On April 11, 2012, George Zimmerman was charged with second-degree murder and manslaughter in the shooting death of Trayvon Martin. Zimmerman's trial began on June 10, 2013, with a White female judge and a six-member, all-female jury, one of whom identified as Puerto Rican and five of whom identified as White. Zimmerman's two attorneys and the state's attorneys all appeared to be White. On July 13, 2013, George Zimmerman was acquitted of all criminal charges in the slaying of Trayvon Martin. On February 24, 2015, the Justice Department announced that it would not bring federal civil rights charges against George Zimmerman.

During the 15 days of televised testimony and 2 days of jury delib-
eration, *The State of Florida v. George Zimmerman*, a criminal trial of
George Zimmerman, effectively became a public trial of Trayvon Martin
and Rachel Jeantel. Martin was described repeatedly as a "thug," and his
hooded sweatshirt was characterized as "thug wear." Jeantel was repeatedly described as "retarded," "stupid," and as an example of the failure
of the American educational system to teach academic literacy. Florida's
Stand-your-Ground law and its ideologies shaped the narrative presented by
Zimmerman's defense team, contributed to the public vilification of Martin
and Jeantel, and were included in the instructions given to the jury.

A DisCrit lens illuminates the racism and ableism at work in this case
as boundary work. George Zimmerman was exonerated because he was
positioned as defending both the physical boundary of his neighborhood
and the social, cultural boundary of White, male, abled privilege. Trayvon
Martin was positioned as a dangerous Black male who stepped *out of place*
in his attempt to transgress those boundaries.

DISCRIT: UNDERSTANDING RACISM
AND ABLEISM AS BOUNDARY WORK

How is it possible that a 17-year-old was intentionally shot dead for simply
walking home *and the admitted shooter was not found culpable of a crime?*
As my DisCrit analysis will show, both ableism and racism were at work in
this case, and their ability to drive its outcome is embedded in the legal and
cultural history of this country.

Fifty-seven years before George Zimmerman killed Trayvon Martin for
being geographically out of place, two vigilante White men in Mississippi
(Roy Bryant and J. W. Milam) publicly bragged about abducting, brutally as-
saulting, and killing a 14-year-old Black boy, Emmett Till, for behavior they
deemed socially out of place—allegedly flirting with a White woman—and
yet they were acquitted of kidnapping and murder charges. After the trial, Bryant and Milam sold their confession story to *Look* magazine. Milam
stated:

> I like niggers—in their place—I know how to work 'em. But I just decided it was
> time a few people got put on notice. As long as I live and can do anything about
> it, *niggers are gonna stay in their place.* Niggers ain't gonna vote where I live.
> If they did, they'd control the government. They ain't gonna go to school with
> my kids. And when a nigger gets close to mentioning sex with a white woman,
> he's tired o' livin.' I'm likely to kill him. (J. W. Milam, as quoted in Huie, 1956,
> emphasis added)

Trayvon Martin, Emmett Till, and countless others have been killed for crossing, or for *appearing* to cross, the boundaries described by Milam—for stepping out of place socially, culturally, or geographically. Indeed, laws, courts, and juries in the United States have always protected police officers, and often those acting as self-appointed individuals, such as Neighborhood Watchmen like Zimmerman, from punishment when killing occurs in the defense of social, cultural, and physical boundaries.

DisCrit theory (Annamma et al., 2013) can help us understand these legally approved killings as part of a historical pattern of sanctioned exclusion and violence in the service of boundary protection. DisCrit examines the ways that perceptions of race and judgments of dis/ability intersect and shape recognition of whose body, mind, language, and/or behavior is acceptable and whose is deserving of incarceration, exclusion, silencing, and/or punishment. The development of DisCrit is critically important to understanding the historical and cultural significance of recent high-profile cases reporting on the unpunished killing, incarceration, or abuse of Black and/or disabled youth for seemingly nonthreatening behaviors.

Each of DisCrit's seven central tenets (Annamma et al., 2013) is important to understanding and disrupting patterns of exclusion, marginalization, and violence against Black, Brown, and disabled people. Most significant to my analysis here, however, are two assertions that I will explain in detail in the following sections.

Racism, Ableism, and the Making of "Normal"

The first tenet is that "racism and ableism circulate interdependently, often in neutralized and invisible ways, to uphold notions of normalcy" (Annamma et al., 2013, pp. 11–12). This tenet of DisCrit underscores ableism and racism as boundary work: In the process of defining, distributing, and upholding what counts as normal, racism and ableism also work to mark, exclude, and extinguish what is different or *abnormal*.

Historically, one of the most fiercely contested sites for this type of boundary work is school. It is not by coincidence that, in his bragging confession of murdering Emmett Till, J. W. Milam emphasized, "They [Black children] ain't gonna go to school with my kids." Milam and Bryant murdered Till on August 28, 1955. Just 3 months earlier, on May 31, 1955, the Supreme Court had followed its historic 1954 *Brown v. the Board of Education of Topeka Kansas* ruling with a second ruling asserting that school desegregation must occur "with all deliberate speed" (*Brown et al. v. Board of Education of Topeka, Kansas II*, 1955).

Shortly thereafter, new "technologies of exclusion" (Ferri & Connor, 2005, p. 470) began to emerge to counter the integration effects of *Brown* and maintain the educational boundary described by Milam. Special education classrooms and academically tracking children according to perceived ability served to provide spaces to contain children marked as out of the bounds of "normal" (such as children with dis/abilities, children of color, children whose first language was not English, children from lower-income families). Although this form of segregation happens within school buildings, the growth of charter schools has served the same sorting purposes and functioned to re-entrench educational segregation between and among different school buildings (Collins, 2015).

Discourse, Law, and Policy: Tools for Boundary Work

The second tenet of DisCrit that guides my analysis points to the importance of considering how laws, policies, and court rulings have worked to enact or challenge racist and ableist ideologies. As noted by the others, identifications of race and dis/ability have changed with time and context, and both have been "used separately and together to deny the rights of some citizens" (Annamma et al., 2013, pp. 14–16). From "ugly laws" to Jim Crow, policies and laws have worked to legalize profiling and to normalize fear of Black, Brown, and dis/abled bodies.

Informed by this tenet of DisCrit, my analysis in this chapter treats policies, laws, and the Zimmerman trial itself as *discourses* and as *texts* (Bacchi, 2000; Ball, 1993a). This perspective asserts that policies and laws are not static; we must understand policy as interpreted and performed by human agents acting within particular contextual affordances and constraints with certain individual interests. Drawing on Foucault (1971, 1974), Ball (1993b) asserts that an understanding of policy as discourse creates recognition of the ideologies that inform and shape policies. This perspective considers the structuring effects of policy and the ways agents take these effects up or resist them (Bacchi, 2000). Similarly, Humphreys (1985) argues for an understanding of law as discourse that recognizes laws as ideological tools which those in power wield to structure and maintain social relationships.

My DisCrit analysis thus considers how ideologies of racism and ableism circulated within the social and legal discourses surrounding *The State of Florida v. George Zimmerman*. DisCrit allows us to ask how social identities are built within discursive interactions and how that building is synergistically both informed by and presented as evidence of the "truth" of larger cultural narratives. In the next section, I begin this analysis with a discussion of how Trayvon Martin was positioned as a potential criminal, as deviant, and as a danger to society by aligning his social identity with the cultural stereotype of the dangerous Black male.

TRAYVON MARTIN: A DANGEROUS BLACK YOUTH

> The only comment that I have right now is that they've killed my son and now they're trying to kill his reputation. —*Sabrina Fulton, Martin's mother, March 26, 2012*

In order to free their client, Zimmerman's defense team needed to create and sustain a narrative wherein the 17-year-old unarmed youth posed such a degree of danger to the older, heavier armed Neighborhood Watch leader that shooting and killing Trayvon could be considered a reasonable response by the jury. On the night George Zimmerman killed Trayvon Martin, Zimmerman outweighed Martin by 30 pounds. Zimmerman was armed with a loaded semi-automatic pistol while Martin carried only a bag of Skittles, a can of AriZona watermelon drink, and his cellphone. Florida's defense law, as reflected in the jury instructions, required only for the jury to agree that "*Based upon appearances*, George Zimmerman must have actually believed that the danger was real" (*The State of Florida v. George Zimmerman,* jury instructions, emphasis added).

The central strategy employed by George Zimmerman's defense team was therefore to portray Trayvon Martin as a threat, as someone potentially violent and capable of provoking fear. They were greatly aided in their efforts to do so by a self-defense law that emphasizes the *appearance of danger* in a country that equates Black males with criminality. As noted by legal scholar Aya Gruber (2014):

> the studies confirming current Americans' cultural adherence to the Black-male-as-criminal stereotype, whether consciously or unconsciously, are so numerous as to be almost banal to the criminal law scholar. (pp. 989–990)

Zimmerman and his defense team had only to activate the jury's internalization of the larger Black-male-as-dangerous-criminal cultural stereotype to make George Zimmerman's decision to kill Trayvon Martin seem reasonable. Critical race scholar Richard Delgado (1995b) calls such stereotypes "stigma pictures," while sociologist Pierre Bourdieu (1977b) describes them as "sincere fictions." They create and sustain a version of Black male identity as criminal that is so ubiquitous as to be taken for granted.

Public Release of 911 Call

The effort to dehumanize and criminalize Trayvon Martin by aligning his personhood with the cultural narrative of the "dangerous Black male" began even before George Zimmerman was charged with murder. The public positioning of Trayvon in the role of dangerous Black male was initiated by the release of Zimmerman's initial phone call to the nonemergency police line on the night of the murder. From this recorded call, we know that from the moment George Zimmerman saw Trayvon Martin, Zimmerman identified Martin as a *dangerous outsider* to the community:

> Hey, we've had some break-ins in my neighborhood, and there's a real suspicious guy [gives street name]. This guy looks like he's up to no good, or he's on drugs or something. It's raining and he's just walking around, looking about.

On what evidence did George Zimmerman base his knowledge-claim that Trayvon Martin was "real suspicious," "up to no good," and "on drugs or something"? The only evidence Zimmerman had access to at this point consisted of Martin's physical characteristics: Black, male, late teens, wearing a hoodie. Zimmerman's initial description is a manifestation of the Black-male-as-criminal cultural narrative, a process commonly referred to as racial profiling.

In continuing to build a narrative description of Martin as the dangerous outsider, the threatening Black male criminal, Zimmerman stated twice to the dispatcher that Martin was Black, once when prompted for a description and later when he said, "He's got his hand in his waistband. And he's a Black male." The juxtaposition of these descriptors was not coincidental or harmless: By discursively aligning the location of Trayvon's hand (implying the presence of a concealed weapon) with the social identity of a Black male, Zimmerman continued to more firmly position Martin in the larger cultural narrative of the dangerous Black male.

Zimmerman continued to align his description of Trayvon with this stigma picture (Delgado, 1995b), emphasizing to the dispatcher, "Something's wrong with him. Yup, he's coming to check me out, he's got something in his hands, I don't know what his deal is." In building the narrative in this manner, Zimmerman aligned himself discursively with his audience, a representative of law enforcement, and distanced himself from Martin, whom he positioned as the deviant threat.

In his call to the nonemergency dispatcher, George Zimmerman thus constructed a narrative depiction of Trayvon Martin as the "other"—as a threat and as deviant or impaired—based solely on the observable evidence that Martin was Black, male, and holding something near or in his waistband. In positioning him as deviant and dangerous, Zimmerman marked Trayvon Martin as *out of place* in the gated community. Identifying Trayvon as out of place allowed Zimmerman to create a narrative that justified the criminalization of behaviors that, absent this narrative, would be considered quite nonthreatening—walking home, talking on the phone, carrying a snack. The release of Zimmerman's narrative to the public marked the beginning of the public alignment of Trayvon Martin's social identity with the dangerous Black male stereotype.

Strategically Leaked Information

The description of Martin as a dangerous Black male was thickened through the release of strategically leaked information that worked to further align his social identity with the dangerous Black male stereotype. The narrative was further supported in the public eye by the release of three pieces of information to the media and the general public: (1) Trayvon Martin's high school disciplinary records; (2) the written statement from Zimmerman to the police, including the original police report, documenting Zimmerman's claim of self-defense; and (3) Trayvon Martin's cellphone records (including texts and photos) and information from his social media accounts.

The *Orlando Sentinel* first reported the story that Trayvon Martin was staying with his father after he had been suspended from school on a drug-related offense; this report was followed quickly by other media outlets (Robles, 2012). Releasing student data to the public is illegal, and furthermore Trayvon's school suspensions were unrelated to what occurred on the night he was killed. Martin's school disciplinary records were made public to justify the racial profiling that contributed to his death and to rationalize Zimmerman's actions. Releasing personal information that can be used to build a public, criminalized biography of Black men killed by law enforcement is not a new strategy; what is significant here is how this strategy is increasing being applied to Black *children and youth* who are killed by law enforcement. Furthermore, Trayvon's school disciplinary records illustrate that even before his encounter with Zimmerman, Trayvon was caught in the web of hyper-surveillance and criminalization that results in a disproportionate number of Black youth being suspended and ultimately pushed out of school (Leonard, 2014).

On June 21, 2012, Zimmerman's defense team used their professional website to publicly release the written statement Zimmerman made to the police shortly after killing Trayvon Martin. In this handwritten statement to police, Zimmerman describes Martin as a "suspect" (rather than "victim") throughout the document, positioning Martin as a dangerous criminal. Zimmerman begins with a brief history of the break-ins at the Retreat at Twin Lakes that led to the formation of the community's Neighborhood Watch program, framing the events of that evening with a story of criminality. He then describes spotting Martin, "casually walking in the rain looking into homes" and notes, "the suspect fled into a darkened area." Zimmerman had clearly already profiled Martin as a suspect—not as a teenager walking home and then running because he fears for his own life.

Zimmerman's narrative continues to position Martin as a dangerous criminal and aggressor. Zimmerman describes an assault where Martin walked up and punched him in the face, climbed on top of him, and slammed his head repeatedly into the concrete sidewalk:

> At this point I felt the suspect reach for my now exposed firearm and say "Your [sic] gonna die tonight Mother Fucker." I unholstered my firearm in fear for my life as he had assured he was going to kill me and fired one shot into his torso. The suspect sat back allowing me to sit up and said "You got me." At this point I slid out from underneath him and got on top of the suspect holding his hands away from his body. (Zimmerman, 2012, pp. 3–4)

Zimmerman uses words and phrases designed to align himself with law enforcement, such as *firearm* rather than *gun*, and his emphasis on the "exposed" nature of the firearm. This phrasing aligns with a narrative often heard in police shootings: "He reached for my weapon." In addition, Zimmerman aligns his narrative with self-defense law, with which he was familiar, by emphasizing that he was "in fear for my life." Releasing Zimmerman's police statement thus allowed the defense team to put forward a story that supported their positioning of Trayvon Martin as a deviant criminal, the dangerous Black male out in the rain casing a quiet community.

Just as Milam drew on the prevalent cultural fears of his time, especially fear of miscegenation and integration, to mark Emmett Till as *out of place* and to justify the brutal murder of an unarmed child, Zimmerman employed the current fear-based narrative of the dangerous Black male to mark Trayvon Martin as *out of place* and to justify killing an unarmed youth. Milam was able to frame his narrative through the cultural fears of miscegenation and integration discursively with the use of the word *nigger*: Milam's use of this word explicitly positioned Till as culturally and socially out of place and reinforced his own role as the powerful White male, the boundary-keeper. Similarly, Zimmerman framed his statement through the fears of Black male criminality by emphasizing perceived threat through words like *suspect* and describing Martin as reaching for his gun. In so doing, Zimmerman positioned Martin as out of place and underscored his own positioning as watchman, defender, keeper of the boundary. As I will discuss later, the word *thug* was later assigned to Martin by the media as a kind of shorthand for the dangerous Black male narrative employed by Zimmerman.

On May 23, 2013, Zimmerman's defense team added an additional layer of "evidence" to support their contention that Trayvon was a threat to Zimmerman through the public release of photos and texts from Trayvon's cellphone as well as photos and tweets from his Twitter account. The release included texts about alleged marijuana use, photos of a Brown-skinned hand holding a gun, and tweets about dating. Zimmerman's attorney claimed this evidence was important for documenting "a different side" of Trayvon Martin. The court ruled that Trayvon Martin's cellphone records, social media accounts, and school records could not be used at trial. However, they had already been released in the court of public opinion.

Heartbreakingly, the narrative of Trayvon Martin as blossoming criminal and a threat was picked up across much of mainstream and social media. Fox News host Geraldo Rivera criminalized both Trayvon's body and his clothing, noting on the July 14, 2013, broadcast of *Fox and Friends Sunday*, "You dress like a thug, people are going to treat you like a thug," and "Aside from the fact that he's dressed in that thug wear—look at the size of him, he's not a little kid." Others argued on social media and blogs that Trayvon's death was a good thing. Right-wing blogger Debbie Schlussel commented on the tweets allegedly sent from Trayvon Martin's account, many of which cited hip-hop lyrics, and asserted:

> With [Trayvon's] criminal record and vile filth, it's becoming more and more apparent that George Zimmerman may have unintentionally performed a service to the world. How many more crime victims and sufferers of his violence would the world endure from this thug had he lived?

George Zimmerman saw Martin not as a teenager walking home on a rainy evening but as a dangerous Black male, a "thug" about to wreak havoc on the community. By strategically activating the ever-present cultural narrative of the dangerous Black male, Zimmerman's defense team was able to position Martin in this role. In so doing, they were successful in legally exonerating the killer of an unarmed 17-year-old boy. Like Emmett Till 57 years before him, Trayvon Martin was killed because he was viewed as *out of place*.

By underscoring how racism and ableism operate as boundary work in cases such as the unpunished killing of Trayvon Martin, a DisCrit perspective invites us to consider how the cultural impulse to "otherize," criminalize, and extinguish Black male children and youth in this manner is also manifested in other contexts. As noted earlier, access to public education for both students of color and students with disabilities in the United States has been legally and culturally contentious and influenced by institutional racism and ableism. Within this system, teachers are positioned as policing the borders of "normal," and in this process they define, identify, and locate the "abnormal" (Collins, 2013). In the following section of this chapter, I examine this process more closely by sharing an analysis of my experiences parenting a Black son marked as out of place in school.

OUT OF PLACE IN SCHOOL:
ABILITY PROFILING, RACIAL PROFILING, AND THE PUSH FOR EXCLUSION

What would you do if that was me, Mom? —Wade, age 7

I write this chapter as a scholar and a teacher but also as the single White mother of a biracial son. Most frequently, my son Wade self-identifies as "Brown" and, sometimes, as either biracial, Black, or African American. He is extremely athletic, funny, kind, and smart. Well over 4 feet tall at age 7, Wade is consistently assumed by strangers to be at least a year or 2 older than he is. All of his teachers, from preschool through 2nd grade, have been White women.

Wade is just beginning to be conscious of and learn to navigate tensions around racial positionings in the worlds outside of our home. However, these tensions have been present since our very first encounters with "formal" education, which began when he started preschool at 15 months old. After a series of microaggressions, I finally removed him from this preschool (breaking a contract) after arriving early one day and discovering that he was alone in a room with one teacher, a spray bottle of water, and a cloth *cleaning lunch tables,* while the other toddlers were in another room having storytime. The teachers explained that Wade was "just too active" for storytime and they saw nothing wrong with excluding him from the literacy community to work in this manner.

Since that time, Wade has continued to encounter regular periods of close scrutiny from classroom teachers and school officials. At different times and in different contexts, he has been officially referred by teachers for speech therapy, occupational therapy, and Title I reading support services. Most recently, his 2nd-grade teacher suggested to me *while Wade was present* that he be treated for attention deficit hyperactivity disorder (ADHD).

Each one of these referrals or "diagnoses," if acted upon, would have removed Wade from the "regular" classroom for at least a portion of the school day and involved me, as his only parent, in a months-long process of negotiation and resistance with various school and district personnel. My position has always been that if my son needs "extra" support, I want him to have it, but I also don't want him unnecessarily scrutinized and labeled. The irony here is that in order to gain access to tools that may help him participate in the manner desired by his teachers—for example, access to lined writing paper in 1st grade to scaffold his printing—I was told I had to consent to having him tested by the school's occupational therapist. Why can't every child simply use lined paper? *Because it's too expensive.*

Each time Wade has changed schools or classrooms I have had to intervene around issues of deficit positioning. One of the most serious sequences of events of this nature occurred in 1st grade. Wade came home upset on the very first day of school, explaining that his teacher made him sit by himself, back at the desks, while everyone else was on the carpet for snack time because a (White, female) classmate "thought she might be allergic" to his snack—a granola bar that he told her "might have nuts in it." Rather than (1) check the snack for nuts (it had none, and it turns out no allergy existed either) or (2) let either the classmate or Wade pick a few friends to sit with, the teacher chose to isolate the only child of color in the classroom.

Over the next 5 weeks, a series of exclusionary incidents like this one occurred (for example, Wade not being allowed to include his grandparents in drawings of his family, because "only a mommy and a daddy count as family"), and the teacher evaded my emails and phone calls. Within a month, Wade no longer wanted to go to school and was having stomach pains so frequently and of such severity that his doctor ordered a series of tests, including abdominal X-rays. The tests were inconclusive, and stress was labeled as the cause of his stomach pain. He was 6 years old.

Back-to-school night was scheduled for the fifth week of the new school year, and I was eager to meet Wade's teacher. Upon entering Wade's classroom, I looked for his desk, and quickly learned that Wade's assigned seat in the classroom was right next to . . . no one. On both sides, my child's desk abutted an empty desk. No other desk in the classroom "U" was isolated in this manner. Wade pulled me over to see his family portrait (depicting just us two) but I stepped away to ask his teacher why his desk was segregated from the others. She looked taken aback, and physically took a step back from me as she faltered, "*You're* Wade's mother?" She paused and looked away from my gaze and over at Wade's desk, saying, "Oh that, that's just by chance." She turned away quickly and greeted another parent before I could respond. Later that night, Wade told me his desk was separated "Because I'm not a good learner, Mom. It's not her fault. I have to be separated from everyone else to learn."

Later that night, I composed a brief but authoritative email to the school principal, citing literature on the overrepresentation of Black boys in segregated educational settings, asserting my belief that Wade's teacher's actions were hurting my son, and insisting on his immediate transfer to another classroom. Unlike my previous attempts, this email was responded to right away. The principal asked me to attend a meeting the very next morning with Wade's teacher. Fortunately, I was able to rearrange my schedule to accommodate this.

When I walked into the principal's conference room, the rectangular table was set up for our meeting with three occupied chairs on one side and a place for me across from them, on the other side of the table. This arrangement of the principal, Wade's classroom teacher, and the director of special education literally felt like three *against* one, not a team of caring educational professionals seeking to reach mutual understanding about the best outcome for a child. When I questioned the need for the presence of the director of special education since my son did not receive special education services, I was told she was required to be there as a "witness." The classroom teacher started speaking and dominated the beginning of the discussion, repeatedly interrupting my attempts to speak of her "behavior modification techniques" for "kids like these" and justifying her use of segregationist approaches. Finally I had had enough:

> "Look, I was a classroom teacher—"
>
> "Oh, so you know what I mean! You understand why we have to separate kids like these—"
>
> "No, I don't understand. You are positioning my son as having a problem. You started excluding him on the very first day of school. The only thing he's learned in 5 weeks of being with you is that he is not a good learner, and that's a quote."
>
> "I never said he wasn't a good learner."
>
> "You didn't need to say it in words. Every action you've made toward him has told him that's what you believe. The bottom line is I wouldn't treat a dog the way you've treated my child. I don't trust you, and I don't want him in your classroom."

After an hour of this, wherein I pointed out that the only child being segregated was also the only child of color in the classroom, the principal finally agreed to move my son to another class.

Wade finished 1st grade without incident. However, 2nd grade has proven even more problematic. In addition to being "diagnosed" by his teacher as having ADHD, I learned that the student teacher in the classroom, with her supervising teacher's approval, has been asking Wade to leave the classroom and do jumping jacks in the hallway during center time to expend some of his "excess" energy. Reluctantly, I have had to recognize the damage inflicted upon my son by the practices and discourses of public schooling within a culture that fears and seeks to contain, remove, and extinguish Black males. With this realization I made the difficult decision to remove Wade from public school.

As a middle-class White woman who excelled in school, I did not undergo the kind of scrutiny my son has to endure. Parenting a child who must bear the weight of having his behavior, learning, and communication constantly under a microscope has been a shock. As an education professional, I have some command of the discourse(s) at work in meetings such as the one described above, as well as command of the relevant research literature. Even with the affordances of these privileges, I have felt overwhelmed and exhausted by every school meeting. It has taken every ounce of energy I have to resist what I have come to know as a united, if largely unconscious, effort to scrutinize my child, mark him as deficient, and exclude him from the main learning community, a process I term *ability profiling* (Collins, 2013).

Despite this exhaustion, I recognize that race, valued cultural capital, and habitus (Bourdieu, 1977a) have afforded me many privileges that are not afforded to all mothers of Black boys. The shock I felt when initially confronted by the racist, ableist, segregationist educational practices directed at my son speaks to my own privilege as a White middle-class woman whose discourses, ways of being, and knowing were always perceived as in alignment with the ableist, racist expectations of school. I have few memories of ever being considered *out of place* in school or in community; I have plenty of memories of being held up by my elementary teachers as the exemplar for classroom behavior and for literate achievement. As a result, I had the privilege of being surprised by the ways that school culture marked my son as out of place and excluded him. I had the privilege of *expecting* an inclusive, equitable, and supportive public schooling experience for my son. I had the privilege of not internalizing fear for my son's physical and psychological well-being during his interactions with authority figures and with law enforcement officials. I was additionally privileged by the social positioning that allowed me to intervene when my son was being pushed *out of place* in school and provided me with the cultural and financial resources with which to seek private educational alternatives when they became necessary. Finally, I am able to speak and write about my experiences parenting a Black male child through school without fear of reprisal. As one Black mother of a Black son said to me recently, "At least you can stand up at this conference [Literacy Research Association] and speak of these things. If I were to talk like you're talking, I would be dismissed as just another angry Black woman."

Though many of these privileges remain, I no longer have the privilege of being shocked by the physical and psychological violence inflicted on children by racist, ableist educational and legal practices guided by cultural narratives such as the *dangerous Black male*. I recognize that this narrative is always present; it floats on the air we breathe in this country and threatens to descend and envelop us at any moment. I've had to acknowledge, as the parent of a male child with Brown skin, that my son will be seen by many as a threatening source of fear before he is seen as a child. Teachers, perhaps many of whom will be well-meaning but misguided, will look for reasons to mark him as deficient. His enthusiasm is more likely to be taken as misbehavior, and his questioning is more likely to be interpreted as defiance. I have to be ever-vigilant and ready to challenge the deficit narratives that circulate and threaten to shape his identity in school. Outside of school, the risk of my son's being seen as a source of danger grows as he grows physically, as do my fears for his safety.

When my son asks, "What would you do if that was me, Mom?" I now know that *it already is him*. His experiences in school, though not physically violent, illustrate the symbolic violence (Bourdieu, 1977a) of exclusion, deficit positioning, and the push to label some ways of knowing, forms of literacy, and bodies as "abnormal." Once a child has come under surveillance for behaviors, literacies, or ways of being that a teacher deems atypical in this manner, segregated special education placements serve as "technologies of exclusion" (Ferri & Connor, 2005, p. 470) and remove the child from the classroom community. This push to homogenize schools and classrooms results in disproportionate numbers of Black children being marked as *out of place* and moved into segregated educational contexts. Students identified as Black or African American "are three times more likely [than non-Black learners] to be diagnosed as intellectually disabled and over 200% more likely to be diagnosed with emotional behavioral disorders" (Artiles, 2013, p. 330).

Once a disability label has been employed as a mechanism to remove children and youth considered "atypical" from the classroom, these children and youth are at even greater risk of being pushed out of school altogether. Behaviors and ways of being deemed out of place are frequently criminalized through school disciplinary procedures; the child is pushed further out of place in school and enters the school-to-prison pipeline (see Fenton, 2013a; Losen, Ee, Hodson, & Martinez, 2015). As I noted earlier, there is evidence from Trayvon Martin's (illegally leaked) school records that he was already experiencing the hyper-surveillance and exclusionary discipline that serve to maintain the school-to-prison pipeline.

CONCLUSION: RACISM, ABLEISM, AND YOUTH OUT OF PLACE

DisCrit uncovers how ideologies of difference as deficit and difference as threat have been and continue to be actualized through the legalized murder, unfounded exclusion, and unwarranted incarceration of Black, Brown, and dis/abled bodies. Such analysis demonstrates how ableism and racism work together to craft the narratives used to justify violence against and incarceration of youth identified as *out of place* in community and school. From this perspective, the symbolic violence of marking some (Black, Brown, and disabled) children out of place within classroom communities must be understood as part of a continuum of state-sanctioned exclusion, marginalization, dehumanization, and physical violence directed at marking some (Black, Brown, disabled) youth as out of place in community and public spaces.

George Zimmerman constructed a narrative depiction of Trayvon Martin as the "other"—as a threat and as deviant or impaired—based solely on the observable evidence that Martin was Black, male, and holding something near or in his waistband. As Jones (2014) argues:

> The racism of the twenty-first century, particularly in the context of racial profiling, is racism dressed up as common sense. While racism as hate could be described as a problem of individual irrationality, the notion that racism

is reasonable appeals to notions of rationality and even science. Thus, the reasonable racist denies that he is acting on emotion. He claims to know something about the Black people who he targets for violence or arrest based on who they are. (p. 1030)

The recognition that racism operates as a knowledge-claim that is then wielded with the authority to exclude (or punish or kill) is an important understanding for ableism as well. This, then, is how racial profiling and ability profiling work synergistically: assignment of a deviant, dangerous, or deficient social identity in response to perceived physical, interactional, or cognitive characteristics that are then used to justify exclusion, incarceration, violence, and/or death. Racism and ableism as knowledge-claims support the "reasonableness" of fear and rationalize exclusion and violence, both discursive and physical.

These knowledge-claims are supported by cultural narratives, such as the "dangerous Black male," and employed to normalize the symbolic and psychological violence of ability profiling, educational exclusion, and symbolic violence just as they are employed to normalize racial profiling, social exclusion, and physical violence. The decision that my son's place is cleaning tables in a room alone or doing jumping jacks in the hallway rather than being part of the classroom community and a teacher's dismissal of her failure to inclusively teach an 11-year-old Black boy with the excuse, "He could so easily get caught up in a gang, or in being a bad-ass again, or, you know, going down that other path" (Collins, 2013, p. 89) reflect the same narrative logic as Zimmerman's statement to the police dispatcher upon first seeing Trayvon Martin: "This guy looks like he's up to no good." These statements also reflect the logic behind Milam's warning to Black youth that they not dare to move *out of place* lest they suffer the same fate as Emmett Till.

Our first challenge, then, is to understand ability profiling and racial profiling, the push to mark some community members as *out of place*, as synergistic and as systemic to American culture and history. Racism and ableism and the violence, both physical and symbolic, that they justify are so prevalent that they are taken for granted as "normal." Because of this, we are all complicit in the damage; we must *choose,* through actions that challenge taken-for-granted notions of normalcy, inclusion, and belonging, to be complicit in the healing.

Martin had a dream that he could see
Once upon a time there was kid like me

CHAPTER 12

Disability Does Not Discriminate

Toward a Theory of Multiple Identity Through Coalition

Zanita E. Fenton

Scholars often erase disability when they focus on other socially subordinating categories (Davis, 2006). Yet, disability is ubiquitous. In its physiological sense, disability will likely affect every individual at some point in his or her lifetime. The term *disability* increasingly is understood as polymorphous (Smith, 2004), and no two disabilities can be equated. Some disabilities are visible; others are imperceptible. Disability may also present challenges to the individual depending on the built or the social environment, although mediated by other social identities, such as race, social class, sexuality, and gender.

Among the various approaches for defining disability, medical definitions predominate. According to Linton (2006), definitions of *disability* often "include incapacity, a disadvantage, deficiency, especially a physical or mental impairment that restricts normal achievement, something that hinders or incapacitates" (p. 162). The medicalization of disability relieves society from its role in the creation, perpetuation, and mitigation of the effects of disability. Acknowledging the role society plays in defining disability does not deny the medical challenges or the experience of pain associated with some impairments (Scarry, 1985). Further,

> disability is much more than a descriptive biological category. . . . Disability could . . . be used to interrogate the normalizing discourses of racism, sexism, and heteronormativity—all of which generate the institutional exclusion of the deviant (read: "disabled") Other. (Erevelles, 2011b, p. 104)

One is not necessarily disabled merely because one has an impairment. Deafness, for instance, would not necessarily be disabling if sign language were routinely taught and therefore normalized in the general population (Groce, 2009). Further, some individuals have greater resources by which to reduce the effects of a disability (Cooper, 2008). Disability, then, is a marker of identity that designates a specific minority group bound by common social and political experience (Linton, 2006).

Under the ADA, "the term 'disability' means . . . a physical or mental impairment that substantially limits one or more major life activities" (ADA, 42 U.S. Code § 12102). Yet, in other legal parlance, *disability* can also serve as a descriptor for a status or circumstance, such as in "disabilities of contract," referring to the limitations imposed by a contract, or as in "legal disability," meaning lack of legal capacity as a result of age, "mental deficiency," or noncitizenship status. In legal representation there are rules of "standing," wherein legal capacity for some individuals with a disability may be met by having a third party speak on their behalf (*Austin Nursing Center Inc. v. Lovato*, 2005). Moreover, because of a legal history of treating (White) women differently, it is not uncommon to refer to "disabilities of gender" as a historical sociolegal status (Kinservik, 2001).

"Nondisabled" individuals have sought protection under the ADA since its inception (Asch, 2004). For example, in *Sutton and Hinton v. United Air Lines, Inc.*, the airline refused to hire as commercial pilots twins with severe myopia who wore corrective lenses. The Court determined that poor vision, without reference to measures that mitigate the impairment, did not substantially limit a major life activity under the ADA. In *Albertson's Inc. v. Kirkingburg*, the Supreme Court ruled that an individual with a physical difficulty was not "disabled" per se under the ADA. Each individual who claims a disability must show that the alleged disability substantially impacts a major life activity and is not mitigated. Asch (2004), contrarily, argues:

> Instead of concluding that a person who uses eyeglasses or blood pressure medication is not a person with a disability for purposes of the Americans with Disabilities Act, it would be much more in keeping with the human variation approach to disability . . . to permit such people to file complaints of employment discrimination as people who are "regarded as" having an impairment. The employer would then bear the burden of [proof and require that] employers ascertain which purported job requirements are truly necessary and which are the result of custom or convenience. (p. 18)

In this chapter, I examine the concept of equal protection and the law's contribution to the concept of disability (as well as other identity categories) as immutable, while simultaneously maintaining hierarchical status quo. Relying primarily on the work of Kimberlé Crenshaw (1989), I show how a critical framework is necessary to understand the multilayered nature of subordination. I then explore society's reproduction of normative, nondisabled bodies as rooted in the history of eugenics and pseudoscience. I show

how reproduction, both metaphorically and literally, continues to be a significant aspect of marginalization or even elimination of nonnormative bodies. I conclude by suggesting ways to build coalition, as suggested by Mari Matsuda (1989), using Derrick Bell's interest convergence theory (1980) and DisCrit (Annamma, Connor, & Ferri, 2013) to show how creating coalitions can subvert dominant hierarchies and transform the status quo.

A CRITICAL FRAMEWORK

Critical Legal Theories (CLTs), including Critical Race Theory, Critical Race Feminism, Queer Theory, Latino/a Critical Legal Theory (LatCrit), and Economic Critical Legal Analysis (ClassCrit), are a few of the burgeoning critical approaches to legal analyses. Each of these approaches examines various forms of social subordination. Disability Studies (DS) articulates a theory and ideological critique of inequitable treatment experienced by persons with disabilities (Davis, 2006). Both DS and the various CLTs expose parallel social imaginings: one created for those meeting normative social expectations and alternative ones for those who, in myriad ways, are not considered as normative. Yet, Disability Studies have been critiqued for assuming Whiteness as an unstated norm (Bell, 2006). Similarly, CLTs have been critiqued for essentialism and for failing to address multiple aspects of identity, most notably, aspects of disability. However, antisubordination activists have engaged in a form of strategic essentialism as a means of resistance (Spivak, 1989). Mimicking conventional strategies of nonsubordinated power holders, strategic essentialism is a move by members of a subordinated category to simplify group identity and counter normative expectations.

Intersectionality, a concept identified by Crenshaw (1989), exposes the inadequacy of legal doctrine for its "focus on the most privileged group members, [which] marginalizes those who are multiply-burdened and obscures claims that cannot be understood as resulting from discrete sources of discrimination" (p. 140). Critical theorists often use intersectionality to describe the ways in which oppressions (such as racism, transphobia, and ableism) are interconnected, mutually constitutive, and cannot therefore be examined separately. Intersectionality is often misunderstood as a subordinated category plus another (for example, race plus gender) (Crenshaw, 1989). Because of the misapplication of intersectionality, even those who are multiply disadvantaged may seek to emphasize a particular aspect of identity that provides the greatest authority in a given context (Fenton, 2007). This practice ultimately serves the dominant group.

Disability is not one-dimensional; neither is race or other socially subordinated identity categories. Identity, in all its forms, implicates multiple variables such as language, culture, and religion (Omi & Winant, 1994).

Social practices play a significant role in shaping how people think about identities (Hamilton, Stroessner, & Driscoll, 1994). Thus, the ways in which multiple identities converge is fluid and diffuse, dependent on context and circumstance. Yet, as Erevelles and Minear (2010) note, "the omission of disability as a critical category in discussions of intersectionality has disastrous and sometimes deadly consequences" (p. 128).

Because hierarchies always exist both between groups and categories, but also between individuals or subgroups, complexity within the various levels of interrelationships must be anticipated (Fenton, 2010). This complexity includes a dissatisfaction with labels of "multiple consciousness" without meaningful redress (Matsuda 1992), and the additional layer of marginalization intendant from the fracturing and atomizing effects of discrete intersectional identities. One must "properly situate the connection between and among competing forms of oppression to understand their relationship" (Obasogie, 2006, p. 483). With this in mind, in the next section, I discuss the social creation of disability, moving between and within multiple communities of oppression.

REPRODUCING NORMS: EUGENICS AND PSEUDOSCIENCE

Legal definitions historically grounded in (pseudo)science further the belief that the categories of identity are stable. Indeed, identities (such as disability, race, sexual orientation) are often considered genetically predetermined rather than socially produced (Cooper, 2006; Fenton, 2013a). An emphasis on the physiological nature of difference has been used to justify differential treatment (Fenton, 2013b).

Although disability is often viewed as inherent (Cooper, 2006), social forces maintain hierarchies based on able-bodied norms. Society also places heavy burdens on Black and Brown bodies under the guise of biological differences, even though these burdens actually stem from social forces that create and maintain hierarchies (Haney López, 1996).

The field of psychology has a history of creating disorders specific to a given subordinated group as a means of ensuring the continuation of that status. "Hysteria," for instance, was once referred to as a medical condition particular to women and understood to be caused by disturbances of the uterus (King, 1993). Drapetomania, a supposed mental disorder, was said to cause Black slaves to run away (White, 2008). Until 1974, the American Psychiatric Association (APA) defined homosexuality as a mental illness, and AIDS was originally known as GRID (Gay-Related Immune Deficiency) (Magnus, 1982). Until recently, transgenderism was listed as a disorder by the APA (Zucker & Spitzer, 2010). Society has a recurring habit of conflating poverty, as well as race and disability, with criminality (Jones, 2002).

In society's pursuit of the "normative," race destabilizes gender ideals (Phillips-Anderson, 2013); abject poverty precipitates banishment from Whiteness (Newitz & Wray, 2013); disability undermines perceptions of normative gender expression (Garland-Thomson, 2004) as well as of sexuality (Chinn, 2004). In a negative convergence, disability is more prevalent in contexts marked by poverty and homelessness (Segal, Silverman, & Temkin, 1997) as well as in so-called "third-world" contexts (Erevelles, 2011b). These intersecting categories help explain why society has gone to such lengths to segregate and eradicate difference.

ELIMINATING/CONTAINING DISABILITY

Once disability, broadly defined, is understood as a foil for the normative ideal and therefore as something to be contained, prevented, or destroyed, reproduction becomes of paramount concern. Gender and race likewise are implicated in concerns over reproducing normative bodies. In fact, the confluence of race and disability was introduced as a consequential aspect of enslavement. According to Nielson (2012), "racist ideologies defined . . . African Americans as fundamentally inferior specimens with deformed bodies and minds who were best confined to slavery" (p. 50). Those bodies were mutilated and killed through the auspices of the institution of slavery, forcing survivors of this brutal institution into submission. Black minds, further manipulated into submission, were kept ignorant through the denial of education and literacy (Genovese, 1974). Capitalism found profit in racially devalued bodies, including those with physical and psychological impairments, even while the "dominant paradigm conceive[d] of disabled bodies as having little economic value" (Erevelles, 2011b, p. 39). Slavery not only created disabled bodies, but also originated an ideology that inferred an entitlement to dominant society to control the reproductive capacities of Black, female, poor, and disabled bodies. Further, this ideology was one that promoted a conflation of these categories in terms of reproduction.

During the same time period as slavery, "most white women remained as *feme coverts*—legal nonentities determined unfit for civic life" (Nielson, 2012, p. 50). Women were not able to vote prior to 1920 and therefore, effectively, were not full citizens (*Minor v. Happersett*, 1875; Ritter, 2002). Coverture erased legal personhood for married women, whereby married women could not enter into legal contracts, could not own property outright, and could not seek state protection from an abusive husband (Eisenberg & Micklow, 1977). Moreover, the origins of rape law were constructed such that a father or husband "owned" his daughter or wife. Therefore, rape could only be seen as an offense against *him* (Brownmiller, 1975). In fact, exemption for claims of marital rape continued in various states until about

1993 (Hasday, 2000). This imagined status of women as property also justified lynching of Black men (Wells, 1892/2013).

Black women, however, were owned through the institution of slavery, and their marriages were not legally recognized (Du Bois, 1935; *Prince v. Cole*, 1859). Thus, "while African American women's sexuality was effectively harnessed for the reproduction of slavery in the service of the colonial state, they were deemed as fit only for a 'dehumanized reproduction'" (Price & Shildrick, 1999, p. 80). The rape of a Black woman, both pre- and postemancipation, was not legally cognizable (Cobb, 1858). Both Black women and men (Fenton, 2013a) were purposed to increase the size of the slave population and thus the economic wealth of their owners. Once the 13th Amendment changed the status of Blacks from property to legal personhood, the social agenda transformed from the reproduction of property to a eugenic one of reduction and elimination—some might say genocide. This rapid shift from a pronatalist to antinatalist position in regard to African American reproduction is reflective of the devaluation of Blackness, consistent with Black people's prior status as property. From this one "disability" of being legally characterized as property (whether through servitude or marriage), practically all other forms of disability emanated. Thus, White women too were also at a social disadvantage regarding their reproductive capacities as a result of legal sterilization (Lombardo, 1985). Under the guise of a loose category of "feeblemindedness," women were sterilized for having the "disability" of being in poverty, unmarried, and pregnant (e.g., *Buck v. Bell*).

The history of forced sterilization impacted poor White women, as well as women of color (Shapiro, 1985). Males were not targeted in the same numbers as females, but they were not immune from being characterized as "feebleminded" or from sterilization. Poor White men were targeted for sterilization (*Skinner v. Oklahoma*), as were Black men (Block, 1983). In fact, Margaret Sanger and other early birth control advocates generally embraced eugenics, encouraging White middle-class women to reproduce, "while discouraging reproduction among nonwhite, immigrant, [poor] and disabled people" (Saxton, 2006, p. 106).

In the United States, nearly 100 eugenic statutes were passed between 1900 and 1970 (Romero-Bosch, 2007), and 60,000 individuals were sterilized for being "feebleminded" (Silver, 2004). Those labeled as feebleminded were sometimes disabled, but often just poor, Black, and/or female. Sterilization epitomized the use of pseudoscientific findings to marginalize entire subpopulations (Romero-Bosch, 2007). By the 1970s and 1980s, many states had repealed sterilization laws, but the effects continued. As Erevelles (2011b) stated, "It is easy to dismiss eugenics as a relic of a bygone era, except that the continued association of race and disability in deficit ways necessitates that we examine how eugenic ideologies continue to reconstitute social hierarchies in contemporary contexts by deploying the ideology of disability" (p. 104). The use of pseudoscience to justify differential treatment remains a pervasive force in American culture and society, responsible for creating, or at least reifying, pervasive social stereotypes (Fenton, 1998).

The specter of eugenics continues today, for instance, through the use of amniocentesis to detect Down syndrome and other fetal genetic "abnormalities." If a physician detects "defects" during the procedure, the woman will likely be encouraged to terminate her pregnancy (Elkins, Stovall, Wilroy, & Dacus, 1986). Today, a number of disability cases address reproductive capacity or rights. Many of these cases concern sterilizations or abortion of a fetus resulting from either consensual sexual activity or rape in facilitative care (Pollack, 2005) or the right of individuals with perceived disabilities to marry (Lindsay, 1998). Pseudoscientific ideology, similar to justifications given for antimiscegenation laws (Wadlington, 1966), is likewise used to justify disability-related marriage restrictions.

Another arm of eugenics has resulted in medical abuses of those deemed expendable. Early gynecological experiments, circa 1845–1849, were performed without anesthetic on three slave women, because of stereotypical beliefs about the increased pain tolerance of Black females (Washington, 2009). Approximately a century later, in 1951, HeLa cells, known as the "immortal cell line," were derived from the cells of an African American woman named Henrietta Lacks, without her consent (Davis, 2006). Between 1932 and 1972, the infamous Tuskegee syphilis experiments were conducted by the U.S. government on Black men. Treatment was withheld from the men so doctors could study the effects of the syphilis (Tuskegee Syphilis Study). History continues to repeat itself. More recently, for instance, the pharmaceutical company NitroMed conducted a race-specific study, garnering 2005 FDA approval of BiDil, a heart disease drug specifically designed for African Americans. Reverby (2008) suggested:

> Both Tuskegee and BiDil remind us of why we must critique, very specifically, how and why race is used as a variable in medical research. Tuskegee could happen in part because racism left a population underfed, undereducated, ill, and in critical need of treatment, and clinical certainty about race—both behavioral and physiological—could be used to explain these conditions. A "natural" study could be constructed to prove what was already assumed, even when contradictory data on purported racial differences and alternative explanations to prevalence rates existed. Statistical manipulations and questionable research at Tuskegee, even in an era when clinical trials were badly organized, protected racialized assumptions about disease. In the face of clinical and autopsy evidence that might undermine that certainty, race and some unknown biological process in the "bad blood" would shore up clinical experience of racial differences— except when race was allowed to disappear to make a larger medical and public health need apparent. (p. 480)

Another instance that highlights society's view of "expendable" people is evidenced by the incarceration rates for Black males, which is seven times that of White men (Carson & Golinelli, 2013). Those deemed mentally ill are also overrepresented in the prison population (Diamond, Wang, Holzer, Thomas, & des Cruser, 2001). The numbers for men of color and for those labeled mentally ill, who are usually in poverty (even taking into account any overlap), are so disproportionate as to indicate that the preference to warehouse these individuals overshadows any attempts to treat them (Lamb & Weinberger, 1998). As Michelle Alexander (2010) wrote, "Rather than rely on race, we use our criminal justice system to label people of color 'criminals' and then engage in all the practices we supposedly left behind" (p. 2). In a similar vein, rather than explicitly acknowledging intellectual disorders, we use the criminal justice system to label these individuals as criminals and thereby avoid treatment, continuing the carceral practices we supposedly left behind.

Incarceration is also an effective means of preventing reproduction (Gelman, 1995), although prison continues to serve as a location for sexual abuse of both men and women (Smith, 2006). Eugenic ideas are infused in ways the state controls the reproductive capacity of certain groups by creating environs that inhibit reproduction, through disease or by undermining the rearing of any resulting children. Poor women and their children are disproportionally placed along with young women of color in juvenile detention facilities. These settings "create the conditions that place young Black, Latina, Native, poor, and working-class women in very dangerous sexual situations . . . many of these young women return infected with an STD or a baby with a disability, who may be placed in foster care" (Erevelles, 2011b, p. 92). The foster system, for the most part, is not one that yields well-adjusted adults (Fanshel, Finch, & Grundy, 1990). Moreover, this sociolegal institution further labels some children as "special needs," which allows for more money to assist with permanent placements. The category of "special needs" includes children with physical and emotional disabilities but also Black children and any child over a certain age (Child Welfare Information Gateway, 2014).

Education and incarceration rates are linked at a systemic level to create and perpetuate subordinated "others." Thus, the education system creates a situation "wherein we punish those labeled as disabled to keep them from an education; we label those in prison as felons to create legal and social disabilities" (Fenton, 2013b, p. 206). Black males have consistently low educational attainment levels. For example, only 16.4% of Black males age 25 to 29 achieve 4 or more years of college (Brault, 2012). For individuals with disabilities, educational attainment rates are even lower. In 2012, approximately 22% of noninstitutionalized persons with disabilities above the age of 21 had an educational attainment that was less than a high school diploma (Cornell University, n.d.).

Just as incarceration has become a form of warehousing, the size of the homeless population demonstrates another example of discarding individuals. Unfortunately, there is also something of a revolving door between incarceration and homelessness (Metraux & Culhane, 2006). Black and Brown men are also disproportionately represented in the population of active service military (U.S. Department of Defense, 2010). Veterans are likewise overrepresented among the homeless population (Rosenheck, Frisman, & Chung, 1994), and the homeless population has a high incidence of mental illness (Folsom et al., 2005). Experts believe between 10% and 30% of veterans from any given war experience post-traumatic stress disorder (PTSD). These rates are even higher among African American and Hispanic service persons (U.S. Department of Veterans Affairs, n.d.).

Discussions of homelessness necessarily implicate individuals and communities in poverty. Further, communities of color experience disproportionally high poverty rates (U.S. Department of Labor, 2014). Not accounting for race, noninstitutionalized disabled persons with less than a high school education experience similar poverty levels (Cornell University, n.d.; Erickson, von Schrader, & Lee, 2012). To complete this circular relationship, people in poverty, comprised disproportionally of people of color and noninstitutionalized disabled persons, accounting for any overlap, are at the greatest risk for homelessness. Another complicating dimension is the economic disadvantage experienced by women, especially those with low educational attainment, including women of color and those with a disability. In fact, "one of the major factors attributed to the cause of women's poverty in the global contexts is their lack of access to education that, in turn, dis-enable[s] women" (Erevelles, 2011b, p. 187).

CONCLUSION

Regrettably, the "social category of disability is prominently missing" from the various CLT analyses, "even though it plays a crucial ideological role in destabilizing normative discourses that construct difference in the first place" (Erevelles, 2011b, p. 97). CLT scholars have not viewed disability as theoretically useful, sometimes relegating its discussion to a passing mention in the text or in footnotes. This is too often the case even though, in aspiration, the CLTs are a set of "collaborative, interdisciplinary inquiry and a self-conscious cultural critique that interrogates how subjects are multiply interpolated: in other words, how the representational systems of gender, race, ethnicity, ability, sexuality, and class mutually construct, inflect, and contradict one another" (Garland-Thomson, 2004, p. 75).

The overlaps, connections, and confluences among social categories are so profound that the routine omission of disability from CLT analyses may stem from a belief that disability is already included. The corresponding regularity with which other socially subordinated categories are omitted from DS may likewise reflect the assumption that disability is already equated with "other" socially subordinated groups. Perhaps these omissions are a result of the stubborn belief that the differences among categories are in fact static and not traversable. Individuals, however, do not experience identity as a fractured reality. If we start instead with this understanding of intersectionality informed by DisCrit, the multivariant nature of experience may be a place for coalition. Asch (2004) argues that one promotes social change but also acknowledges that the social consequences emanating from different social categories may not be equated. Regardless of the reasons and realities prompting the disconnect among subordinated communities, similarities in theory, experience, and objectives for transformation point to a more collaborative effort to counteract misunderstandings, mischaracterizations, outright misrepresentations, and stereotypes. Seeking a convergence of relevant dominant interests (Bell, 1980) along with the voices of those with disability is one significant means of achieving this transformation.

DisCrit is a useful framework for envisioning a unifying and comprehensive theory. On its own terms, DS struggles with internal stratification. Already, DS is a field that by necessity must engender flexibility because of the range of experiences included under the umbrella of disability. It also has the historical benefit of its relation to other subordinated categories. For example, learning and intellectual disabilities are something that may potentially affect any individual, but the subjective nature of their diagnoses and identification is such that overwhelmingly Black boys are identified with this disability (Fenton, 2013b). In this vein, the most important, yet most challenging aspect of antisubordination coalition building is understanding that subordination arises from the same structure, with each subhierarchy reinforcing the others. The lessons learned from the various civil rights struggles are therefore instructive if only because of the overlap among categories. A convergence of interests promotes cohesion within a single group and enables coalition building among disparate groups. However, finding common interest, much less agreeing on form and approach, is challenging. Recognizing that collaboration is neither a single event nor a zero-sum game is a helpful starting point.

In a broad sense, this chapter is an attempt to identify multiple layers of converging interests. The point is to further destabilize identity so as to enable activists to find unity of purpose across difference. Such destabilization requires finding common interest within subgroups' internal hierarchy, points of cohesion among subordinated groups, as well as important interest points with the overriding power structure.

Critical Conversations Across Race and Ability

Beth A. Ferri
Subini Ancy Annamma
David J. Connor

If this book demonstrates anything, it is that we have much to talk about. Necessary dialogues must engage our most critical and complex thinking around longstanding inequities that present themselves in educational contexts, such as (1) opportunity gaps and education debt, (2) overrepresentation of students of color in special education and underrepresentation in gifted and advanced placement options, (3) the school-to-prison pipeline and overly harsh disciplinary sanctions, and (4) racialized economy of smartness and goodness, to name but a few. The impetus of this book began with the idea that untangling these and other persistent problems would require a more intersectional approach—one that could fully account for race/ethnicity and dis/ability, as well as social class and the many other systems of oppression that students experience in schools.

We thought about this book as an expansion, beginning where DisCrit left off by engaging a wider constituency. We envisioned both DisCrit and this text as a new starting point, allowing us to move beyond an oversimplified, additive analysis of race to existing frameworks within Disability Studies or adding disability to existing analyses of race. Early in the process of thinking about the shape this text would take, we decided to "go big or go home" by creating a sort of dream team list of some of the most impressive educational thinkers in the fields of Disability Studies and Critical Race Theory to be contributors. Sharing our growing excitement about the project, contributors eagerly responded to our call, fostering a new dialogue around some of the most intractable problems in education by placing their own work in conversation (or even in contestation) with element(s) of DisCrit. We were careful to communicate to all of the contributors that we welcomed any form of engagement—whether it involved critique, expansion, or adaptation of the DisCrit framework—as we envisioned a book that would improve, extend, and grow DisCrit's utility. What followed were some of the most amazingly thoughtful, articulate, and provocative chapters we have had the pleasure to assemble within these pages. In the remaining part of this chapter, we summarize what we see as their most important and useful insights. We then conclude with directions the collection points to as the next steps for DisCrit.

ISSUES, INSIGHTS, INTERPRETATIONS

Perceptions of Race, Class, and Ability

In the first section of the book, "Race, Class, and Ability," Gillborn et al. (Chapter 1) present findings from their qualitative research study with Black middle-class parents. This work represents an important next step in teasing out the experiences and complexities underlying the persistent problem of overrepresentation of students of color in special education. The authors go beyond simply documenting overrepresentation to illustrate how particular labels are deployed in particular ways to serve specific interests. They demonstrate the importance of being attuned to and fully accounting for a range of intersecting oppressive forces within scholarly work, even when these forces are not immediately apparent. For instance, although they initially expected to tell a story about the interworkings of race, class, and gender, they were nonetheless attentive to the ways that disability, too, was an inescapable feature of the participants' (and their children's) marginalization.

Broderick and Leonardo (Chapter 2) build on their germinal work on "smartness" as property (Leonardo & Broderick, 2011) to explore how "goodness" also operates as a form of property in schools. Specifically, they illustrate how the discourse of goodness serves to construct students as either intrinsically "good" or "bad," based on perceived social and cultural capital. Various forms of inequities in schools are then based on those identity positions—assigned most often by White, mostly female teachers who serve as the arbiters of goodness. Students then learn to internalize particular subject positions, thinking of themselves (and others) as "good" or "bad." Moreover, those students who are afforded "goodness" come to see their subject position as innate or earned via meritocracy.

Both of these chapters explore how relative privilege is constructed and maintained for some while being restricted for others in schools. In the case of middle-class Black parents from professional backgrounds, race, as mutually constituted in and through disability, serves to cancel out class privilege these parents may leverage on behalf of their children. Broderick, like Collins (Chapter 11), must acknowledge how her own child (and his classmates) are actively positioned within these discourses in creating a problem identity for the targeted child as well as a positive identity for her own young son. In each of these chapters, we are invited into the ways the young children (both White and of color) and their parents navigate these very disparate discourses to make sense of the world and their positioning within it. In each instance, driven by confluences of race, class, and gender, schools affix disability labels in racially distinct ways—these labels then function either to further cement marginality or to confer privilege on particular bodies. Because behavior is not simply pathologized but increasingly also criminalized, being able to claim "goodness" is a high-stakes form of social capital—perhaps, we might argue, even more consequential than being able to claim "smartness." Finally, because the intersections of identities permeate schooling and, indeed, our everyday lives in complex ways, these chapters remind us that our methods of analysis must also be capable of accounting for multiple systems of oppression.

Achievement/Opportunity Gap

In Chapter 3, Mendoza et al. point to ways that teacher education can serve as an important site of interruption and transformation—helping to disrupt teachers' common sense notions about race, ability, and culture and to "foster equity-oriented practices." Drawing on cultural historical activity theory (CH/AT), Mendoza and colleagues elucidate how learning must be intentionally designed to disrupt non-tensions, that is, to rupture everyday common sense notions about racial privilege, supremacy, and ableism. These authors demonstrate the usefulness of engaging tension as a resource for learning, growth, and change as a form of critical praxis that can help teacher candidates begin to question previously unexplored assumptions that perpetuate deficit thinking about minoritized youth.

In the second chapter in this section, King Thorius and Tan (Chapter 4) illustrate how typical framings of the achievement gap are problematic in that they ignore structural inequities, promote deficit thinking, focus on narrow conceptualizations of achievement, and position White students as the norm against which all other groups are measured. They then expand Ladson-Billings's notion of educational debt by documenting the various kinds of educational debt owed to students with disabilities and considering students at the intersections of race and disability. They propose ways to address a range of structural, attitudinal, and pedagogical inequities in order to begin to pay back the debt owed to these children.

The chapters in this section (and indeed the entire book) are aimed at disruption. Engaging with teachers who, as Broderick and Leonardo (Chapter 2) remind us, are often the arbiters of both smartness and goodness remains a vitally important project of DisCrit. Both chapters in this section demonstrate how engaging simultaneously with race and disability within teacher education can help reframe students' taken-for-granted practices and ways of knowing. This work requires that we examine the processes that perpetuate inequities in daily interactions. Linking achievement/opportunity gaps, educational debt, deficit thinking, overrepresentation, and ableism will require more nuanced intersectional work like these chapters offer.

Overrepresentation

In Chapter 5, Kozleski provides a much-needed critical analysis of the very measurement tools that are used to document disproportionate representation of students of color in special education. Drawing on infrastructural inversion, she deftly explicates the inherent irony and absurdity involved in the federal government and national agencies using tools that reduce and erase personhood and context and in so doing perpetuating the very problem they aim to address. Specifically, she uncovers the suppositions both in the ways that these big data sets are constructed and in the ways that limits researchers.

In the second chapter in this section (Chapter 6), Fergus interrogates what might be fueling overrepresentation and contemplates what can be done to change it. Using large-scale quantitative methods, Fergus looks at the role of school structures and teacher dispositions as embedded in larger societal structures of race, class, and dis/ability that work in tandem to maintain overrepresentation. Fergus's findings indicate that teacher perceptions about race and culture do, in fact, contribute to deficit thinking about students from minoritized groups and should therefore constitute a key site for intervention and transformation.

The chapters in this section (and indeed the entire book) illustrate how DisCrit can be put to use in a range of research formats and types, including quantitative research. Although DisCrit insists on the value of narrative, it is important to acknowledge that the framework is not limited in any way to a particular research paradigm or approach, as long as a critical and intersectional analysis that questions power is employed. Both chapters contribute to the larger conversation about the need to help practitioners and teachers see how various systems and institutional processes as well as individual perceptions and ideologies work in tandem to maintain inequity. Both chapters draw out the potential for DisCrit to impact policy as well as praxis.

School-to-Prison Pipeline

In Chapter 7, Adams and Erevelles examine how oppressive and intersecting discourses of disability and race are deployed in ways that justify the dis-location of particular student bodies via the school-to-prison pipeline. Conceiving Black and Brown bodies as matter out of place and presuming that incarceration is an eventual inevitability, teacher perceptions and school practices reflect a pathologizing, dehumanizing, and criminalizing of racial difference. Adams and Erevelles eschew reducing overrepresentation or racialized violence to statistics, thereby insisting on humanizing lives that are all too often dehumanized in the courts, in our schools, and in the wider society. Though their findings from teacher interviews are disheartening, they do identify possible points of entry for disrupting deficit discourses and influencing teacher dispositions and practices.

In the second chapter in this section (Chapter 8), Mahon-Reynolds and Parker use the concept of working identity to highlight forms of implicit bias as mechanisms through which overrepresentation occurs. In other words, they help elucidate how implicit forms of racism and ableism, because they are so engrained in the everyday practices of schools, are not necessarily conscious or overt, particularly to those in the dominant group. Their work suggests that schools must therefore consciously take up practices that are calibrated to work against normalization, marginalization, and discrimination. A first step in this process must include developing a critical consciousness of the various forms of bias that lead to overrepresentation, deficit thinking, and the school-to-prison pipeline.

Chapters in this section are in keeping with others that highlight the need to both acknowledge and disrupt deficit thinking—whether these perceptions are conscious or not. Most urgently, these chapters point to the importance of actively counteracting pedagogical and representational practices that position students vis-à-vis racism and ableism. Moreover, we must acknowledge that special education labels and practices often foster (rather than mitigate) oppressive and intersecting deficit discourses of race, which are then deployed to justify further segregation and dis-location of student bodies via the school-to-prison pipeline. DisCrit helps us be further mindful of ways that even those services that may prove helpful in particular ways for dominant groups may have very different consequences for minoritized groups.

School Reform

In Chapter 9, Tomlinson expands her longstanding work on race, class, and ability to examine the prevalence of overrepresentation and achievement gaps beyond any one national context. Looking specifically at school reforms within the United Kingdom and the United States, which have been driven by neoliberal market-based ideologies, Tomlinson shows how minoritized students across these and other contexts are similarly subject to disproportionate placement in special education, in lower academic tracks, and among those labeled disruptive or behaviorally disordered. Her work highlights the marked disjuncture between the rhetoric of inclusivity and the embodied experiences of inequities that are hallmarks of contemporary educational reforms, but are a part of a longer history of educational reforms bound up in eugenic ideologies.

In the second chapter in this section, Baglieri (Chapter 10) looks at schooling as a form of property—one that is unequally distributed by race, class, and ability and that positions both students of color and students with disabilities as "at risk"—that centers deficits within marginalized children and communities. She skillfully illustrates how school policy has colluded with economic policy to co-construct race and ability in ways that produce inequity. Moving beyond a critique of current practices, she proposes a unified DisCrit approach to school reform, which combines elements of multicultural education, inclusive education, and urban education. This multifaceted approach would work against meritocratic practices of schooling and normative assessment practices, assume that all norming practices are problematic, view curriculum as a service to communities, and insist on local-based control of schools and services. By continuing to work against the intersecting and pathologizing discourses of racism and ableism and the material implications of inequitable schooling, Baglieri suggests that there is an opportunity to leverage our collective efforts toward a more equitable education for all.

The chapters in this section are broadly sweeping in their scope and deeply concentrated in their focus on the need to simultaneously tackle racism, classism, and ableism in school reform and policy. Recognizing the ways in which school policy is both a product of and an active (or at least complicit) contributor to inequality, Tomlinson and Baglieri illustrate the complexity of the problem at hand. Both highlight the impact that neoliberal, market-based school reforms have had in exacerbating inequities based on race, ability, and class and show how they have only solidified gaps in opportunity and achievement between students who are more and less privileged. Deeply critical, these chapters are resolutely hopeful that productive points of connection can begin to be leveraged in the service of equity. Both point to some of the necessary dialogues and strategic alliances that will be required to shift the discourse.

Race, Disability, and the Law

In the final section of the book, Collins (Chapter 11) critically analyzes court documents, media accounts, and videotaped trial testimony from *The State of Florida v. George Zimmerman* murder trial. She connects this horrifying case backwards and forwards—placing it within a longer historical continuum of state violence. Her analysis shows how Trayvon Martin was positioned by the defense team in ways that called forth familiar cultural tropes of the dangerous Black male—a designation that relies upon the synergistic comingling of racism and ableism. Finally, she refuses to allow history to stay in place or research to remain in abstraction by connecting the symbolic dots between the lynching of Emmett Till, the murder of Trayvon Martin, and the seeds of aggression wielded at her own much younger biracial son, who is likewise positioned via deficit discourses, social and physical exclusions, and hyper-surveillance. By inserting her own very personal story into the larger cultural, historical, and legal narrative, she (like Broderick and Leonardo) offers us a child's point of view, as her own Black child struggles to make sense of the world he must occupy, as the world makes (non) sense out of him and in so doing provides a way forward, toward an as-yet-unrealized dream of healing.

In the second chapter in this section, Fenton (Chapter 12) traces historical and legal parallels between race and disability. She points to how the law, by emphasizing biological difference, has been used historically (and presently) as a tool to legitimize the unequal treatment of marginalized groups. Connecting ways that differences are deployed within the law to the legacies of eugenics and pseudoscience, Fenton shows how the law, like special education, though often seen as a tool for civil rights (or educational access), has been used as a tool for rendering marginalized groups (based on race, class, gender, and disability) as disposable. Finally, she offers an invitation for scholars to further engage with DisCrit and intersectionality as critical resources from which to forge coalitions.

Taken together, the chapters in this section illustrate that despite the rhetoric of civil rights and assurances of equal protection, the law, like science, is always inside culture and therefore reflects the biases of its particular cultural, social, and historical milieu. In other words, laws and policies reflect taken-for-granted ways of perceiving difference, affording the most protection to those most privileged in a given context and conversely punishing bodies furthest from those identity statuses. Both chapters point to the importance of seeing the past reflected in the present and using coalition to forge a different, more equitable, and just future.

MOVING FORWARD FROM A DIFFERENT STARTING POINT

We finish this book in the context of an alarming number of highly publicized incidents of racialized violence enacted on Black children and youth by police and those serving to "police" White neighborhoods. The public outcry, which began after 17-year-old Trayvon Martin was gunned down in 2012 by a White male neighborhood watch volunteer, took the form of protests, marches, and social media campaigns, like *Black Lives Matter* and *Say Her Name*. Sadly, depressingly, horribly, other Black lives in the years following this flashpoint event didn't seem to matter either. Recently a 14-year-old young Black girl was violently wrestled to the ground by a clearly out-of-control White police officer who proceeded to point his gun at two other young Black boys who were at a suburban pool party. Watching the video, which was recorded by a White peer, one cannot help but fear for these children's lives. How close were we to one more young life being senselessly lost? How terrifying was the incident for each and every child at that pool party? How many nightmares will they, their parents, or we have, and for how long? Then in June 2015, we experienced a massacre in the Emanuel AME Church in Charleston, South Carolina. A White supremacist entered the church, attended services for an hour, and then killed nine people at the prayer meeting. Juxtaposing his arrest (he was given a bulletproof vest and not cuffed) versus that of the young Black girl in a bikini who was thrown to the ground by her hair, we could not help but see the stark differences in the way Black and White bodies are treated by the system. Moreover, this massacre took the lives of nine Black people because of the murderer's commitment to White supremacy and his goal to start a race war. From hyper-criminalization to actual murder, what will it take to shift the course from these 21st-century forms of lynching?

While these horrific events were taking place, other lives, too, were deemed not to matter. A recent amicus brief issued by the ACLU reports that over half of the individuals who are killed by police have some form of mental health–related disability. Police who are called in to help frequently escalate situations or overreact, leading to increased violence and often death. In 2013, for instance, a 26-year-old man with Down syndrome died of asphyxiation after being handcuffed and restrained on the ground for not paying to watch a second feature in a local cinema. In the brief, the ACLU reports that "hundreds of Americans with disabilities die every year in police encounters and many more are seriously injured" (Center, Coles, Mizner, Shapiro, & Schlosser, 2015, p. 9). Individuals who have failed to hear or understand or who are unable to comply with police orders in a timely manner are all at a higher risk of being injured or killed by police who may mistake their failure to act as insubordination. Others are injured, sometimes gravely or fatally, in the process of being physically detained by police. Beyond these and other forms of state-sponsored murders, a shocking number of young people with disabilities are also killed by caregivers each year, leading self-advocates to host what has become a yearly *National Day of Mourning* to bring awareness to this disturbing issue.

Each November advocates also hold vigils, teach-ins, and marches as part of the Transgender Day of Remembrance. The yearly event honors transgender and gender-nonconforming people who have been murdered as a result of transgender bigotry and violence. The event was first started after the murder of Rita Hester, a transgender woman who was killed in 1998. Each year, this event is a shocking reminder of the danger associated with gender nonconformity, even as celebrities such as Laverne Cox, Janet Mock, and Caitlyn Jenner are celebrated in the national media. Though these three women have done so much to improve visibility and acceptance for transgender people, the community remains particularly vulnerable, with hundreds being murdered every year around the world (Trans Murder Monitoring Project, 2015).

How should we think about these instances of hate crimes leveled at minoritized groups of young people and adults? How do the intersections of race, class, disability, gender, and sexuality put people of color with disabilities and transgender people of color in even more vulnerable positions? What is the relationship between these crimes and the forms of marginalization that are now embedded in the fabric of schooling, such as the overrepresentation of students of color in special education or the school-to-prison pipeline? Although many scholars advancing CRT argue that race is a central and unifying axis upon which all these other forms of marginalization are grounded, scholars in DS and DSE have made the opposite claim that disability has primacy. No doubt some queer and transgender advocates see sexuality and gender nonconformity as central. Yet, as Baglieri (Chapter 10) argues, DisCrit offers us "a way to unravel the experiential and conceptual histories that have distanced disability studies from critical race studies and inclusive education from multicultural education. It provides a theoretical framework that instructs us in what we must learn about ourselves from one another."

Our motivation in first wanting to articulate DisCrit was fueled by what we see as the need to continue to work toward a truly intersectional starting point for our collective work—refusing primacy of either race or dis/ability or gender or any other aspect of identity without failing to also acknowledge that schooling as an institution has been deeply invested in creating and maintaining hierarchies based on race, class, and gender. We wanted to consider what new insights might emerge if our analyses *began* with the assumption that these and other systems of oppression are mutually constituted and interconnected at the deepest and most fundamental level. How might these new insights inform our politics and our practices? In crafting this book, we have brought some of the most impressive minds from interdisciplinary fields of study to the task of helping to do just that.

Contributors brought a range of diverse theories and constructs from Bell's (1980) interest convergence, to Saltman's (2007) disaster capitalism, to Rawls's *A Theory of Justice* (1971), to Crenshaw's intersectionality (1989), to Collins's (2003) ability profiling, to cultural historical activity theory (CH/AT), and more, and placed those constructs in conversation with DisCrit. They also employed a range of methodologies and analyses, including both qualitative and quantitative methods and analyses of large data sets, narrative, and discourse analysis. Reading each of these contributors as part of a larger conversation, we can begin to see synergies forming across their analyses and their aims. Whether taking on teacher beliefs, law and policy, curriculum or classroom practices, or causes of and contributors to overrepresentation, contributors situate DisCrit historically, contextually, and internationally. They mine the past to envision a different future. Whether explicitly or implicitly, contributors also engaged with, clarified, provided examples of, and expanded on all seven tenets of DisCrit. We couldn't be more pleased with the level of their analysis, the thoughtfulness of their critique, and the quality of their insights. Collectively, they have given us much to think about, have prodded us to be, and do, better in the service of a more expansive vision of educational equity for all.

In closing, we (David and Beth) feel indebted to Subini for pushing us forward in our own thinking. Without the audacity and boldness of her vision and confidence as a young scholar, I do not think we would have set out to claim a new theoretical framework. She should be credited with coining the term *DisCrit,* and we are simply pleased to have been able to help realize her initial vision for what great work could come as a result of pushing both of our respective fields in these important ways.

References

Abbas, J. (2012). A legacy of exploitation: Intellectual disability, unpaid labor, and disability services. *New Politics, 14*(1), 22–26.

Adams, M., Bell, L. A., & Griffin, P. (Eds.). (2007). *Teaching for diversity and social justice*. New York, NY: Routledge.

Adichie, C. A. (2014). *Americanah*. London, England: HarperCollins.

Agosto, V. (2012, June). A scripted curriculum: What movies teach us about disability and Black males. Paper presented at the 6th Annual Conference of the Critical Race Studies in Education Association, Teachers College, Columbia University, New York.

Ahern, L., & Rosenthal, E. (2010). Torture not treatment: Electric shock and long-term restraint in the United States on children and adults with disabilities at the Judge Rotenberg Center: Urgent appeal to the United Nations special rapporteur on torture. *Mental Disability Rights International*.

Ahram, R., Fergus, E., & Noguera, P. (2011). Addressing racial/ethnic disproportionality in special education: Case studies of suburban school districts. *Teachers College Record, 113*(10), 2233–2266.

Akiba, M., LeTendre, G. K., & Scribner, J. P. (2007). Teacher quality, opportunity gap, and national achievement in 46 countries. *Educational Researcher, 36*(7), 369–387. doi:10.3102/0013189X07308739

Albertson's Inc. v. Kirkingburg, 527 U.S. 555 (1999).

Alcoff, L. M. (2005). *Visible identities: Race, gender, and the self*. Oxford, England: Oxford University Press.

Alexander, M. (2010). *The new Jim Crow: Mass incarceration in the age of colorblindness*. New York, NY: The New Press.

Althusser, L. (1969). *For Marx* (B. Brewster, Trans.). New York, NY: Verso.

Althusser, L. (1971a). Ideology and ideological state apparatuses. In *Lenin and philosophy and other essays*. Monthly Free Press.

Althusser, L. (1971b). *Lenin and philosophy* (B. Brewster, Trans.). New York, NY: Monthly Review Press.

Althusser, L. (2003). *The humanist controversy and other writings* (F. Matheron, Ed. and Trans. & G. M. Goshgarian, Trans.). London, England: Verso.

American Anthropological Association Response to OMB Directive 15: Race and Ethnic Standards for Federal Statistics and Administrative Reporting. (1997). Retrieved from www.aaanet.org/gvt/ombdraft.htm

American Bar Association & the National Bar Association. (2001). *Justice by gender: The lack of appropriate prevention, diversion and treatment alternatives for girls in the juvenile justice system*. Washington, DC: American Bar Association and the National Bar Association.

Americans with Disabilities Act (42 U.S.C. § 12101-12213).

Anderson, E. (2010). *The imperative of integration*. Princeton, NJ: Princeton University Press.

Annamma, S. A. (2014). Whiteness as property: Innocence and ability in teacher education. *Urban Review*. doi: 10.1007/s11256-014-0293-6

Annamma, S. A., Connor, D., & Ferri, B. (2013). Dis/ability critical race studies (DisCrit): Theorizing at the intersections of race and dis/ability. *Journal of Race, Ethnicity, and Education, 16*(1), 1–31.

Araujo, M. (2007). "Modernising the comprehensive principle": Selection, setting and the institutionalisation of educational failure. *British Journal of Sociology of Education, 28*(2), 241–257.

Artiles, A. J. (2003). Special education's changing identity: Paradoxes and dilemmas in views of culture and space. *Harvard Educational Review, 73*, 164–202.

Artiles, A. J. (2009). Re-framing disproportionality research: Outline of a cultural historical paradigm. *Multiple Voices for Ethnically Diverse Exceptional Learners, 11*(2), 24–37.

Artiles, A. J. (2011). Toward an interdisciplinary understanding of educational equity and difference: The case of the racialization of ability. *Educational Researcher, 40*(9), 431–445.

Artiles, A. J. (2013). Untangling the racialization of disabilities. *Du Bois Review: Social Science Research on Race, 10*(02), 329–347.

Artiles, A. J. (2014a). Beyond responsiveness to identity badges: Future research on culture in disability and implications for Response to Intervention. *Educational Review*, 1–22. doi:10.1080/00131911.2014.934322

Artiles, A. J. (2014b). Future research on the intersections of ability, race, and language differences: Re-framing the roles of history and poverty. Inaugural lecture. University of Birmingham. Birmingham, England.

Artiles, A. J., & Bal, A. (2008). The next generation of disproportionality research: Toward a comparative model in the study of equity in ability differences. *The Journal of Special Education, 42*(1), 4–14.

Artiles, A. J., Bal, A., & Thorius, K. A. K. (2010). Back to the future: A critique of Response to Intervention's social justice views. *Theory into Practice, 49*, 250–257.

Artiles, A. J., & Dyson, A. (2005). Inclusive education in the globalization age: The promise of comparative cultural historical analysis. In D. Mitchell (Ed.), *Contextualizing inclusive education* (pp. 37–62). London, England: Routledge.

Artiles, A. J., Harry, B., Reschly, D. J., & Chinn, P. C. (2002). Over-identification of students of color in special education: A critical overview. *Multicultural Perspectives, 4*(1), 3–10.

Artiles, A. J., Kozleski, E. B., Trent, S. C., Osher, D., & Ortiz, A. (2010). Justifying and explaining disproportionality, 1968–2008: A critique of underlying views of culture. *Exceptional Children, 76*(2), 279–299.

Artiles, A. J., Kozleski, E., Waitoller, F. R., & Lukinbeal, C. L. (2011). Inclusive education and the interlocking of ability and race in the United States: Notes for an educational equality programme. In A. J. Artiles, E. Kozleski, & F. R. Waitoller (Eds.), *Inclusive education* (pp. 45–68). Cambridge, MA: Harvard Educational Press.

Artiles, A. J., Rueda, R., Salazar, J., & Higardea, I. (2005). Within-group diversity in minority disproportionate representation: English language learners in urban school districts. *Exceptional Children, 71*, 283–300.

Artiles, A., & Trent, S. C. (1994). Overrepresentation of minority students in special education: A continuing debate. *Journal of Special Education, 27*(4), 410–437.

Artiles, A., Trent, S. C., & Palmer, J. D. (2004). Culturally diverse students in special education: Legacies and prospects. In J. A. Banks & C. A. McGee Banks (Eds.), *Handbook of research on multicultural education* (pp. 716–735). San Francisco, CA: Jossey-Bass.

Arzubiaga, A. E., Artiles, A. J., King, K., & Harris-Murri, N. (2008). Beyond research on cultural minorities: Challenges and implications of research as situated cultural practice. *Exceptional Children, 74*(3), 309–327.

Asante, M. K. (1991). Afrocentric curriculum. *Educational Leadership, 49*(4), 28–31.

Asbury, K., & Plomin, R. (2014). *G is for genes: The impact of genetics on education and achievement.* Chichester: Wiley and Sons.

Asch, A. (2001). Critical Race Theory, feminism, and disability: Reflections on social justice and personal identity. *Ohio State Law Journal, 62*, 1–17.

Asch, A. (2004). Critical race theory, feminism, and disability: Reflections on social justice and personal identity. In B. G. Smith & B. Hutchison (Eds.), *Gendering disability* (pp. 9–44). New Brunswick, NJ: Rutgers University Press.

Austin Nursing Center Inc. v. Lovato, 171 S.W. 3d. 845 (Tex. 2005).

Baca, L., & Cervantes, H. (2004). *The bilingual special education interface* (4th ed.). Columbus, OH: Merrill/Prentice Hall.

Bacchi, C. (2000). Policy as discourse: What does it mean? Where does it get us? *Discourse: Studies in the Cultural Politics of Education, 21*(1), 45–57.

Baglieri, S., Bejoian, L., Broderick, A., Connor, D. J., & Valle, J. (2011). Creating alliances against exclusivity: A pathway to educational reform. *Teachers College Record, 113*(10), 2282–2308.

Baglieri, S., & Knopf, J. H. (2004). Normalizing difference in inclusive teaching. *Journal of Learning Disabilities, 37*(6), 525–529.

Baglieri, S., & Shapiro, A. (2012). *Disability studies and the inclusive classroom: Critical practices for creating least restrictive attitudes.* New York, NY: Routledge.

Bahena, S., Cooc, N., Currie-Rubin, R., Kuttner, P., & Ng, M. (2012). *Disrupting the school-to-prison pipeline.* Cambridge, MA: Harvard Education Press.

Baker, B. (2002). The hunt for disability: The new eugenics and the normalization of school children. *Teachers College Record, 104*, 663–703.

Baker, C. (2001). *Foundations of bilingual education and bilingualism* (3rd ed.). Clevedon: Multilingual Matters.

Bal, A., Sullivan, A. L., & Harper, J. (2013). A situated analysis of special education disproportionality for systemic transformation in an urban school district. *Remedial and Special Education.* 0741932513507754.

Ball, E. W., & Harry, B. (2010). Assessment and the policing of the norm. In C. Dudley-Marling & A. Gurn (Eds.), *The myth of the normal curve* (pp. 105–122). New York, NY: Peter Lang.

Ball, S. J. (1981). *Beachside comprehensive: A case-study of secondary schooling.* Cambridge, England: Cambridge University Press.

Ball, S. J. (1993a). The teacher's soul and the terrors of performativity. *Journal of Educational Policy, 18*(3), 215–228. Retrieved from dx.doi.org/10.1080/0268093022000043065

Ball, S. J. (1993b). What is policy? Texts, trajectories, and toolboxes. *Discourse: Studies in the Cultural Politics of Education, 13*(2), 10–17.

Banks, J. A. (1993). The cannon debate, knowledge construction, and multicultural education. *Educational Researcher, 22*(5), 4–14.

Banks, J. A. (1995). *Handbook of research on multicultural education.* San Francisco, CA: Jossey-Bass.

Banks, J. A. (2002). Race, knowledge construction, and education in the USA: Lessons from history. *Journal of Race, Ethnicity and Education, 5*(1), 7–28.

Baxter, L. A. (2011). *Voicing relationships: A dialogic perspective.* Thousand Oaks, CA: Sage.

Baynton, D. (2001). Disability and the justification of inequality in American history. In P. K. Longmore & L. Umansky (Eds.), *The new disability history: American perspectives* (pp. 33–57). New York, NY: New York University Press.

Beck, A., & Muschkin, C. (2012). The enduring impact of race: Understanding disparities in student disciplinary infractions and achievement. *Sociological Perspectives, 55*(4), 637–662.

Bell, C. M. (2006). Introducing *White* disability studies: A modest proposal. In L. J. Davis (Ed.), *The disability studies reader* (2nd ed., pp. 275–282). New York, NY: Routledge.

Bell, C. M. (2011). Introduction: Doing representational detective work. In C. Bell (Ed.), *Blackness and disability: Critical examinations and cultural interventions* (Vol. 21, pp. 1–8). Münster, Germany: LIT Verlag.

Bell, D. (1980). *Brown v. Board of the Education* and the interest convergence dilemma. *Harvard Law Review, 93*, 518–533.

Bell, D. (1987). *And we are not saved: The elusive quest for racial justice.* New York, NY: Basic Books.

Bell, D. (2004). *Silent covenants: Brown v. Board of Education and the unfulfilled hopes for racial reform.* Oxford, England: Oxford University Press.

Ben-Moshe, L. (2013). Disabling incarceration: Connecting disability to divergent confinements in the USA. *Critical Sociology, 39*(3), 385–403.

Ben-Moshe, L., Chapman, C., & Carey, A. (Eds.). (2014). *Disability incarcerated: Imprisonment and disability in the United States and Canada.* Basingstoke: Palgrave Macmillan.

Beratan, G. (2008). The song remains the same: Transposition and the disproportionate representation of minority students in special education. *Journal of Race, Ethnicity, and Education, 11*(4), 337–354.

Bernal, D. D., Alemán Jr., E., & Garavito, A. (2009). Latina/o undergraduate students mentoring Latina/o elementary students: A borderlands analysis of shifting identities and first-year experiences. *Harvard Educational Review, 79,* 560–586.

Berry, T. R. (2010). Engaged pedagogy and critical race feminism. *Educational Foundations, 24,* 19–26.

Bhopal, K., & Preston, J. (Eds.). (2012). *Intersectionality and "race" in education.* London, England: Routledge.

Biklen, D., & Kliewer, C. (2006). Constructing competence: Autism, voice and the "disordered" body. *International Journal of Inclusive Education, 10,* 169–188.

BillyJam. (2012). Latest Krip-Hop compilation addresses police brutality against people with disabilities. *Amoeblog.* Retrieved from www.amoeba.com/blog/2012/06/jamoeblog/latest-krip-hop-compilation-addresses-police-brutality-against-people-with-disabilities.html

Blackorby, J., & Wagner, M. (1996). Longitudinal postschool outcomes of youth with disabilities: Findings from the National Longitudinal Study. *Exceptional Children, 62*(5), 399–413.

Blair, M. (2001). *Why pick on me? School exclusions and Black youth.* Stoke-on-Trent, England: Trentham.

Blanchett, W. J. (2006). Disproportionate representation of African Americans in special education: Acknowledging the role of White privilege and racism. *Remedial and Special Education, 35*(6), 24–28.

Blanchett, W. (2008). Educational inequities: The intersection of disability, race, and social class [Foreword]. In D. J. Connor, *Urban narratives: Life at the intersections of learning disability, race, & social class* (pp. x–xvii). New York, NY: Peter Lang.

Blanchett, W. J. (2009). A retrospective examination of urban education from Brown to the resegregation of African Americans in special education—It is time to "Go for broke." *Urban Education, 44*(4), 370–388. doi:10.1177/0042085909338688

Blanchett, W. J. (2010). Telling it like it is: The role of race, class, and culture in the perpetuation of learning disability as a privileged category for the White middle class. *Disability Studies Quarterly, 30*(2), 1230–1277.

Blanchett, W. J., Brantlinger, E., & Shealey, M. W. (2005). Brown 50 years later—Exclusion, segregation, and inclusion. *Symposium, 26*(2), 66–121. doi:10.1177/07419325050260020101

Blanchett, W. J., Klingner, J. K., & Harry, B. (2009). The intersection of race, culture, language, and disability: Implications for urban education. *Urban Education, 44*(4), 389–409. doi:10.1177/0042085909338686

Blanchett, W. J., Mumford, V., & Beachum, F. (2005). Urban school failure and disproportionality in a post-Brown era: Benign neglect of the constitutional rights of students of color. *Remedial & Special Education, 26*(2), 70–81. doi:10.1177/07419325050260020201

Block, G. (1983). Racism and sexism in Nazi Germany: Motherhood, compulsory sterilization, and the state. *Signs, 8*(3), 400–421.

Blood, M. R. (2014, July 10). Disabled people denied voting rights, group says. *Associated Press.* Retrieved from bigstory.ap.org/article/ap-exclusive-disabled-often-banned-voting

Bobo, L., & Smith, R. (1998). From Jim Crow racism to laissez-faire racism: The transformation of racial attitudes. In W. F. Katkin, N. Landsman, & A. Tyree (Eds.), *Beyond pluralism*. Chicago, IL: University of Illinois Press.

Bonilla-Silva, E. (2006). *Racism without racists: Colorblind racism and the persistence of racial inequality in the United States*. Lanham, MD: Rowman & Littlefield.

Boudon, R. (1974). *Education opportunity and social inequality*. New York, NY: Wiley.

Bourdieu, P. (1977a). Cultural reproduction and social reproduction. In *Power and ideology in education*. London, England: Oxford University Press.

Bourdieu, P. (1977b). *Outline of a theory of practice*. Cambridge, England: Cambridge University Press.

Bourdieu, P., & Wacquant, L. J. D. (1992). *An invitation to reflexive sociology*. Chicago, IL: University of Chicago Press.

Bowker, G. C., Baker, K., Millerand, F., & Ribes, D. (2010). Toward information infrastructure studies: Ways of knowing in a networked environment. In J. Hunsinger, L. Klastup, & M. Allen (Eds.), *International handbook of Internet research* (pp. 97–117). New York, NY: Springer Science + Business Media. doi:10.1007/978-1-4020-9789-8_5

Bowker, G. C., & Star, S. L. (1999). *Sorting things out*. Cambridge, MA: MIT Press.

Bowles, S., & Gintis, H. (1976). *Schooling in capitalist America*. New York, NY: Basic Books.

Brantlinger, E. (1997). Using ideology: Cases of nonrecognition of the politics of research and practice in special education. *Review of Educational Research, 67*(4), 425–459.

Brantlinger, E. (2003). *Dividing classes: How the middle class negotiates and rationalizes school advantage*. New York, NY: Routledge Falmer.

Brantlinger, E. (Ed.). (2006). *Who benefits from special education? Remediating (fixing) other people's children*. Mahwah, NJ: Erlbaum.

Brault, M. W. (2012). *Americans with disabilities: 2010*. U.S. Department of Commerce, U.S. Census Bureau.

Brayboy, B. M. J. (2006). Toward a tribal Critical Race Theory in education. *The Urban Review, 37*(5), 425–446.

Brew-Parrish, V. (1997, March/April). Whether their perpetrators believe it or not, Disability Awareness Days send the wrong message. *Ragged Edge Magazine*. Retrieved from www.raggededgemagazine.com

Brown, J. K. (2013, November 21; updated September 8, 2014). In Miami Gardens, store video catches cops in the act. *Miami Herald*. Retrieved from www.miamiherald.com/news/local/community/miami-dade/article1957716.html

Brown-Jeffy, S., & Cooper, J. E. (2011). Toward a conceptual framework of culturally relevant pedagogy: An overview of the conceptual and theoretical literature. *Teacher Education Quarterly, 38*(1), 65–84.

Brown et al. v. Board of Education of Topeka, Kansas, et al., 347 U.S. 483 (1954), 349 U.S. 294 (1955).

Brownmiller, S. (1975). *Against our will: Men, women and rape*. New York, NY: Simon & Schuster.

Bryan, J., Day-Vnes, N. L., Griffin, D., & Moore-Thomas, C. (2012). The dispro-portionality dilemma: Patterns of teacher referrals to school counselors for dis-ruptive behavior. *Journal of Counseling & Development, 90*(2), 177–190.

Buck v. Bell, 143 Va. 310 (Va. Ct. App. 1925).

Burt, C. (1937). *The backward child.* London, England: London University Press.

Caldwell, J. (2011). Disability identity of leaders in the self-advocacy movement. *Intellectual and Developmental Disabilities, 49*(5), 315–326.

Campbell, F. K. (2009). *Contours of abelism: The production of disability and able-ness.* New York, NY: Palgrave McMillan.

Caps, R., Fix, M., Murray, J., Ost, J., Passel, J. S., & Herwantoro, S. (2005). The new demography of America's schools: Immigration and the No Child Left Behind Act. *Urban Institute Research.* Retrieved from www.urban.org/UploadedPDF/311230_new_demography.pdf

Carbado, D. W., & Gulati, M. (2000). Working identity. *Cornell Law Review, 85*(5), 1260–1308.

Carbado, D. W., & Gulati, M. (2013). *Acting White?: Rethinking race in post-racial America.* New York, NY: Oxford University Press.

Carlson, L. (2001). Cognitive ableism and disability studies: Feminist reflections on the history of mental retardation. *Hypatia, 16*(4), 124–146.

Carson, E. A., & Golinelli, D. (2013). *BJS statisticians, prisoners in 2012—Advance counts.* U.S. Department of Justice, Office of Justice Programs, Bureau of Justice Statistics.

Center, C., Coles, M., Mizner, S. P., Shapiro, S. R., & Schlosser, A. L. (2015, February 12). Amicus curiae of the ACLU, the American Diabetes Assoc., the Epilepsy Foundation, Mental Health America, the National Disability Rights Network, the ARC, et al., to the U.S. Court of Appeals for the Ninth Circuit (No. 13-1412). Retrieved from www.aclu.org/sites/default/files/assets/13-1412_bsac_the_american_civil_liberties_union.pdf

Chapman, P. D. (1988). *Schools as sorters: Lewis M. Terman, applied psychology, and the intelligence testing movement, 1890–1930.* New York, NY: New York University Press.

Charlton, J. I. (2000). *Nothing about us without us: Disability oppression and em-powerment.* Berkeley, CA: University of California Press.

Charlton, J. I. (2006). The dimensions of disability oppression: An overview. In L. J. Davis (Ed.), *The disability studies reader* (2nd ed., pp. 217–227). New York, NY: Routledge.

Chen, M. (2013). *Animacies: Bio-politics, racial mattering, and queer affect.* Durham, NC: Duke University Press.

Child Welfare Information Gateway, Administration for Children and Families, U.S. Department of Health and Human Services. (2014). "Special needs" adoption: What does it mean? Retrieved from www.childwelfare.gov/pubs/factsheets/specialneeds

Chinn, S. E. (2004). Feeling her way: Audre Lorde and the power of touch. In B. G. Smith & B. Hutchison (Eds.), *Gendering disability* (pp. 192–215). New Brunswick, NJ: Rutgers University Press.

Chirico, J. (2014, August). Police use taser on mentally disabled man; accused of racial profiling. *CBS 42 News.* Retrieved from www.cbs46.com/story/26367814/police-tase-mentally-disabled-man-accused-of-racial-profiling

Chowdhry, G. (2007). Edward Said and contrapuntal reading: Implications for critical interventions in international relations. *Millennium—Journal of International Studies, 36,* 101–116.

City of Cleburne v. Cleburne Living Center, Inc., 473 U.S. 432 (1985).

Civil Rights Data Collection (CRDC). (2012). *User guide.* Washington, DC: U.S. Department of Education, Office for Civil Rights. Retrieved from ocrdata.ed.gov/downloads/UserGuide.pdf

CNS News. (2012, March 23). Retrieved from cnsnews.com/news/article/obama-if-i-had-son-he-d-look-trayvon

Coard, B. (2005). How the West Indian child is made educationally subnormal in the British school system. In B. Richardson (Ed.), *Tell it like it is: How our schools fail Black children* (pp. 27–59). London, England: Bookmarks. (Original work published in 1971)

Cobb, R.R.T. (1858). *A inquiry into the law of negro slavery in the United States of America: To which is prefixed, an historical sketch of slavery.* Philadelphia, PA: T. & J. W. Johnson & Company.

Cochran-Smith, M. (1995). Color blindness and basket making are not the answers: Confronting the dilemmas of race, culture, and language diversity in teacher education. *American Educational Research Journal, 32*(3), 493–522.

Cohen, J., & Cohen, P. (1983). *Applied multiple regression/correlation analysis for the behavioral sciences.* Hillsdale, NJ: Erlbaum.

Cole, M. (n.d.). The illusion of culture-free intelligence testing. Retrieved from www.lchc.ucsd.edu/mca/paper/cole.iq.html

Cole, M. (1996). *Cultural psychology: A once and future discipline.* Cambridge, MA: Harvard University Press.

Cole, M. (1998). Can cultural psychology help us think about diversity? *Mind, Culture, and Activity, 5*(4), 291–304.

Cole, M. (2003). *Cultural psychology: A once and future discipline* (6th ed.). Cambridge, MA: Harvard University.

Cole, M., & Gajdamashko, N. (2009). Development in cultural-historical activity. In A. Sannino, H. Daniels, & K. D. Gutiérrez (Eds.), *Learning and expanding with activity theory* (pp. 129–143). New York, NY: Cambridge University Press.

Cole, M., & Griffin, P. (1983). A socio-historical approach to re-mediation. *The Quarterly Newsletter of the Laboratory of Comparative Human Cognition, 5*(4), 69–74.

Cole, M., & Levitin, K. (2000). A cultural-historical view of human nature. In N. Roughley (Ed.), *Being humans: Anthropological universality and particularity in transdisciplinary perspectives* (pp. 64–80). New York, NY: deGruyter.

Cole, M., & The Distributed Literacy Consortium. (2006). *The Fifth Dimension: An after-school program built on diversity.* Beverly Hills, CA: Sage.

Cole, P. G. (1999). The structure of arguments used to support or oppose inclusion policies for students with disabilities. *Journal of Intellectual and Developmental Disability, 24*(3), 215–225.

Collins, K. M. (2003). *Ability profiling and school failure: One child's struggle to be seen as competent.* New York, NY: Routledge.

Collins, K. M. (2013). *Ability profiling and school failure: One child's struggle to be seen as competent* (2nd ed.). New York, NY: Routledge.

Collins, K. M. (2015). A disability studies in education analysis of corporate-based educational reform: Lessons from New Orleans. In D. J. Connor, J. W. Valle, & C. Hale (Eds.), *Practicing disability studies in education: Acting toward social change* (pp. 217–233). New York: Peter Lang.

Collins, P. H. (1990). *Black feminist thought: Knowledge, consciousness, and the politics of empowerment.* New York, NY: Routledge.

Coloma, R. (2011). White gazes, Brown breasts: Imperial feminism and disciplining desires and bodies in colonial encounters. *Paedagogica Historica.* doi:10.1080/00309230.2010.547511

Commission for Racial Equality (CRE). (1992). *Set to fail? Setting and banding in secondary schools.* London, England: Commission for Racial Equality.

Communities Empowerment Network. (2005). Zero tolerance and school exclusions. *Special Issue of the CEN Newsletter, 5*(6).

Compass. (2011). *Anatomy of a riot.* London, England: Compass (Direction for the Democratic Left).

Connor, D. J. (2008a). Not so strange bedfellows: The promise of disability studies and Critical Race Theory. In S. L. Gabel & S. Danforth (Eds.), *Disability and the politics of education: An international reader* (pp. 451–476). New York, NY: Peter Lang.

Connor, D. J. (2008b). *Urban narratives: Portraits-in-progress—Life at the intersections of learning disability, race, and social class.* New York, NY: Peter Lang.

Connor, D. J. (2012). Does dis/ability now sit at the table(s) of social justice and multicultural education? A descriptive survey of three recent anthologies. *Disability Studies Quarterly, 32*(3).

Connor, D. J., & Baglieri, S. (2009). Tipping the scales: Disability studies asks "How much diversity can you take?" In S. Steinberg (Ed.), *Diversity and multiculturalism: A reader* (pp. 341–361). New York, NY: Peter Lang.

Connor, D. J., & Ferri, B. A. (2007). The conflict within: Resistance to inclusion and other paradoxes in special education. *Disability & Society, 22,* 63–77.

Connor, D. J., & Gabel, S. (2013). "Cripping" the curriculum through academic activism: Working toward increasing global exchanges to reframe (dis)ability and education. *Equity and Excellence in Education, 46*(1), 100–118.

Cooper, B. (2008). *Beethoven.* Oxford, England: Oxford University Press.

Cooper, F. R. (2006). Against bipolar Black masculinity: Intersectionality, assimilation, identity performance, and hierarchy. *University of California Davis Law Review, 39,* 853–904.

Cornell University. (n.d.). Find U.S. disability statistics in 3 easy steps. *Disability statistics.* Retrieved from www.disabilitystatistics.org/reports/acs.cfm?statistic=9

Coutinho, M. J., & Oswald, D. P. (2000). Disproportionate representation in special education: A synthesis and recommendations. *Journal of Child and Family Studies, 9*(2), 135–156.

Crenshaw, K. (1989). Demarginalizing the intersection of race and sex: A Black feminist critique of antidiscrimination doctrine, feminist theory and antiracist politics. *The University of Chicago Legal Forum, 140,* 139–167.

Crenshaw, K. (1993). Mapping the margins: Intersectionality, identity politics, and violence against women of color. *Stanford Law Review, 43,* 1241–1299.

Crenshaw, K. (1995). The intersection of race and gender. In K. Crenshaw, N. Gotanda, G. Peller, & K. Thomas (Eds.), *Critical Race Theory: The key writings that formed the movement* (pp. 357–381). New York, NY: The New Press.

Crenshaw, K., Gotanda, N., Peller, G., & Thomas, K. (1995). *Critical Race Theory: The key writings that formed the movement.* New York, NY: The New Press.

Crunkadelic. (2014, October 16). Reflections of respectability. *Crunk feminist collective.* Retrieved from www.crunkfeministcollective.com/tag/respectability-politics/

Cummings D. (2013, August). Some thoughts on education and political priorities. Paper presented to Michael Gove, Secretary of State for Education, by his advisor. London, England: Department for Education.

Dalton, H. L. (1987). The clouded prism. *Harvard Law Review, 22*(435), 439–440.

Danforth, S., Taff, S., & Ferguson, P. M. (2006). Place, profession, and program in the history of special education curriculum. In E. Brantlinger (Ed.), *Who benefits from special education? Remediating (fixing) other people's children* (pp. 1–26). New York, NY: Routledge.

Darrow School. (n.d.). Admissions. *Darrow School.* Retrieved from www.darrow school.org/admissions/admissions

da Silva, C. D., Huguley, J. P., Kakli, Z., & Rao, R. (2007). *The opportunity gap: Achievement and inequality in education.* Cambridge, MA: Harvard Educational Review.

Davila, B. (2012). Disability micro aggressions and Latino/a student responses. Paper presented at the 6th Annual Conference of the Critical Race Studies in Education Association, May 31–June 2, Teachers College, Columbia University, New York.

Davis, A. (2003). *Are prisons obsolete?* New York, NY: Seven Stories Press.

Davis, K. (2008). Intersectionality as buzzword, *Feminist Theory, 9*(1), 67–85.

Davis, L. J. (2002). *Bending over backwards: Disability, dismodernism and other difficult positions.* New York, NY: New York University Press.

Davis, L. J. (2006). Constructing normalcy. In L. J. Davis (Ed.), *The disability studies reader* (pp. 3–16). New York, NY: Routledge.

Delgado, R. (1995a). *Critical Race Theory: The cutting edge.* Philadelphia, PA: Temple University Press.

Delgado, R. (1995b). *The Rodrigo chronicles: Conversations about America and race.* New York, NY: New York University Press.

Delgado, R. (2012). Rodrigo's reconsideration: Intersectionality and the future of Critical Race Theory. *Iowa Law Review, 96,* 1247–1288.

Delgado, R., & Stefancic, J. (2001). *Critical Race Theory: An introduction.* New York, NY: New York University Press.

Delgado Bernal, D. (2002). Critical Race Theory, LatCrit theory, and critical race-gendered epistemologies: Recognizing students of color as holders and creators of knowledge. *Qualitative Inquiry, 8*(1), 105–126.

Deloria, P. J. (1999). *Playing Indian.* New Haven, CT: Yale University.

DeNavas-Walt, C., Proctor, B. D., & Smith, J. C. (2012). *Income, poverty, and health insurance coverage in the United States: 2012, U.S. Census Bureau, Current Population Reports P60-245, Table 3: People in Poverty by Selected Characteristics: 2011 and 2012.* Washington, DC: Government Printing Office.

Denzine, G. M., Cooney, J. B., & McKenzie, R. (2005). Confirmatory factor analysis of the teacher efficacy scale for prospective teachers. *British Journal of Educational Psychology, 75*(4), 689–708.

Department for Children, Schools and Families. (2010). Special educational needs (SEN)—A guide for parents and carers. A commitment from The Children's Plan. DCSF-00639-2008BKT-EN. Nottingham, England: DCSF.

Department for Education. (2010). *The importance of teaching* (White Paper. Cmnd 7980). London, England: Author.

DES. (1978). *Special educational needs (The Warnock report).* London, England: HMSO.

DES. (1985). *Education for all: Report of the committee of inquiry into the education of children from ethnic minority groups.* London, England: HMSO.

Developmental Adult Neuro-Diversity Association (DANDA). (2011). What is neuro-diversity? Retrieved from www.danda.org.uk/pages/neuro-diversity.php

DfCS. (2010). *Breaking the link between special educational needs and low attainment.* London, England: Department for Children, Schools and Families.

DfEE. (1997). *Excellence for all children: Meeting special educational needs.* London, England: Department for Education and Employment.

DfES. (2005). *Ethnicity and education: The evidence on minority ethnic pupils* (Research topic paper RTP01-05). London, England: Department for Education and Skills.

Diamond, P. M., Wang, E. W., Holzer III, C. E., Thomas, C., & des Cruser, A. (2001). The prevalence of mental illness in prison. *Administration and Policy in Mental Health and Mental Health Services Research, 29*(1), 21–40.

Dixson, A. D., & Rousseau, C. K. (2005). And we are still not saved: Critical Race Theory in education ten years later. *Journal of Race Ethnicity and Education, 8*(1), 7–27.

Donoghue, C. (2003). Challenging the authority of the medical definition of disability: An analysis of the resistance to the social constructionist paradigm. *Disability & Society, 18*(2), 199–208.

Donovan, M. S., & Cross, C. T. (2002). *Minority students in special and gifted education.* Washington, DC: National Research Council.

Douglas, M. (1966). *Purity and danger: An analysis of the concepts of pollution and taboo.* New York, NY: Routledge.

Du Bois, W. E. B. (1989). *The souls of Black folk.* New York, NY: Penguin Books. (Original work published 1904)

Du Bois, W. E. B. (1920). Race intelligence. *The Crisis, 20*(3).

Du Bois, W. E. B. (1935). *Black reconstruction in America: Toward a history of the part which Black folk played in the attempt to reconstruct democracy in America, 1860–1880.* New York, NY: The Free Press.

Dudley-Marling, C., & Gurn, A. (Eds.). (2010). *The myth of the normal curve*. New York, NY: Peter Lang.

Dunn, L. M. (1968). Special education for the mildly retarded: Is much of it justifiable? *Exceptional Children, 35*(1), 75–83.

Dyson, A., & Kozleski, E. B. (2008). Disproportionality in special education: A transatlantic phenomenon. In L. Florian & M. McLaughlin (Eds.), *Dilemmas and alternatives in the classification of children with disabilities: New perspectives* (pp. 170–190). Thousand Oaks, CA: Corwin Press.

Eisenberg, S. E., & P. L. Micklow. (1977, Spring/summer). The assaulted wife: "Catch 22" revisited. *Women's Rights Law Reporter*, 151–153.

Elkins, T. E., Stovall, T. G., Wilroy, S., & Dacus, J. V. (1986). Attitudes of mothers of children with Down Syndrome concerning amniocentesis, abortion, and prenatal genetic counseling techniques. *Obstetrics & Gynecology, 68*(2), 181–184.

Elmore, R. F., & Fuhrman, S. H. (1995). Opportunity-to-learn standards and the state role in education. *Teachers College Record, 96*(3), 433–458.

Engeström, Y. (2001). Expansive learning at work: Toward an activity theoretical reconceptualization. *Journal of Education and Work, 16*(1), 133–156.

Engeström, Y., & Sannino, A. (2010). Studies of expansive learning: Foundations, findings and future challenges. *Educational Research Review, 5*(1), 1–24.

Erevelles, N. (2000). Educating unruly bodies: Critical pedagogy, disability studies, and the politics of schooling. *Educational Theory, 50*(1), 25–47.

Erevelles, N. (2011a). "Coming out Crip" in inclusive education. *Teachers College Record, 113*(10), 2155–2185.

Erevelles, N. (2011b). *Disability and difference in global contexts: Enabling a transformative body politic*. New York, NY: Palgrave MacMillan.

Erevelles, N. (2012). *Disability and difference in global context: Towards a transformative body politic*. New York, NY: Palgrave.

Erevelles, N. (2014). Crippin' Jim Crow: Disability and the school to prison pipeline. In L. Ben-Moshe, C. Chapman, & A. Carey (Eds.), *Disability incarcerated: Imprisonment and disability in the United States and Canada* (pp. 81–99). Basingstoke: Palgrave Macmillan.

Erevelles, N., Kanga, A., & Middleton, R. (2006). How does it feel to be a problem? Race, disability, and exclusion in educational policy. In E. Brantlinger (Ed.), *Who benefits from special education? Remediating (fixing) other people's children* (pp. 77–99). New York, NY: Routledge.

Erevelles, N., & Minear, A. (2010). Unspeakable offenses: Untangling race and disability in discourses of intersectionality. *Journal of Literary & Cultural Disability Studies, 4*(2), 127–145.

Erevelles, N., & Mutua, N. K., (2005). "I am a woman now!" Rewriting cartographies of girlhood from the critical standpoint of disability. In P. Bettis & N. Adams (Eds.), *Geographies of girlhood: Identity in-between* (pp. 253–270). Mahwah, NJ: Erlbaum.

Erickson, W., von Schrader, S., & Lee, C. (2012). *2010 Disability status report: The United States*. Ithaca, NY: Cornell University.

Eysenck, H. J. (1971). *Race, intelligence and education*. London, England: Temple-Smith.

Fabelo, T., Thompson, M., Plotkin, M., Carmichael, D., Marchbanks, M., & Booth, E. (2012). *Breaking school rules: A statewide study of how school discipline relates to students' success and juvenile justice involvement.* Washington, DC: The Council of State Governments Justice Center.

Fanshel, D., Finch, S. J., & Grundy, J. F. (1990). *Foster children in a life course perspective.* New York, NY: Columbia University.

Faulkner, W. (1955, September 10). Faulkner pictures Till case as test of survival of White man, America. *Jackson Daily News*, p. 1.

Feinberg, W. (1998). *Common schools/uncommon identities: National unity and cultural difference.* New Haven, CT: Yale University Press.

Fenton, Z. E. (1998). Domestic violence in Black and White: Racialized gender stereotypes in gender violence. *Columbia Journal of Gender and Law, 8*, 1–65.

Fenton, Z. E. (2007). The paradox of hierarchy—Or why we always choose the tools of the master's house. *New York University Review of Law & Social Change, 31*, 627–637.

Fenton, Z. E. (2010). No witch is a bad witch: A commentary on the erasure of Matilda Joslyn Gage. *Southern California Law Journal of Interdisciplinary Studies, 20*(10), 21–38.

Fenton, Z. E. (2013a). Bastards! . . . and the welfare plantation. *Iowa Journal of Gender, Race & Justice, 17*, 9–34.

Fenton, Z. E. (2013b). Disabling racial repetition. In A. Kanter & B. Ferri (Eds.), *Righting educational wrongs: Disability studies in law and education* (pp. 174–206). Syracuse, NY: Syracuse University Press.

Ferguson, A. (2001). *Bad boys: Public schools in the making of Black masculinity.* Ann Arbor, MI: University of Michigan Press.

Ferguson, P. M. (2008). The doubting dance: Contributions to a history of parent/professional interactions in early 20th century America. *Research and Practice for Persons with Severe Disabilities, 33*(1–2), 48–58.

FERPA. (1974). 20 U.S.C. 1232g.

Ferri, B. A. (2010). A dialogue we've yet to have: Race and disability studies. In C. Dudley-Marling & A. Gurn (Eds.), *The myth of the normal curve.* New York, NY: Peter Lang.

Ferri, B. A. (2011). Disability life writing and the politics of knowing. *Teachers College Record, 113*(10), 2267–2282.

Ferri, B. A., & Connor, D. J. (2005). In the shadow of *Brown*: Special education and overrepresentation of students of color. *Remedial and Special Education, 26*, 93–100.

Ferri, B. A., & Connor, D. J. (2006). *Reading resistance: Discourses of exclusion in desegregation and inclusion debates.* New York, NY: Peter Lang.

Ferri, B. A., & Connor, D. J. (2010). "I was the special ed. girl": Urban working-class young women of colour. *Journal of Gender and Education, 22*(1), 105–121.

Ferri, B. A., & Connor, D. J. (2014). Talking (and not talking) about race, social class and dis/ability: Working margin to margin. *Race Ethnicity and Education, 17*(4), 471–493.

Fierros, E. G., & Conroy, J. W. (2002). Double jeopardy: An exploration of restrictiveness and race in special education. In D. J. Losen & G. Orfield (Eds.), *Racial inequity in special education* (pp. 39–70). Cambridge, MA: Harvard Education Press.

Fitzgerald, T. D. (2009). Controlling the Black school age male: Psychotropic medications and the circumvention of public law 94-142 and section 504. *Urban Education, 44*, 225–247.

Foley, R. J. (2013, May 1). Abused disabled Iowa plant workers awarded $240M. *Associated Press*. Retrieved from bigstory.ap.org/article/abused-disabled-iowa-plant-workers-awarded-240m

Folsom, D. P., Hawthorne, W., Lindamer, L., Gilmer, T., Bailey, A., Golshan, S., . . . Jeste, D. V. (2005). Prevalence and risk factors for homelessness and utilization of mental health services among 10,340 patients with serious mental illness in a large public mental health system. *American Journal of Psychiatry, 162*, 370–376.

Foster, M. (1999). Race, class, and gender in education research: Surveying the political terrain. *Educational Policy, 13*(1–2), 77–85.

Foucault, M. (1971). *The order of discourse*. Paris, France: Gallimard.

Foucault, M. (1972). *The archaeology of knowledge* (A. M. Smith, Trans.). New York, NY: Pantheon Books.

Foucault, M. (1974). *The order of things*. London, England: Tavistock.

Foucault, M. (1977). *Discipline and punish: The birth of the prison* (A. Sheridan, Trans.). New York, NY: Vintage Books.

Frankenberg, R. (1993). *The social construction of Whiteness: White women, race matters*. Minneapolis, MN: University of Minnesota Press.

Franklin, B. M. (1987). *Learning disability: Dissenting essays*. New York, NY: Falmer Press.

Fraser, N. (2007). Re-framing justice in a globalizing world. In T. Lovell (Ed.), *(Mis)recognition, social inequality, and social justice* (pp. 17–35). London, England: Routledge.

Frattura, E. M., & Topinka, C. (2006). Theoretical underpinnings of separate educational programs: The social justice challenge continues. *Education and Urban Society, 38*(3), 327–344.

Freire, P. (1970/2002). *Pedagogy of the oppressed*. New York, NY: Continuum.

Freire, P. (2005). *Teachers as cultural workers: Letters to those who dare teach* (expanded version). Boulder, CO: Westview.

Friend, M., & Bursuck, W. (2012). *Including students with special needs: A practical guide for classroom teachers* (6th ed.). Boston, MA: Beacon.

Frontiero v. Richardson, 411 US 677 (1973).

Gabel, S. (2002). Some conceptual problems with critical pedagogy. *Curriculum Inquiry, 32*(2), 177.

Gallagher, D. (2010). Educational researchers and the making of normal people. In C. Dudley-Marling & A. Gurn (Eds.), *The myth of the normal curve* (pp. 25–38). New York, NY: Peter Lang.

Garland-Thomson, R. (2004). Integrating disability, transforming feminist theory. In B. G. Smith & B. Hutchison (Eds.), *Gendering disability* (pp. 73–103). New Brunswick, NJ: Rutgers University Press.

Gay, G. (2010). *Culturally responsive teaching* (2nd ed.). New York, NY: Teachers College Press.

Gelman, S. (1995). The biological alteration cases. *William and Mary Law Review*, *36*(4), 1203–1301.

Genovese, E. D. (1974). *Roll, Jordan, roll: The world the slaves made*. New York, NY: Random House.

Gildersleeve, R. E. (2010). *Fracturing opportunity: Mexican migrant students and college-going literacy*. New York, NY: Peter Lang.

Gillborn, D. (2006). Critical Race Theory and education: Racism and antiracism in educational theory and praxis. *Discourse: Studies in the Cultural Politics of Education*, *27*(1), 11–32.

Gillborn, D. (2008). *Racism and education: Coincidence or conspiracy?* London, England: Routledge.

Gillborn, D. (2012). Intersectionality and the primacy of racism: Race, class, gender and disability in education. Keynote address presented at the 6th Annual Conference of the Critical Race Studies in Education Association, May 31–June 2, Teachers College, Columbia University, New York City.

Gillborn, D., & Gipps, C. (1996). *Recent research into the achievement of ethnic minority pupils* London, England: Office for Standards in Education.

Gillborn, D., & Mirza, H. (2000). *Educational inequality: Mapping race, class and gender*. London, England: Office for Standards in Education.

Gillborn, D., Rollock, N., Vincent, C., & Ball, S. J. (2012). "You got a pass, so what more do you want?": Race, class and gender intersections in the educational experiences of the Black middle class. *Race Ethnicity and Education*, *15*(1), 121–139.

Gillies, V., & Robinson, Y. (2012). "Including" while excluding: Race, class and behaviour support units. *Race Ethnicity and Education*, *15*(2), 157–174.

Giroux, H. (1983). Theories of reproduction and resistance in the new sociology of education: A critical analysis. *Harvard Educational Review*, *53*(3), 257–293.

Good, T. L. (2011). Reflections on editing the *Elementary School Journal* in an era of constant reform. *The Elementary School Journal*, *112*(1), 1–15.

Goodwin, M. (2003). Gender, race, and mental illness: The case of Wanda Jean Allen. In A. K. Wing (Ed.), *Critical race feminism: A reader* (2nd ed., pp. 228–237). New York, NY: New York University Press.

Gould, S. J. (1996). *The mismeasure of man*. New York, NY: Norton.

Graham, L., & Slee, R. (2007). An illusory interiority: Interrogating the discourses of inclusion. *Educational Philosophy and Theory*, *40*(2), 277–293.

Gramsci, A. (1999). *Selections from the prison notebooks*. New York, NY: International.

Gravois, T. A., & Rosenfield. S. A. (2006). Impact of instructional consultation teams on the disproportionate referral and placement of minority students in special education. *Remedial and Special Education*, *27*(1), 42–52.

Green, A. (2013). *Education and state formation* (2nd ed.). London, England: Palgrave Macmillan.

Gregory, A., & Mosely, P. M. (2004). The discipline gap: Teachers' views on the over-representation of African American students in the discipline system. *Equity & Excellence in Education, 37*(1), 18–30.

Gregory, A., Skiba, R. J., & Noguera, P. A. (2010). The achievement gap and the discipline gap: Two sides of the same coin? *Educational Researcher, 39*(1), 59–68.

Gregory, A., & Weinstein, R. S. (2008). The discipline gap and African Americans: Defiance or cooperation in the high school classroom. *Journal of School Psychology, 46*(4), 455–475.

Groce, N. E. (2009). *Everyone here spoke sign language: Hereditary deafness on Martha's Vineyard.* Cambridge, MA: Harvard University Press.

Gruber, A. (2014). Race to incarcerate: Punitive impulse and the bid to repeal Stand Your Ground. *University of Miami Law Review, 68*(4), 961–1024.

Guinier, L., & Torres, R. (2002). *The miner's canary: Enlisting race, resisting power, transforming democracy.* Cambridge, MA: Harvard University Press.

Gutiérrez, K. D., (2008). Developing a sociocritical literacy in the Third Space. *Reading Research Quarterly, 43*(2), 148–164.

Gutiérrez, K. D., Hunter, S., & Arzubiaga, A. (2009). Re-mediating the university. *Pedagogies: An International Journal, 4*(1) 1–23.

Gutiérrez, K. D., & Stone, L. D. (1997). A cultural-historical view of learning and learning disabilities: Participating in a community of learners. *Learning Disabilities Research & Practice 12*(2), 123–131.

Gutiérrez, K. D., & Rogoff, B. (2003). Cultural ways of learning. *Educational Researcher, 32*(5), 19–25.

Gutiérrez, K. D., & Vossoughi, S. (2010). "Lifting off the ground to return anew": Documenting and designing for equity and transformation through social design experiments. *Journal of Teacher Education, 61*(1–2), 100–117.

Gutiérrez, R. (2008). A "gap-gazing" fetish in mathematics education? Problematizing research on the achievement gap. *Journal for Research in Mathematics Education, 39*(4), 357–364.

Gutman, M., & Tienabeso, S. (2012). Trayvon Martin shooter told cops teenager went for his gun. *ABC News online.* Retrieved from abcnews.go.com/US/trayvon-martin-shooter-teenager-gun/story?id=16000239

Habib, D. (Producer). (2008). *Including Samuel* [DVD]. Retrieved from www.includingsamuel.com/home.aspx

Hallam, S. (2002). *Ability grouping in schools: A literature review.* London, England: Institute of Education, University of London.

Hallam, S., & Toutounji, I. (1996). *What do we know about the grouping of pupils by ability? A research review.* London, England: Institute of Education, University of London.

Hamer, D. (2011). *Science of desire: The gay gene and the biology of behavior.* New York, NY: Simon & Schuster.

Hamilton, D. L., Stroessner, S., & Driscoll, D. M. (1994). Social cognition and the study of stereotyping. In P. G. Devine, P. L. Hamilton, & P. M. Ostrom (Eds.), *Social cognition: Impact on social psychology* (pp. 291–321). New York, NY: Academic Press.

Haney López, I. (1996). *White by law: The legal construction of race.* New York, NY: New York University Press.

Haney Lopez, I. (2003). *Racism on trial, the Chicano fight for justice.* Cambridge, MA: Belknap.

Harper, S. (2013). Am I my brother's teacher? Black undergraduates, racial socialization, and peer pedagogies in predominantly White postsecondary contexts. *Review of Research in Education, 37,* 183–211.

Harris, C. (1993). Whiteness as property. *Harvard Law Review, 106,* 1709–1791.

Harris, T. W. (2012). No disrespect: Black women and the burden of respectability. *Bitch media.* Retrieved from bitchmagazine.org/article/no-disrespect

Harry, B., & Anderson, M. G. (1994). The disproportionate placement of African-American males in special education programs: A critique of the process. *Journal of Negro Education, 63*(4), 602–619.

Harry, B., & Anderson, M. G. (1999). The social construction of high-incidence disabilities: The effect on African American males. In V. C. Polite & J. E. Davis (Eds.), *African American males in school and society: Policies and practices for effective education* (pp. 32–50). New York, NY: Teacher College Press.

Harry, B., & Klingner, J. (2014). *Why are so many minority students in special education?* (2nd ed.). New York, NY: Teachers College Press.

Hart, J., Cramer, L., Harry, B., Klingner, J., & Sturges, K. (2009). The continuum of troubling to troubled behavior: Exploratory case studies of African American students in programs for emotional disturbance. *Remedial and Special Education, 31*(3), 148–162.

Hasday, J. E. (2000). Contest and consent: A legal history of marital rape. *California Law Review, 88,* 1373–1505.

Hatt, B. (2011). Smartness as a cultural practice in schools. *American Educational Research Journal, 49*(3), 438–460.

Hawkins, J. D., Doueck, H. J., & Lishner, D. M. (1988). Changing teaching practices in mainstream classrooms to improve bonding and behavior of low achievers. *American Educational Research Journal, 25*(1), 31–50.

Hayman Jr., R. L. (1998). *The smart culture: Society, intelligence, and law.* New York, NY: New York University Press.

Heller, K. A., Holtzman, W. H., & Messick, S. (1982). *Placing children in special education: A strategy for equity.* Washington, DC: National Academy Press.

Helms, A. D. (2013, July 27). NC eugenics payments bring hope for some victims. *News & Observer.* Retrieved from www.newsobserver.com/2013/07/27/3062619/nc-eugenics-payments-bring-hope.html

Helms, A. D., & Tomlinson, T. (2011, September 26). Wallace Kuralt's era of sterilization. *Charlotte Observer.* Retrieved from www.charlotteobserver.com/2011/09/26/2637820/wallace-kuralts-era-of-sterilization.html#.U9PKr-NdWSo

Henderson, C. (2001). *College freshman with disabilities. 2001: A biennial statistical profile.* Washington, DC: American Council on Education.

Herrnstein, R., & Murray, C. (1994). *The bell curve.* New York, NY: Free Press.

Hershey, L. (1991). You get proud by practicing. Retrieved from www.cripcommentary.com/poetry.html#PROUD

Hess, R. S., Molina, A. M., & Kozleski, E. B. (2006). Until somebody hears me: Parent voice and advocacy in special educational decision making. *British Journal of Special Education, 33*(3), 148–157.

Hills, A. (2012). Interview with Leroy Moore. *Disability Right Now*. Retrieved from disabilityrightnow.wordpress.com/2012/05/14/interview-with-leroy-moore-2/

Holloway, S. D. (2011). Attitudes toward prenatal testing and pregnancy termination among a diverse population of parents of children with intellectual disabilities. *Prenatal Diagnosis, 31*(13), 1251–1258.

House of Commons. (1976). *The West Indian community. Report of the Select Committee on Race Relations and Immigration* (3 vols.). London, England: HMSO.

Huie, W. B. (1956, January 24). The shocking story of approved killing in Mississippi. *Look*, 46–48. Retrieved from www.pbs.org/wgbh/amex/till/sfeature/sf_look_confession.html

Hull, G., & Rose, M. (1990). "This wooden shack place": The logic of an unconventional reading. *College Composition and Communication, 41*(3), 287–298.

Humphreys, S. (1985). *Law as discourse. History and Anthropology, 1*(2), 241–264.

Hursh, D. (2005). The growth of high-stakes testing in the USA: Accountability, markets and the decline in educational equality. *British Educational Research Journal, 31*(5), 605–622.

Individuals With Disabilities Education Act (IDEA), 20 U.S.C. § 1400 (2004).

Inquisitr. (2014, November 6). Kaldrick Donald police shooting: Cop arrives to help mentally ill man, kills him in own home instead. *Inquisitr*. Retrieved from www.inquisitr.com/1589172/cop-shoots-mentally-ill-man/

Ioffe, J. (2014, August 15). White St. Louis has some awful things to say about Ferguson. *The New Republic*. Retrieved from www.newrepublic.com/article/119102/what-white-st-louis-thinks-about-ferguson

Irvine, J. J. (2010). Foreword. In H. R. Milner (Ed.), *Culture, curriculum, and identity in education*. New York, NY: Palgrave Macmillan.

Irvine, J. J. (2012). Complex relationships between multicultural education and special education: An African American perspective. *Journal of Teacher Education, 63*(4), 268–274.

Jayakumar, U. M. (2008). Can higher education meet the needs of an increasingly diverse and global society? Campus diversity and cross-cultural workforce competencies. *Harvard Education Review, 78*(4), 615–651.

Jean, E., & Samuels, E. (2002). Critical divides: Judith Butler's body theory and the question of disability critical divides. *NWSA Journal, 14*(3), 58–76.

Jensen, A. (1969). How much can we boost IQ and scholastic ability? *Education Review, 39*, 1–23.

John, G. (2006). *Taking a stand: Gus John speaks on education, race, social action & civil unrest 1980–2005*. Manchester, England: The Gus John Partnership.

Johnson, J. R. (2004). Universal instructional design and critical (communication) pedagogy: Strategies for voice, inclusion, and social justice/change. *Equity & Excellence in Education, 37*(2), 145–153.

Johnson, K. (1998). Immigration and Latino identity. *Chicago Law Review, 19*, 197–212.

Jones, D. M. (2014). "He's a Black male . . . something is wrong with him!" The role of race in the Stand Your Ground debate. 68 U. *Miami L. Rev.* 1025 (No. 4, Summer -1050 2014).

Jones, M. (2002). Overcoming the myth of free will in criminal law: The true impact of the genetic revolution. *Duke Law Journal, 52*, 1031–1053.

Jones, N. (2010). *Between good and ghetto: African American girls and inner-city violence.* New Brunswick, NJ: Rutgers University Press.

Kang, J., & Lane, K. (2010). Seeing through colorblinds: Implicit bias and the law. *UCLA Law Review, 58*(2), 466–520.

Kaplan, A., Gheen, M., & Midgley, C. (2002). Classroom goal structure and student disruptive behaviour. *British Journal of Educational Psychology, 72*(2), 191–211.

Katsiyannis, A., Yell, M. L., & Bradley, R. (2001). Reflections on the 25th anniversary of the Individuals with Disabilities Education Act. *Remedial and Special Education, 22*(6), 324–334.

Keep, E. (2014, March). *What does a skills policy look like now the money has run out?* Oxford, England: SKOPE (Centre on Skills, Knowledge and Organisational Performance), University of Oxford.

Kim, C. Y., Losen, D. J., & Hewitt, D. T. (2010). *The school-to-prison pipeline: Structuring legal reform.* New York, NY: New York University Press.

King, H. (1993). Once upon a text: Hysteria from Hippocrates. In S. L. Gilman & H. King (Eds.), *Hysteria beyond Freud* (pp. 3–90). Berkeley, CA: University of California Press.

Kinservik, M. J. (2001). Beyond romanticism: New books on late eighteenth and early nineteenth-century British drama. *Eighteenth-Century Studies, 35*(1), 109–162.

Kliebard, H. (1995). *The struggle for the American curriculum.* London, England: Routledge.

Kliewer, C., Biklen, D., & Kasa-Hendrickson, C. (2006). Who may be literate? Disability and resistance to the cultural denial of competence. *American Educational Research Journal, 43*, 163–192.

Klingner, J. K., & Harry, B. (2006). The special education referral and decision-making process for English language learners: Child study team meetings and placement conferences. *Teachers College Record, 108*, 2247–2281.

Kohn, A. (2004). NCLB and the effort to privatize public education. In D. Meier & G. Wood (Eds.), *Many children left behind* (pp. 79–100). Boston, MA: Beacon Press.

Kozleski, E. B. (2011). How systems construct ability and create disproportionality. Paper presented at the American Educational Research Association, April 8–12, New Orleans, LA.

Kozleski, E. B., & Artiles, A. J. (2012). Technical assistance as inquiry: Using activity theory methods to engage equity in educational practice communities. In S. Steinberg & G. Canella (Eds.), *Handbook on critical qualitative research* (pp. 431–445). New York, NY: Peter Lang.

Kozleski, E. B., Artiles, A. J., & Waitoller, F. (2011). Equity in inclusive education. In A. J. Artiles, E. B. Kozleski, & F. Waitoller (Eds.), *Inclusive education:*

Examining equity on five continents (pp. 1–14). Cambridge, MA: Harvard Education Press.

Kozleski, E. B., & Thorius, K. A. K. (2013). Making policy sticky: Distributed networks of reform. In E. B. Kozleski & K. A. K. Thorius (Eds.), *Ability, equity, and culture: Sustaining inclusive urban education reform*. New York, NY: Teachers College Press.

Kozol, J. (2005). *The shame of the nation: The restoration of apartheid schooling in America*. New York, NY: Crown.

Kudlick, C. J. (2003). Review essay on disability history: Why we need another "Other." *American Historical Review, 108*(3), 763–793.

Kumashiro, K. K. (2012). *Bad teacher! How blaming teachers distorts the bigger picture*. New York, NY: Teachers College Press.

Kuppermann, M., Nakagawa, S., Cohen, S. R., Dominguez-Pareto, I., Shaffer, B. L., & Ladson-Billings, G. (1995). Toward a theory of culturally relevant pedagogy. *American Education Research Journal, 32*(3), 465–491.

Ladson-Billings, G. (1995). Toward a theory of culturally relevant pedagogy. *American Education Research Journal, 32*(3), 465–491.

Ladson-Billings, G. (1998). Just what is Critical Race Theory and what's it doing in a nice field like education? *Qualitative Studies in Education, 11*(1), 7–24.

Ladson-Billings, G. (1999). Preparing teachers for diverse student populations: A Critical Race Theory perspective. In A. Iran-Nejad & P. D. Pearson (Eds.), *Review of research in education, 24* (pp. 211–247). Washington, DC: American Educational Research Association.

Ladson-Billings, G. (2006). From the achievement gap to the education debt: Understanding achievement in U.S. schools. *Educational Researcher, 35*(7), 3–12.

Ladson-Billings, G. (2009). Race *still* matters: Critical Race Theory in education. In M. W. Apple, W. Au, & L. A. Gandin (Eds.), *Routledge international handbook of critical education* (pp. 110–122). New York, NY: Routledge.

Ladson-Billings, G., & Tate, W. (1995). Toward a Critical Race Theory of education. *Teachers College Record, 97*(1), 47–68.

Lamb, H. R., & Weinberger, L. E. (1998). Persons with severe mental illness in jails and prisons: A review. *Psychiatric Services, 49*(4), 483–492.

Lane, H. (2002). Do deaf people have a disability? *Sign Language Studies, 2*(4), 356–379.

Larson, E. J. (1996). *Sex, race, and science: Eugenics in the Deep South*. Baltimore, MD: Johns Hopkins University Press.

Lawrence, C. R. (2008). Unconscious racism revisited: Reflections on the impact and origins of "The id, the ego, and equal protection." *Connecticut Law Review, 40*(4), 931–978.

Lazerson, M. (1983). The origins of special education. In D. J. Chambers & W. T. Hartman (Eds.), *Special education policies: Their history, implementation and finance* (pp. 15–47). Philadelphia, PA: Temple-Smith.

Lee, S. (2009). *Unraveling the model-minority stereotype: Listening to Asian American youth* (2nd ed.). New York, NY: Teachers College Press.

Leonard, D. J. (2014). Rotten to its core: Trayvon Martin as a microcosm of American racism. In V. E. Evans-Winters & M. C. Bethune (Eds.), *Re-teaching*

Trayvon: Education for racial justice and human freedom (pp. 133–142). Boston, MA: Sense Publishers.

Leonardo, Z. (2004). Critical social theory and transformative knowledge: The functions of criticism in quality education. *Educational Researcher, 33*(6), 11–18.

Leonardo, Z. (2007). The war on schools: NCLB, nation creation, and the educational construction of Whiteness. *Journal of Race, Ethnicity and Education, 10*(3), 261–278.

Leonardo, Z. (2013). *Race frameworks: A multidimensional theory of racism and education*. New York, NY: Teachers College Press.

Leonardo, Z., & Boas, E. (2013). Other kids' teachers: What children of color learn from white women and what this says about race, whiteness, and gender. *Handbook of critical race theory and education* (pp. 313–324). New York, NY: Routledge.

Leonardo, Z., & Broderick, A. (2011). Smartness as property: A critical exploration of intersections between Whiteness and disability studies. *Teachers College Record, 113*(10). Retrieved from www.tcrecord.org—ID 16431

Leonardo, Z., & Grubb, W. N. (2014). *Education and racism: A primer on issues and dilemmas*. New York, NY: Routledge.

Lindsay, G., Pather, S., & Strand, S. (2006). *Special educational needs and ethnicity: Issues of over- and under-representation*. Research Report RR757. London, England: Department for Education and Skills.

Lindsay, M. J. (1998). Reproducing a fit citizenry: Dependency, eugenics, and the law of marriage in the United States, 1860–1920. *Law and Social Inquiry, 23*(3), 541–585.

Linton, S. (1998a). *Claiming disability*. New York, NY: New York University Press.

Linton, S. (1998b). Disability studies/not disability studies. *Disability & Society, 13*(4), 525–540.

Linton, S. (2006). Reassigning meaning. In L. J. Davis (Ed.), *The disability studies reader* (pp. 161–172). New York, NY: Routledge.

Lloyd, T. O. (1984). *The British Empire 1558–1983*. Oxford, England: Oxford University Press.

Lombardo, P. A. (1985). Three generations, no imbeciles: New light on Buck v. Bell. *New York Law Review, 60*(1), 30–62.

Lombardo, P. A., & Hardin, P. L. (2013, August 21). Compensate eugenic sterilization victims: Column. *USA Today*. Retrieved from www.usatoday.com/story/opinion/2013/08/21/eugenics-north-carolina- column/2662317/

Longmore, P. K., & Umansky, L. (Eds.). (2001). *The new disability history: American perspectives*. New York, NY: New York University Press.

Lorde, A. (2007). *Sister outsider: Essays and speeches*. Chicago, IL: Random House.

Los Angeles Times. Retrieved from documents.latimes.com/trayvon-martin-and-george-zimmerman/

Losen, D., Ee, J., Hodson, C., & Martinez, T. (2015). Disturbing inequities: Exploring the relationship between racial disparities in special education identification and discipline. In D. Losen (Ed.), *Closing the school discipline gap: Equitable remedies for excessive exclusion* (pp. 89–117). New York, NY: Teachers College Press.

Losen, D. J., & Orfield, G. (2002). (Eds.). *Racial inequality in special education*. Cambridge, MA: Harvard Education Press.

Losen, D. J., & Skiba, R. J. (2010). *Suspended education: Urban middle schools in crisis*. Montgomery, AL: Southern Poverty Law Center.

MacKinnon, C. A. (1998/2011). Are women human? In J. L. Lee & S. M. Shaw (Eds.), *Women worldwide: Transnational feminist perspectives on women* (pp. 48–49). New York, NY: McGraw-Hill.

Madon, S., Jussim, L., & Eccles, J. (1997). In search of the powerful self-fulfilling prophecy. *Journal of Personality and Social Psychology, 72*(4), 791–809.

Madon, S., Jussim, L., Keiper, S., Eccles, J., Smith, A., & Palumbo, P. (1998). The accuracy and power of sex, social class, and ethnic stereotypes: A naturalistic study in person perception. *Personality & Social Psychology Bulletin, 24*(12), 1304–1318.

Madon, S., Smith, A., Jussim, L., Russell, D. W., Eccles, J., Palumbo, P., & Walkiewicz, M. (2001). Am I as you see me or do you see me as I am? Self-fulfilling prophecies and self-verification. *Personality and Social Psychology Bulletin, 27*(9), 1214–1224.

Magnus, M. (1982). A cluster of Kaposi's sarcoma and pneumocystis carinii pneumonia among homosexual male residents of Los Angeles and Orange Counties, California. *Morbidity and Mortality Weekly Report, 31*(23), 305–307.

Mandell, D. S., Wiggins, L. D., Yeargin-Allsopp, M., Carpenter, L. A., Daniels, J., Thomas, K. C., . . . Kirby, R. S. (2009). Racial/ethnic disparities in the identification of children with autism spectrum disorders. *American Journal of Public Health, 99*(3), 493–498. doi:10.2105/AJPH.2007.131243

Martin, T., & Fulton, S. (2012). Prosecute the killer of our son, 17-year-old Trayvon Martin. Retrieved from www.change.org/p/prosecute-the-killer-of-our-son-17-year-old-trayvon-martin

Matsuda, M. J. (1987). Looking to the bottom: Critical legal studies and reparations. *Harvard Civil Rights–Civil Liberties Law Review, 72*, 30–164.

Matsuda, M. J. (1989). When the first quail calls: Multiple consciousness as jurisprudential method. *Women's Rights Law Reporter, 11*, 7–10.

Matsuda, M. J. (1992). When the first quail calls: Multiple consciousness as jurisprudential method. *Women's Rights Law Reporter, 14*, 297–300.

May, V. M., & Ferri, B. A. (2005). Fixated on ability: Questioning ableist metaphors in feminist theories of resistance. *Prose Studies, 27*(1–2), 120–140.

McDermott, R. (1993). The acquisition of a child by a learning disability. In S. Chaiklin & J. Lave (Eds.), *Understanding practice: Perspectives on activity and context* (pp. 269–305). New York, NY: Cambridge University Press.

McDermott, R., Goldman, S., & Varenne, H. (2006). The cultural work of learning disabilities. *Educational Researcher, 35*(6), 12–17.

McDonnell, L. M. (1995). Opportunity to learn as a research concept and a policy instrument. *Educational Evaluation and Policy Analysis, 17*(3), 305–322.

McKenley, J. (2005). *Seven Black men: An ecological study of education and parenting*. Bristol, England: Aduma Books.

Meiners, E. R. (2007). *Right to be hostile: Schools, prisons, and the making of public enemies*. New York, NY: Routledge.

Menchaca, M. (1997). Early racist discourses: Roots of deficit thinking. In R. Valencia (Ed.), *The evolution of deficit thinking: Educational thought and practice*
(pp. 113–131). London, England: Routledge Falmer.

Mendez, L. M. R., & Knoff, H. M. (2003). Who gets suspended from school and
why: A demographic analysis of schools and disciplinary infractions in a large
school district. *Education and Treatment of Children, 26*(1), 30–51.

Mendoza, E. (2014). *Disrupting common sense notions through transformative education: Understanding purposeful organization and movement toward mediated praxis* (Doctoral dissertation). Retrieved from ProQuest Dissertations and
Theses Database (UMI No. 3635879).

Mercer, J. R. (1973). *Labeling the mentally retarded* (pp. 197–221). Berkeley: University of California Press.

Metraux, S., & D. P. Culhane. (2006). Recent incarceration history among a sheltered homeless population. *Crime & Delinquency, 52*(3), 504–517.

Meyer, H. D., & Benavot, A. (2013). *Pisa, power and policy: The emergence of global educational governance*. Didcot, England: Symposium Books.

Milner, H. R. (2006). Classroom management in urban classrooms. In C. M. Evert-
son & C. S. Weinstein (Eds.), *The handbook of classroom management: Research, practice & contemporary issues* (pp. 491–522). Mahwah, NJ: Erlbaum.

Minor v. Happersett, 88 U.S. 162, 166 (1875).

Mirza, H. S. (1998). Race, gender and IQ: The social consequence of a pseudo-
scientific Discourse. *Journal of Race, Ethnicity, and Education, 1*(1), 109–126.

Mitchell, D. T., & Snyder, S. L. (Eds.). (2000). *Narrative prosthesis: Disability and
the dependencies of discourse*. Ann Arbor, Michigan: University of Michigan
Press.

Moll, L. C. (1998). Turning to the world: Bilingualism, literacy and the cultural mediation of thinking. *National Reading Conference Yearbook, 47*, 59–75.

Mooney, J. (2008). *The short bus*. New York, NY: Henry Holt.

Morris, J. (1991). *Pride against prejudice*. London, England: Women's Press.

Moses, R. P., & Cobb, C. E. (2001). *Radical equations: Civil rights from Mississippi
to the Algebra Project*. Boston, MA: Beacon Press.

Muhammad, K. G. (2010). *The condemnation of Blackness; Race, crime and the
making of modern urban America*. Cambridge, MA: Harvard University Press.

National Disability Rights Network. (2011). Segregated and exploited: The failure
of the disability service system to provide quality work. Retrieved from www.
napas.org/images/Documents/Resources/Publications/Reports/Segregated-and-
Exploited.pdf

National Forum on Education Statistics, Race/Ethnicity Data Implementation Task
Force. (2008). *Managing an Identity Crisis: Forum Guide to Implementing
New Federal Race and Ethnicity Categories* (NFES 2008-802). Washington,
DC: National Center for Education Statistics, Institute of Education Sciences,
U.S. Department of Education.

Newitz, A., & Wray, M. (2013). Introduction. In M. Wray & A. Newitz (Eds.),
White trash: Race and class in America (pp. 1–14). New York, NY: Routledge.

Newman, L., Wagner, M., Knokey, A. M., Marder, C., Nagle, K., Shaver, D., & Wei,
X. (2011). The post-high school outcomes of young adults with disabilities

up to 8 years after high school: A report from the National Longitudinal Transition Study-2 (NLTS2). NCSER 2011-3005. *National Center for Special Education Research*. Retrieved from ies.ed.gov/ncser/pubs/20113004/pdf/20113004.pdf

New York State Office of Children and Family Services, Division of Juvenile Justice and Opportunities for Youth. Youth in care report. (2012). Retrieved from ocfs.ny.gov/main/reports/2012%20Youth%20in%20Care.pdf

New York State Unified Court System. (n.d.). *Persons in need of supervision (PINS)*. Retrieved from www.nycourts.gov/courts/nyc/family/faqs_pins.shtml

Nicholson-Crotty, S., Birchmeier, Z., & Valentine, D. (2009). Exploring the impact of school discipline on racial disproportion in the juvenile justice system. *Social Science Quarterly, 90*(4), 1003–1018.

Nielson, K. E. (2012). *A disability history of the United States*. Boston, MA: Beacon Press.

Nieto, S. (1995). From brown heroes and holidays to assimilationist agendas: Reconsidering the critiques of multicultural education. In C. E. Sleeter & P. McLaren (Eds.), *Multicultural education, critical pedagogy, and the politics of difference* (pp. 191–220). Albany, NY: State University of New York Press.

Noguera, P. A. (2003). Schools, prisons, and social implications of punishment: Rethinking disciplinary practices. *Theory into Practice, 42*(4), 341–350.

Oakes, J. (1995). Two cities' tracking and within school segregation. *Teachers College Record, 96*(4), 681–690.

Oates, G. (2003). Teacher–student racial congruence, teacher perceptions, and test performance. *Social Science Inquiry, 84*(3), 508–525.

Obasogie, O. (2006). Anything but a hypocrite: Interactional musings on race, colorblindness, and the redemption of Strom Thurmond. *Yale Journal of Law and Feminism, 18*, 451–488.

O'Connor, M., Hales, E., Davies, J., & Tomlinson, S. (1999). *Hackney Downs: The school that dared to fight*. London, England: Cassell.

Oliver, M. (1996). *Understanding disability: From theory to practice*. London, England: Macmillan.

Oliver, M. J. (1999). Capitalism, disability, and ideology. In R. J. Flynn & R. A. Lemay (Eds.), *A quarter-century of normalization and social role valorization: Evolution and impact* (pp. 163–174). Toronto, Canada: University of Ottawa Press.

Olivos, E. M., & Quintana de Vallidolid, C. E. (2005). Entre la espada y la pared: Critical educators, bilingual education, and education reform. *Journal of Latinos and Education, 4*(4), 283–293.

Omi, M., & Winant, H. (1994). *Racial formation in the United States: From the 1960s to the 1990s*. New York, NY: Routledge.

Orfield, G., & Lee, C. (2006). *Racial transformation and the changing nature of segregation*. Cambridge, MA: The Civil Rights Project at Harvard University.

Oswald, D. P., Coutinho, M. J., & Best, A. M. (2002). Community and school predictors of overrepresentation of minority children in special education. In D. Losen & G. Orfield (Eds.), *Racial inequality in special education*. Cambridge, MA: Harvard Education Press.

Parrish, T. (2002). Racial disparities in the identification, funding, and provision of special education. In D. J. Losen & G. Orfield (Eds.), *Racial inequality in special education* (pp. 15–37). Cambridge, MA: Harvard Education Press.

Patton, J. M. (1998). The disproportionate representation of African Americans in special education: Looking behind the curtain for understanding and possible solutions. *Journal of Special Education, 32,* 25–31.

Patton, S. (2012, October 29). From cellblock to campus, one Black man defies the data. *Chronicle of Higher Education-Diversity in Academe, 2013,* 1–12.

Peck, F. (Forthcoming). *The intertwinement of activity and artifacts: A cultural perspective on realistic mathematics education* (Unpublished doctoral dissertation). University of Colorado Boulder, Boulder, CO.

Penuel, W. R. (2010). A dialogical epistemology for educational evaluation. *Yearbook of the National Society for the Study of Education, 109*(1), 128–143.

Pérez-Huber, L. (2009). Challenging racist nativist framing: Acknowledging the community cultural wealth of undocumented Chicana college students to reframe the immigration debate. *Harvard Education Review, 79*(4), 704–729.

Peterson, A. (2009). "Ain't nobody gonna get me down": An examination of the educational experiences of four African American women labeled with disabilities. *Equity & Excellence in Education, 42*(4), 428–442.

Phillips-Anderson, M. (2013). Sojourner Truth. Address at the Woman's Rights Convention in Akron, Ohio. (May 29, 1851).

Plomin, R., De Vries, J. C., Knopik, V. S., & Neiderhier, J. M. (2013). *Behavioural genetics* (6th ed.). New York, NY: Worth Publications.

Pollack, D. (2005). The capacity of a mentally challenged person to consent to abortion and sterilization. *Health & Social Work, 30*(3), 253–257.

Price, J., & Shildrick, M. (Eds.). (1999). *Feminist theory and the body: A reader.* New York, NY: Taylor & Francis.

Prince v. Cole, 28 Mo. 486, 487 (1859).

Proctor, C. P. (1984). Teacher expectations: A model for school improvement. *The Elementary School Journal, 84*(4), 468–481.

Pugach, M. C., & Warger, C. L. (1996). *Curriculum trends, special education, and reform: Refocusing the conversation.* New York, NY: Teachers College Press.

Rawls, J. (1971). *A theory of justice.* Cambridge, MA: Harvard University Press.

RCCCFM. (1908). *Royal-Commission on the care and control of the feeble-minded* (8 vols.). London, England: HMSO.

Reid, D. K., & Knight, M. G. (2006). Disability justifies exclusion of minority students: A critical history grounded in disability studies. *Educational Researcher, 35*(6), 18–23.

Reid, D. K., & Valle, J. W. (2004). The discursive practice of learning disability: Implications for instruction and parent–school relations. *Journal of Learning Disabilities, 37*(6), 466–481.

Reverby, S. M. (2008). "Special treatment": Bidil, Tuskegee, and the logic of race. *Journal of Law, Medicine & Ethics, 36*(3), 478–484.

Reynolds, T. (2009). Exploring the absent/present dilemma: Black fathers, family relationships and social capital in Britain. *Annals of the American Academy of Political and Social Science, 624,* 12–28.

Richardson, J. G., & Powell, J. W. (2011). *Comparing special education: From origins to contemporary paradoxes.* Palo Alto, CA: Stanford University Press.

Ritter, G. (2002). Jury service and women's citizenship before and after the nineteenth amendment. *Law & History Review, 20*(3), 479–515.

Rivkin, D. H. (2009/2010). Decriminalizing students with disabilities. *New York Law School Review, 54,* 909–952.

Roberts, D. (2011). *Fatal invention: How science, politics, and big business re-create race in the twenty-first century.* New York, NY: The New Press.

Robles, F. (2012, March 26). Multiple suspensions paint complicated portrait of Trayvon Martin. *Miami Herald.* Retrieved from www.palmbeachpost.com/news/news/state-regional/multiple-suspensions-paint-complicated-portrait--1/nLhx2/#__federated=1

Rodriguez, D. (2010). Abolition as pedagogy. *Radical Teacher, 88,* 7–17.

Roediger, D. (1991). *The wages of Whiteness.* London, England: Verso.

Rogers, R. (2002). Through the eyes of the institution: A critical discourse analysis of decision making in two special education meetings. *Anthropology & Education Quarterly, 33*(2), 213–237.

Rogoff, B., Paradise, R., Arauz, R., Correa-Chavez, M., & Angelillo, C. (2003). Firsthand learning through intent participation. *Annual Review of Psychology, 54,*175–203.

Rollock, N., Gillborn, D., Vincent, C., & Ball, S. J. (2015). *The colour of class: The educational strategies of the Black middle classes.* London, England: Routledge.

Rollock, N., Vincent, C., Gillborn, D., & Ball, S. (2013). "Middle class by profession": Class status and identification amongst the Black middle classes. *Ethnicities, 13*(3), 253–275.

Romer v. Evans, 517 U.S. 620 (1996).

Romero-Bosch, A. (2007). Lessons in legal history: Eugenics and genetics. *Michigan State University Journal of Medicine & Law, 11,* 89–114.

Rose, S. (2014, January 24). Is genius in the genes? *Times Educational Supplement,* 27–30.

Rosenheck, R., Frisman, L., & Chung, A. M. (1994). The proportion of veterans among homeless men. *American Journal of Public Health, 84*(3), 466–469.

Rubin, B. C., & Noguera, P. (2004). Tracking detracking: Sorting through the dilemmas and possibilities of detracking in practice. *Equity & Excellence in Education, 37*(1), 92–101. doi:10.1080/10665680490422142

Sadker, M., & Sadker, D. (1995). *Failing at fairness: How our schools cheat girls.* New York, NY: Touchstone Press.

Sailor, W., & Stowe, M. (2003). School vouchers and students with disabilities. *National Council on Disability.* Retrieved from www.ncd.gov/publications/2003/April152003

Saltman, K. J. (2007). *Capitalizing on disaster: Taking and breaking public schools.* Herndon, VA: Paradigm.

Samuels, C. A. (2014, March 31). Pre-K suspension data prompt focus on intervention. *Education Week.* Retrieved from www.edweek.org/ew/articles/2014/04/02/27ocrprek.h33.html

Samuels, E. (2013). *Fantasies of identification: Disability, gender, race.* New York, NY: New York University Press.

Saxton, M. (2006). Disability rights and selective abortion. In L. J. Davis (Ed.), *The disability studies reader* (pp. 105–116). New York, NY: Routledge.

Saxton, M. (2013). Disability rights and selective abortion. In L. J. Davis (Ed.), *The disability studies reader* (4th ed., pp. 87–99). New York, NY: Routledge

Scarry, E. (1985). *The body in pain: The making and unmaking of the world.* New York, NY: Oxford University Press.

Schiraldi, V., & Ziedenberg, J. (2002, September 1). *Cellblocks or classrooms? The funding of higher education and corrections and its impact on African American men.* Justice Policy Institute report. Retrieved from www.justicepolicy.org/research/2046

Schoorman, D., & Bogotch, I. (2010). Moving beyond "diversity" to "social justice": The challenge to re-conceptualize multicultural education. *Intercultural Education, 21*(1), 79–85.

Schriner, K., Ochs, L., & Shields, T. (2000). Democratic dilemmas: Notes on the ADA and voting rights of people with cognitive and emotional impairments. *Berkeley Journal of Employment and Labor Law, 21,* 437.

Schweik, S. (2009). *The ugly laws: Disability in public.* New York, NY: New York University Press.

Segal, S. P., Silverman, C., & Temkin, T. (1997). Social networks and psychological disability among housed and homeless users of self-help agencies. *Social Work in Health Care, 25*(3), 49–61.

Selden, S. (1999). *Inheriting shame: The story of eugenics and racism in America.* New York, NY: Teachers College Press.

Shakespeare, T. (1996). Disability, identity, and difference. In C. Barnes & G. Mercer (Eds.), *Exploring the divide* (pp. 94–113). Leeds: The Disability Press.

Shapiro, J. (2002, October 3). Deaf Michigan boys. *National Public Radio.* Retrieved from www.npr.org/templates/story/story.php?storyId=1151042

Shapiro, J. P. (1994). *No pity: People with disabilities forging a new civil rights movement.* New York, NY: Random House.

Shapiro, T. M. (1985). *Population control politics: Women sterilization and reproductive choice.* Philadelphia, PA: Temple University Press.

Shifrer, D., Callahan, R. M., & Muller, C. (2013). Equity or marginalization? The high school course-taking of students labeled with a learning disability. *American Educational Research Journal, 50*(4), 546–682.

Shim, J. (2014). A Bourdieuian analysis: Teachers' beliefs about English language learners' academic challenges. *International Journal of Multicultural Education, 16*(1), 40–55.

Silver, M. G. (2004). Eugenics and compulsory sterilization laws: Providing redress for the victims of a shameful era in United States history. *George Washington Law Review, 72*(4), 862–892.

Simmons, A. S. (2011). I saw the sign, but did we really need a sign? Slutwalk and racism. *Crunk Feminist Collective.* Retrieved from crunkfeministcollective.wordpress.com/2011/10/06/i-saw-the-sign-but-did-we-really-need-a-sign-slutwalk-and-racism/

Sivanandan, A. (1990). *Communities of resistance: Writings on Black struggles for socialism*. London, England: Verso.

Skiba, R. J., Horner, R. H., Chung, C. G., Karega Rausch, M., May, S. L., & Tobin, T. (2011). Race is not neutral: A national investigation of African American and Latino disproportionality in school discipline. *School Psychology Review*, 40(1), 85–107.

Skiba, R. J., Michael, R. S., Nardo, A. C., & Peterson, R. L. (2002). The color of discipline: Sources of racial and gender disproportionality in school punishment. *The Urban Review*, 34(4), 317–342.

Skiba, R. J., Middelberg, L., & McClain, M. (2014). Multicultural issues for schools and EBD students: Disproportionality in discipline and special education. In H. M. Walker & F. M. Gresham (Eds.), *Handbook of evidence-based practices for emotional and behavioral disorders: Applications in schools* (pp. 54–70). New York, NY: Guilford Press.

Skiba, R. J., Peterson, R. L., & Williams, T. (1997). Office referrals and suspension: Disciplinary intervention in middle schools. *Education and Treatment of Children*, 20(3), 295–315.

Skiba, R. J., Poloni-Staudinger, L., Simmons, A. B., Feggins, L. R., & Chung, C. G. (2005). Unproven links: Can poverty explain ethnic disproportionality in special education? *The Journal of Special Education*, 39(3), 130–144.

Skiba, R. J., Simmons, A. D., Ritter, S., Gibb, A., Rausch, M. K., Cuadrado, J., & Chung, C. G. (2008). Achieving equity in special education: History, status, and current challenges. *Exceptional Children*, 74(3), 264–288.

Skiba, R., Simmons, A., Ritter, S., Kohler, K., Henderson, M., & Wu, T. (2006). The context of minority disproportionality: Practitioner perspectives on special education referral. *Teachers College Record*, 108, 1424–1459.

Skinner v. Oklahoma, 316 U.S. 535 (1942).

Slee, R. (2011). *The irregular school*. New York, NY: Routledge.

Sleeter, C. E. (1987). Why is there learning disabilities? A critical analysis of the birth of the field in its social context. In T. S. Popkewitz (Ed.), *The formation of the school subjects: The struggle for creating an American institution* (pp. 210–237). Philadelphia, PA: Falmer Press.

Sleeter, C. E. (1995). Foreword. In B. B. Swadener & S. Lubeck (Eds.), *Children and families "at promise"* (pp. ix–xi). Albany, NY: State University of New York Press.

Sleeter, C. E. (1998). Yes, learning disabilities is political; what isn't? *Learning Disability Quarterly*, 21(4), 289–296.

Sleeter, C. E., & Grant, C. A. (2007). *Making choices for multicultural education: Five approaches to race, class and gender* (6th ed.). Hoboken, NJ: Wiley.

Smith, B. G. (2004). Introduction. In B. G. Smith & B. Hutchison (Eds.), *Gendering disability*. New Brunswick, NJ: Rutgers University Press.

Smith, B. V. (2006). Prison and punishment: Rethinking prison sex: Self-expression and safety. *Columbia Journal of Gender and Law*, 15, 185–234.

Smith, P. (Ed.). (2009). *What ever happened to inclusion: The place of students with intellectual disabilities in education*. New York, NY: Peter Lang.

Solorzano, D. G. (1998). Critical Race Theory, race and gender microaggressions, and the experience of Chicana and Chicano scholars. *International Journal of Qualitative Studies in Education, 11*(1), 121–136.

Solorzano, D. G., & Bernal, D. D. (2001). Examining transformational resistance through a critical race and LatCrit theory framework: Chicana and Chicano students in an urban context. *Urban Education, 36*(3), 308–342. doi:10.1177/0042085901363002

Solorzano, D. G., Ceja, M., & Yosso, T. (2000). Critical Race Theory, racial micro-aggressions and campus racial climate: The experiences of African American college students. *Journal of Negro Education, 69*(1–2), 60–73.

Solorzano, D. G., & Yosso, T. (2001). Critical race and LatCrit theory and method: Counterstorytelling, Chicana and Chicano graduate school experiences. *International Journal of Qualitative Studies in Education, 4,* 471–495.

Spelman, E. (1990). *Inessential woman: Problems of exclusion in feminist thought.* Boston, MA: Beacon Press.

Spivak, G. (1989). *Outside the teaching machine.* Padstow, England: TJ International.

Star, L., & Ruhleder, K. (1996). Steps toward an ecology of infrastructure: Complex problems in design and access for large-scale collaborative systems. *Proceedings of the Conference on Computer Supported Cooperative Work* (CSCW 94—Transcending Boundaries). New York, NY: ACM Press.

Steinberg, S. R., & Kincheloe, J. L. (2009). Smoke and mirrors: More than one way to be diverse and multicultural. In S. R. Steinberg & J. L. Kincheloe (Eds.), *Diversity and multiculturalism: A reader* (pp. 3–22). New York, NY: Peter Lang.

Stovall, D. O. (2006). Forging community in race and class: Critical Race Theory and the quest for social justice in education. *Race Ethnicity and Education, 9*(3), 243–259.

Strand, S. (2011). The White British–Black Caribbean achievement gap: Tests, tiers and teacher expectations. *British Educational Research Journal, 38*(1), 75–101.

Strand, S., & Lindsay, G. (2009). Evidence of ethnic disproportionality in special education in an English population. *The Journal of Special Education, 43*(3), 174–190.

Stubblefield, A. (2005). *Ethics along the color line.* Ithaca, NY: Cornell University Press.

Sue, D. W. (2010). Microaggressions, marginality and oppression. In D. W. Sue (Ed.), *Microaggressions and marginality* (pp. 3–22). Hoboken, NJ: Wiley.

Sukhnandan, L., & Lee, B. (1998). *Streaming, setting and grouping by ability.* Slough: NFER.

Sullivan, A. L. (2013). Beyond behavior: Multilevel analysis of the influence of sociodemographics and school characteristics on students' risk of suspension. *School Psychology Review, 42*(1), 99–114.

Sullivan, A. L., & Artiles, A. J. (2011). Theorizing racial inequity in special education: Applying structural theory to disproportionality. *Urban Education, 46*(6), 1526–1552.

Sussman, A. (2012). Learning in lockdown: School police, race and the limits of law. *UCLA Law Review, 54,* 788–846.

Sutton and Hinton v. United Air Lines, Inc., 527 U.S. 471 (1999).

Swadener, B. B., & Lubeck, S. (1995). The social construction of children and families "at Risk": An introduction. In B. B. Swadener & S. Lubeck (Eds.), *Children
and families "At promise"* (pp. 1–16). Albany, NY: State University of New
York Press, Albany.

Tate, W. F. (1997). Critical Race Theory and education: History, theory, and implications. In M. Apple (Ed.), *Review of research in education* (pp. 195–247),
Washington, DC: AERA.

Tate, W. F., Ladson-Billings, G., & Grant, C. (1996). The Brown decision revisited:
Mathematizing a social problem. In M. J. Shujaa (Ed.), *Beyond desegregation:
The politics of quality in African American schooling* (pp. 29–50). Thousand
Oaks, CA: Corwin Press.

Taylor, H., Krane, D., & Orkis, K. (2010). The ADA, 20 years later. *Kessler Foundation and National Organization*. New York, NY: Harris Interactive. Retrieved
from www.2010disabilitysurveys.org/pdfs/surveysummary.pdf

Taylor, S. J. (1988). Caught in the continuum: A critical analysis of the principle of
the least restrictive environment. *Journal of the Association for Persons with
Severe Handicaps, 13*(1), 41–53.

Terman, L. M. (1916). *The measurement of intelligence*. Boston, MA: Houghton
Mifflin.

Terman, L. M. (1917). Feeble-minded children in the public schools of California.
School and Society, 5.

Terry, J., & Urla, J. (Eds.). (1995). *Deviant bodies*. Bloomington: Indiana University
Press.

Thorius, K. A. K., & Scribner, S. M. P. (2013). Teacher learning in urban schools. In
E. B. Kozleski & K. A. K. Thorius (Eds.), *Ability, equity, and culture: Sustain-
ing inclusive urban education reform* (pp. 134–150). New York, NY: Teachers
College Press.

Thorius, K. A. K., & Stephenson, J. (2012). Racial and ethnic disproportionality
in special education. In A. L. Noltemeyer & C. Mcloughlin (Eds.), *Disproportionality in education and special education: A guide to creating more equitable
learning environments* (pp. 25–44). Springfield, IL: Charles C Thomas.

Tikly, L., Haynes, J., Caballero, C., Hill, J., & Gillborn, D. (2006). *Evaluation of
aiming high: African Caribbean achievement project*. Research Report RR801.
London, England: DfES.

Tincani, M., Travers, J., & Boutot, A. (2009). Race, culture, and autism spectrum
disorder: Understanding the role of diversity in successful educational interventions. *Research & Practice for Persons With Severe Disabilities, 34*(3/4), 81–90.

Tomlinson, S. (1981). *Educational subnormality: A study in decision-making*. London, England: Routledge & Kegan Paul.

Tomlinson, S. (1982). *A sociology of special education*. London, England: Routledge
& Kegan Paul.

Tomlinson, S. (2012a). The irresistible rise of the SEN industry. *Oxford Review of
Education, 38*(3), 267–283.

Tomlinson, S. (2012b). *A sociology of special education (RLE Edu M)*. New York,
NY: Routledge.

Tomlinson, S. (2013). *Ignorant yobs? Low attainers in a global knowledge economy*. London, England: Routledge.

Trainor, A. A. (2010). Diverse approaches to parent advocacy during special education home–school interactions identification and use of cultural and social capital. *Remedial and Special Education, 31*(1), 34–47.

Trans Murder Monitoring Project. (2015). Retrieved from www.transrespect-trans phobia.org/en_US/tvt-project/tmm-results/idahot-2015.htm

Trent, J. W. (1998). Defectives at the world's fair: Constructing dis/ability in 1904. *Remedial and Special Education, 19*(4), 201–211. Retrieved from rse.sagepub.com/cgi/content/abstract/19/4/201

Tuck, E. (2012). *Urban youth and school pushout: Gateways, Get-aways, and the GED*. New York, NY: Routledge.

Tulman, J. B., & Weck, D. M. (2009/2010). Shutting off the school to prison pipeline for status offenders with education related disabilities. *New York Law School Review, 54*, 875–907.

Turnbull, A., Turnbull, H. R., Wehmeyer, M., & Shogren, K. (2012). *Exceptional lives: Special education in today's schools*. Upper Saddle River, NJ: Pearson.

Tyack, D. (1974). *The one best system: A history of American urban education*. Cambridge, MA: Harvard University Press.

U.S. Department of Defense. (2010). Demographics: Profile of the military community, DOD. Retrieved from www.militaryonesource.mil/12038/MOS/Reports/2010_Demographics_Report.pdf

U.S. Department of Education, Office of Civil Rights. (2014, March 21). *Expansive survey of America's public schools reveals troubling racial disparities*. Retrieved from www.ed.gov/news/press-releases/expansive-survey-americas-public-schools-reveals-troubling-racial-disparities

U.S. Department of Education, Office of Special Education and Rehabilitative Services, Office of Special Education Programs. (2007). *27th Annual Report to Congress on the Implementation the Individuals with Disabilities Education Act, 2005*. Washington, DC: Author.

U.S. Department of Education, Office of Special Education and Rehabilitative Services, Office of Special Education Programs. (2009). *28th Annual Report to Congress on the Implementation of the Individuals with Disabilities Education Act, 2006*. Washington, DC: Author.

U.S. Department of Education, Office of Special Education and Rehabilitative Services, Office of Special Education Programs. (2010). *29th Annual Report to Congress on the Implementation of the Individuals with Disabilities Education Act, 2007*, Vol. 1. Washington, DC: Author.

U.S. Department of Education, Office of Special Education and Rehabilitative Services, Office of Special Education Programs. (2011). *30th Annual Report to Congress on the Implementation the Individuals with Disabilities Education Act, 2008*. Washington, DC: Author.

U.S. Department of Education, Office of Special Education and Rehabilitative Services, Office of Special Education Programs. (2012). *31st Annual Report to Congress on the Implementation the Individuals with Disabilities Education Act, 2009*. Washington, DC: Author.

U.S. Department of Labor. (2014). Bureau of Labor Statistics, Economic News Release, Table A-2. Retrieved from www.bls.gov/news.release/empsit.t02.htm

U.S. Department of Veterans Affairs. (n.d.). PTSD: National Center for PTSD. Retrieved from www.ptsd.va.gov/public/PTSD-overview/basics/how-common-is-ptsd.asp

Utley, C. A., Obiakor, F. E., & Bakken, J. P. (2011). Culturally responsive practices for culturally and linguistically diverse students with learning disabilities. *Learning Disabilities: A Contemporary Journal, 9*(1), 5–18.

Valencia, R. R. (1997). Conceptualizing the notion of deficit thinking. In R. R. Valencia (Ed.), *The evolution of deficit thinking: Educational thought and practice* (pp. 113–131). London, England: Routledge Falmer.

Valencia, R. R. (2010). *Dismantling contemporary deficit thinking: Educational thought and practice.* New York, NY: Routledge.

Valencia, R. R., & Suzuki, L. A. (2001). *Intelligence testing and minority students: Foundations, performance factors, and assessment issues.* Thousand Oaks, CA: Sage.

Valles, E. C. (1998). The disproportionate representation of minority students in special education: Responding to the problem. *Journal of Special Education, 32*(1), 52–54. doi:10.1177/002246699803200110

VanDeBurg, W. L. (1992). *New day in Babylon: The Black power movement and American culture, 1965–1975.* Chicago, IL: The University of Chicago Press.

Vargas, T. (2010, July 11). Stafford County woman confronts issues of race, autism after son's arrest. *The Washington Post.* Retrieved from www.washingtonpost.com/wp-dyn/content/article/2010/07/10/AR2010071002633.html

Vaught, S. E. (2011). *Racism, public schooling, and the entrenchment of White supremacy: A critical race ethnography.* Albany, NY: State University of New York Press.

Vega, T., Williams, T., & Eckholm, E. (2014, August 15). Emotions flare in Missouri amid police statements. *New York Times.* Retrieved from www.nytimes.com/2014/08/16/us/darren-wilson-identified-as-officer-in-fatal-shooting-in-ferguson-missouri.html?_r=0

Villazor, R. C. (2008). Blood quantum land laws and the race versus political identity dilemma. *California Law Review, 96*(3), 801–837.

Vincent, C., Rollock, N., Ball, S. J., & Gillborn, D. (2012). Being strategic, being watchful, being determined: Black middle-class parents and schooling. *British Journal of Sociology of Education, 33*(3), 337–354.

Vincent, C., Tobin, T., Hawken, L., & Frank, J. (2012). Discipline referrals and access to secondary level of support in elementary and middle schools: Patterns across African American, Hispanic American, and White students. *Education and Treatment of Children, 35*(3), 431–458.

Vives, R., Mather, K., & Winton, R. (2014). LAPD shooting of mentally ill man stirs criticism, questions. *Los Angeles Times.* Retrieved from www.latimes.com/local/lanow/la-me-ln-lapd-shooting-of-mentally-ill-man-stirs-criticism-questions-20140813-story.html

Voulgarides, C. (2012). Fragmented harm: "We don't have a problem." The story of Townsville. Paper presented at the 12th Annual International Disability Studies in Education Conference, May 25–27, Hunter College, CUNY, New York.

Vygotsky, L. (1978). *Mind in society*. Cambridge, MA: Harvard University Press.

Wadlington, W. (1966). The loving case: Virginia's anti-miscegenation statute in historical perspective. *Virginia Law Review, 52*, 1189–1223.

Waitoller, F. R., Artiles, A. J., & Cheney, D. A. (2010a). The miner's canary: A review of overrepresentation research and explanations. *Journal of Special Education, 44*, 29–49.

Waitoller, F. R., Artiles, A. J., & Cheney, D. A. (2010b). A review of overrepresentation research and explanations. *The Journal of Special Education, 44*(1), 29–49.

Waitoller, F. R., & Kozleski, E. B. (2013). Working in boundary practices: Identity development and learning in partnerships for inclusive education. *Teaching and Teacher Education, 31*(1), 35–45.

Wald, J., & Losen, D. J. (2003). Defining and redirecting a school to prison pipeline. *New Directions for Youth Development, 99*, 9–15.

Warmington, P. (2014). *Black British intellectuals and education: Multiculturalism's hidden history*. London, England: Routledge.

Warner, M. (1999). *The trouble with normal: Sex, politics, and the ethics of queer life*. New York, NY: Simon & Schuster.

Washington, D. A. (2009). Critical race feminist bioethics: Telling stories in law school and medical school in pursuit of "cultural competency." *Albany Law Review, 72*, 961–998.

Watson, W., Oyler, C., Schlessinger, S., & Chako. M. (2012). Toward a praxis of critical inclusivity. Paper session presented at the 6th Annual Conference of the Critical Race Studies in Education Association, May 31–June 2, Teachers College, Columbia University, New York.

Watts, I. E., & Erevelles, N. (2004). These deadly times: Reconceptualizing school violence by using Critical Race Theory and disability studies. *American Educational Research Journal, 41*(2), 271–299.

Weber, M. C. (2004). *Understanding disability law*. Danvers, MA: Matthew Bender.

Weedon, C. (1997). *Feminist practice & poststructuralist theory* (2nd ed.). Cambridge, MA: Blackwell.

Weinstein, C. S., Thomlinson-Clarke, S., & Curran, M. (2003). Culturally responsive classroom management: Awareness into action. *Theory into Practice, 42*(4), 269–276.

Wells, I. B. (1892/2013). *Southern horrors: Lynch law in all its phases*. Goodridge, England: Dodo Press.

Wendell, S. (1993). Feminism, disability and the transcendence of the body. *Canadian Women's Studies, 13*(4), 116–122.

Wertsch, J. V., & Toma, C. (1995). Discourse and learning in the classroom: A sociocultural approach. In L. P. Steffe & J. Gale (Eds.), *Constructivism in education* (pp. 159–174). Hillsdale, NJ: Erlbaum.

White, K. (2008). *An introduction to the sociology of health and illness*. New York, NY: Sage.

Wiliam, D., & Bartholomew, H. (2004). It's not which school but which set you're in that matters: The influence of ability grouping practices on student progress in mathematics. *British Educational Research Journal, 30*(2), 279–293.

Wilkinson, R., & Pickett, K. (2009). *The spirit level: Why more equal societies almost always do better.* London, England: Allen Lane.

Wright, C., Weekes, D., & McGlaughlin, A. (2000). *"Race," class and gender in exclusion from school.* London, England: Routledge.

Yell, M. L., Rogers, D., & Lodge-Rodgers, E. (1998). The legal history of special education: What a long strange trip it's been. *Remedial and Special Education, 19*(4), 219–228.

Youdell, D. (2010). Performativity: Making the subjects of education. In Z. Leonardo, *Handbook of cultural politics and education* (pp. 219–236). Rotterdam; Boston: Sense.

Young, K. S. (2011). Institutional separation in schools of education: Understanding the functions of space in general and special education teacher preparation. *Teaching and Teacher Education, 27*(2), 483–493.

Yuval-Davis, N. (2006). Intersectionality and feminist politics. *European Journal of Women's Studies, 13,* 193–209.

Zhang, D., Katsyannis, A., Ju, S., & Roberts, E. (2014). Minority representation in special education: 5 year trends. *Journal of Child and Family Studies, 23*(1), 118–127.

Zimmerman, G. (2012, February 26). Handwritten statement to police, as submitted to Officer D. Singleton. Retrieved from gzlegalcase.com/index.php/court-documents?start=108

Zola, I. K. (1993). Disability statistics, what we count and what it tells us: A personal and political analysis. *Journal of Disability Policy Studies, 4*(2), 9–39.

Zucker, K. J. (2002). Intersexuality and gender identity differentiation. *Journal of Pediatric and Adolescent Gynecology, 15*(1), 3–13.

Zucker, K. J., & Spitzer, R. L. (2010). Was the gender identity disorder of childhood diagnosis introduced into DSM-III as a backdoor maneuver to replace homosexuality? *Journal of Sex and Marital Therapy, 31*(1), 31–42.

About the Contributors

D. L. Adams, PhD, graduated from Syracuse University interdisciplinary program in Special Education, Disability Studies, and Women and Gender Studies. She has coauthored chapters on the use of adversives to modify behavior, as well as the intersection of disability and the school-to-prison pipeline. Her current research covers the topics of schoolwide positive behavior supports as a tool for ending the suspensions of students of color, as well as educational reform in urban schools' connection to school closure. She is currently an instructor in Women and Gender Studies at University of Toledo.

Subini Ancy Annamma, PhD, is an assistant professor in the Department of Special Education at the University of Kansas. Her research and pedagogy focus on increasing access to equitable education for historically marginalized students and communities. Her commitments emphasize an interdisciplinary approach drawing from the fields of urban education, sociology, criminology, and geography. Specifically, she examines the social construction of race and ability: how the two are interdependent, how they intersect with other identity markers, and how their mutually constitutive nature impacts education experiences. She centers this research in urban education settings and focuses on how student voice can identify exemplary educational practices.

Susan Baglieri, EdD, is an associate professor in the Department of Secondary and Special Education at Montclair State University in Montclair, New Jersey. Her areas of interest and inquiry are in Disability Studies in Education (DSE), inclusive education, and teacher education. She is coauthor of the book *Disability Studies and the Inclusive Classroom.*

Stephen J. Ball, PhD, is the Karl Mannheim Professor of Sociology of Education at the Institute of Education, University College London. He was elected fellow of the British Academy in 2006, is also fellow of the Academy of Social Sciences, and has honorary doctorates from the Universities of Turku (Finland) and Leicester. He was cofounder and is managing editor of the *Journal of Education Policy*. His main areas of interest are in sociologically informed education policy analysis and the relationships between education, education policy, and social class. He has written 20 books and had published more than 140 journal articles. Recent books include *How Schools Do Policy* (2012), *Global Education Inc.* (2012), *Networks, New Governance and Education* (with Carolina Junemann) (2012), and *Foucault, Power and Education* (2013).

Alicia A. Broderick, PhD, is an associate professor of Education in the Inclusive Education graduate programs of the College of Education and Human Services at Montclair State University, New Jersey. Alicia's program of research aims to explore the implications for teacher education of Disability Studies in Education (DSE) work, as well as to engage in DSE scholarship through a specific exploration of the workings of ableism in media and cultural representations of autism. This collaborative piece of work with Zeus Leonardo in the current text builds upon their previous essay, "Smartness as Property," which appeared in *Teachers College Record* in 2011. Alicia's other research has appeared in journals such as *Education, Citizenship, and Social Justice; International Journal of Inclusive Education; Disability and Society; Disability Studies Quarterly; Equity & Excellence in Education; Theory into Practice;* and other journals, as well as in contributed chapters in numerous books and handbooks.

Kathleen M. Collins, PhD, is an associate professor of Language, Culture and Society and codirector of the Center for Disability Studies in the College of Education at Pennsylvania State University, University Park. Through analysis of the processes and consequences of dis/ability identification, Kathleen's program of research aims to identify and interrupt deficit discourses surrounding children who are positioned as struggling in school. Kathleen is the author of *Ability Profiling and School Failure: One Child's Struggle to Be Seen as Competent* (2nd ed., 2013). Her research has also appeared in *Equity & Excellence in Education; English Journal; International Journal of Inclusive Education; Language Arts; Language, Speech, and Hearing Services in Schools; Learning Disabilities Quarterly; Research in the Teaching of English; Teachers College Record; Urban Education;* and *Young Children.* Kathleen was the 2012 recipient of the Ellen Brantlinger Junior Scholar Award for outstanding work within Disability Studies in Education.

David J. Connor, EdD, is a professor and chairperson of the Special Education Department, Hunter College, part of the City University of New York (CUNY). He is also a faculty member at large in the Urban Education doctoral program at CUNY's Graduate Center. David is the author/editor of several books: *Reading Resistance: Discourses of Exclusion in Desegregation and Inclusion Debates,* coauthored with Beth A. Ferri (2006); *Urban Narratives:*

Portraits-in-Progress—Life at the Intersections of Learning Disability, Race, and Social Class (2008); *Rethinking Disability: A Disability Studies Guide to Inclusive Practices,* coauthored with Jan Valle (2011); *Teaching and Disability,* coauthored with Susan Gabel (2014); and *Practicing Disability Studies in Education: Acting Toward Social Change,* coedited with Jan Valle and Chris Hale (2015). His research interests include learning disabilities, inclusive education, and intersectional understandings of disability. For more information, see hunter-cuny.academia.edu/DavidJConnor.

Nirmala Erevelles, PhD, is professor of Social and Cultural Studies in Education at the University of Alabama. Her teaching and research interests lie in the areas of disability studies, Critical Race Theory, transnational feminism, sociology of education, and postcolonial studies. Erevelles has published articles in the *American Educational Research Journal, Educational Theory, Studies in Education and Philosophy,* the *Journal of Curriculum Studies, Teachers College Record, Disability & Society, Disability Studies Quarterly,* and the *Journal of Literary and Cultural Disability Studies,* among others. Her book, *Disability and Difference in Global Contexts: Enabling a Transformative Body Politic,* was published in 2012.

Zanita E. Fenton, JD, is a professor of law, University of Miami School of Law, where she teaches courses in Constitutional Law, Family Law, Torts, Race and the Law, and seminars on Critical Race Feminism and Women and the Law Stories. Professor Fenton's research interests cover issues of structural inequality and forms of subordination, including those of disability, race, gender, and class. Fenton's publications include "Disabling Racial Repetition" in *Righting Educational Wrongs: Disability Studies in Law and Education* (edited by Kanter & Ferri, 2013); "Town of Castle Rock v. Gonzales: A Tale of State Enabled Violence," in *Women & the Law Stories* (edited by Schneider & Wildman, 2011), and "Bastards! And the Welfare Plantation," in the *Iowa Journal of Gender, Race & Justice.*

Edward Fergus, PhD, is assistant professor of Educational Leadership and Policy at Steinhardt School of Culture, Education and Human Development at New York University. Dr. Fergus's current work is on the educational outcomes of Black and Latino boys, disproportionality in special education and suspensions, and school climate conditions for low-income and marginalized populations. He has published numerous articles and is the author of *Skin Color and Identity Formation: Perceptions of Opportunity and Academic Orientation among Mexican and Puerto Rican Youth* (2004), coeditor of *Invisible No More: Disenfranchisement of Latino Men and Boys* (2011), and coauthor of *Schooling for Resilience: Improving Trajectory of Black and Latino Boys* (2014).

Beth A. Ferri, PhD, is a professor of Inclusive Education and Disability Studies at Syracuse University, where she also coordinates the doctoral program in special education. Professor Ferri has published widely on the intersection of race, gender, and disability, including more than 30 journal articles in *Teachers College Record, Race Ethnicity & Education, International Journal of Inclusive Education, Remedial & Special Education, Journal of Learning Disabilities, Gender & Education, Disability Studies Quarterly, Disability & Society,* the *Journal of African American History,* and more. Her first book, coauthored with David J. Connor, titled *Reading Resistance: Discourses of Exclusion in Desegregation and Inclusion Debates,* was published in 2006. The second, a coedited book with Arlene Kanter, titled *Righting Educational Wrongs: Disability Studies in Law & Education,* was published in 2013. She has also coedited a recent issue of *Disability Studies Quarterly* (with David J. Connor) and a special double issue of *Learning Disability Quarterly* (with David J. Connor & Deborah Gallagher). She was recognized in 2003 as an Outstanding Young Scholar in Disability Studies in Education.

David Gillborn, PhD, is professor of Critical Race Studies and director of the Centre for Research in Race & Education (CRRE) at the University of Birmingham, United Kingdom. He is founding editor of the peer-reviewed journal *Race Ethnicity and Education.* David is twice winner of the Book of the Year award by the Society for Educational Studies (SES), most recently for *Racism and Education: Coincidence or Conspiracy* (2008), and is coeditor, with Edward Taylor and Gloria Ladson-Billings, of the collection *Foundations of Critical Race Theory in Education* (2015). David received the Derrick Bell Legacy Award from the Critical Race Studies in Education Association (CRSEA) for career accomplishments that demonstrate "personal courage and professional commitment to supporting and advocating race equality in education"; and was recently named to the Laureate Chapter of the *Kappa Delta Pi* international honor society, limited to 60 living educators who have made a significant and lasting impact on the profession of education.

Kris Gutiérrez, PhD, is professor of Language, Literacy and Culture in the Graduate School of Education at the University of California, Berkeley. She was most recently a professor of Learning Sciences/Literacy and Inaugural Provost's Chair, University of Colorado, Boulder, and Professor Emerita of Social Research Methodology at GSE&IS at UCLA. Her research examines learning in designed learning environments, with attention to students from nondominant communities. Professor Gutiérrez's work on Third Spaces examines the affordances of hybrid and syncretic approaches to literacy, new media literacies, STEM learning, and the remediation of functional systems of learning. Her work in social design experiments seeks to leverage students' everyday concepts and practices to ratchet up expansive forms of learning. Gutiérrez is past president of the American Educational Research Association and the National Conference on Research in Language and Literacy and was appointed by President Obama to the National Board for the Institute of Education Sciences.

Elizabeth B. Kozleski, PhD, chair of Special Education at the University of Kansas, engages systems change for equity and justice, inclusive education, and professional learning. Recent awards include the UNESCO Chair in Inclusive International Research in 2005, the TED-Merrill award for leadership in special education teacher education in 2011, and the Scholar of the Century award from the University of Northern Colorado in 2013. Her research interests include the analysis of systems change in education, how teachers learn in practice in complex, diverse school settings, as well how educational practices improve student learning. Professor Kozleski coedits a book series for Teachers College Press on Disability, Culture, and Equity with Professor Alfredo J. Artiles. Her recent books include *Ability, Equity, and Culture* (with coauthor Kathleen King Thorius), published by Teachers College Press in 2014, and *Equity on Five Continents* (with Alfredo J. Artiles and Federico Waitoller), published in 2011 by Harvard Education Press.

Zeus Leonardo, PhD, is professor of education and faculty of the Critical Theory Designated Emphasis at the University of California, Berkeley. In addition to many articles, he is the author of *Race Frameworks*; *Race, Whiteness and Education*, and with Norton Grubb, *Education and Racism*. He has received several recognitions, including being named an American Educational Research Association (AERA) Fellow, the American Educational Studies Association's R. Freeman Butts Endowed Lecturer, the Barbara Powell Humanities Lecturer at the University of Regina, Canada, and the Early Career Award from AERA's Division G. Dr. Leonardo has delivered keynote lectures domestically and internationally. His research interests involve the study of ideologies and discourses in education. Much of his work is interdisciplinary and draws insights from sociology, contemporary philosophy, and cultural studies. In particular, he engages critical theories to inform his analysis of the relationship between schooling and social relations, such as race, class, and culture. His research is informed by the premise that educational knowledge should promote the democratization of schools and society.

Claustina Mahon-Reynolds is a doctoral student in the College of Education, Special Education Department at the University of Utah. She also works for the Salt Lake City School District as an assistant principal of an urban middle school. Her research interests include disability Critical Race Theory, overrepresentation of students of color, restorative justice, multitiered system of supports implementation, and creating and incentivizing multiclassroom school leaders.

Elizabeth Mendoza, PhD, is currently a postdoctoral research fellow in the Psychology Department at the University of California, Santa Cruz. Her work is grounded in Participatory Action Research and Design-Based Research, specifically social design experiments using a cultural historical activity theory (CH/AT) framework. She explores how to research and design spaces that leverage everyday knowledge and academic content to redefine who is—or is allowed to be—smart, bring together theory and practice, and work centrally toward educational equity. She focuses on educational spaces that seek to increase college access, in particular for nondominant youth, as well as the pedagogical practices implemented in teacher education and higher education that support teachers and practitioners in developing practices that challenge dominant and unexamined ideologies and re-imagine new practices. Mendoza was both a Miramontes Fellow and an American Education Research Association Minority Dissertation Fellow.

Christina Paguyo, PhD, is a postdoctoral research fellow in the College of Engineering at Colorado State University. Her research interests focus on mixed methods approaches for examining diversity initiatives and designing educational environments grounded in research, theory, and equity. Paguyo has coauthored peer-reviewed articles published in the *Peabody Journal of Education* and the *Encyclopedia of Diversity in Education.*

Laurence Parker, PhD, is a professor in the Department of Educational Leadership & Policy at the University of Utah. His primary research interests are in Critical Race Theory and its connection to education leadership and policy issues in K–12 and higher education. His most recent work appears in a 2015 issue of *Qualitative Inquiry* as guest editor on Critical Race Theory and qualitative methodologies/new directions in education research.

Nicola Rollock, PhD, is senior lecturer in Equalities and deputy director of the Centre for Research in Race & Education (CRRE) at the University of Birmingham, United Kingdom. Her interests lie in examining race inequalities in society and in understanding how racially minoritized groups navigate and survive racism. Theoretically, she is particularly interested in Bourdieu and Critical Race Theory and in how these theories might work together to foster a greater understanding of how race and class intersect. She is lead author of *The Colour of Class: The Educational Strategies of the Black Middle Classes* (2014).

Paulo Tan, PhD, is an assistant professor of Urban Education at the University of Tulsa. He is passionately committed to equity and social justice for individuals with disabilities. His research focuses on teacher learning, inclusive practices, and mathematics education. He is actively involved in supporting pre- and inservice teachers to lead safe, inclusive, and high-quality learning environments. Prior to joining the University of Tulsa, he served as a technical assistance coordinator and a graduate assistant for the Great Lakes Equity Center, where he planned and coordinated network/outreach and center-hosted professional learning activities. Dr. Tan was a mathematics teacher in the public schools in Kansas and Indiana for 10 years where supported students from culturally and linguistically diverse backgrounds and supported students with a range of dis/abilities and English language learners in inclusive mathematics classrooms.

Kathleen A. King Thorius, PhD, is an assistant professor of special education in Indiana University's School of Education and principal investigator for the Great Lakes Equity Center, funded by the U.S. Department of Education to address school desegregation in relation to race, gender, and national origin. Dr. Thorius has a strong record of facilitating partnerships with state departments of education and school districts to create inclusive educational systems. In her research she explores ways educational policy and local practices converge to shape experiences and outcomes for historically underserved students. Dr. Thorius's work has been published in *Exceptional Children*, *Remedial and Special Education*, and *Theory into Practice*, as well as other dis/ability-related and interdisciplinary journals. She is co-editor (with Dr. Elizabeth B. Kozleski) of *Ability, Equity, and Culture: Sustaining Inclusive Urban Education Reform*, also published by Teachers College Press as part of this Disability, Equity, and Culture series.

Sally Tomlinson, PhD, is emeritus professor at Goldsmiths College, London University, and an honorary research fellow in the Department of Education, University of Oxford. She has taught, researched, and published for over 30 years in the areas of education policy, special education and disability, and race, ethnicity and education. Her most recent books are *Ignorant Yobs? Low Attainers in a Global Knowledge Economy"* (2013) and *The Politics of Race, Class and Special Education: The Selected Works of Sally Tomlinson* (2014). Papers from group research on *Special Education and Globalisation, Continuities and Contrasts Across the Developed World* (Riddell, Danforth, Graham, Hjorne, Sip-Jan Pijl, Tomlinson, & Weedon), will be published in a special issue of the journal *Discourse* in 2016.

Carol Vincent, PhD, is professor of Sociology of Education at University College London, Institute of Education. The areas in which she writes and researches include parents' interactions with educational institutions and how these are shaped by class and race; parenting, especially mothering; and education policy. Her current project examines the friendships children and adults, living in diverse urban areas, make (or avoid), focusing in particular on friendship across class and ethnic difference.

Index

Asbury, K., 163
Asch, A., 25, 204, 212
Asians
  as "model minority," 16, 64
  risk ratios for learning disabilities/special
    education, 119
Assessment
  as basis of school reform, 157, 160–161,
    177–178
  "blaming" impact of, 157, 165
  "failing schools," 160–161
  high-stakes testing in the U.S., 25, 84,
    158, 175, 215
  IQ testing, 11, 73–75, 76, 90, 94–95, 113,
    160, 163–164
  psychometric tradition, 163–164
  for special education needs (SEN, UK),
    40, 43, 45, 46–48, 53, 159–160
Assimilationist practices, 133–134
At-risk students, 11, 19, 170–172, 175, 176,
  177–178, 218
Attention deficit hyperactivity disorder
  (ADHD), 41–42, 196, 198
Austin Nursing Center Inc. v. Lovato, 204
Autistic spectrum, 10, 43, 46–48, 50, 53,
  132, 133, 137, 162

Baca, L., 23
Bacchi, C., 190
Baglieri, Susan, 5, 18, 65, 147, 167–179,
  173, 218, 221
Bahena, S., 145–146
Bailey, A., 211
Baker, B., 26, 177
Baker, C., 23
Baker, K., 101–102, 111
Bal, A., 30, 31, 90, 101
Baldwin, James, 1
Ball, E. W., 30, 177
Ball, Stephen J., 3–4, 35–54, 36, 37, 40, 51,
  54, 190
Banking model of education (Freire), 82–83
Banks, J. A., 18, 173, 174
Bartholomew, H., 51
Baxter, L. A., 103
Baynton, D., 23, 24, 26–27, 134
Beachum, F., 145
Beck, A., 117–118
Behavior disorders, 10, 15, 113, 135, 137,
  161–162, 196, 198, 200
Behavior management systems, 61, 62–63,
  136–144
  labeling students, 136, 137–138, 147

Positive Behavior Intervention Supports
  (PBIS), 118, 138–141
zero-tolerance policies, 65, 118, 137
Bejoian, L., 65
Bell, Chris M., 2, 3, 11, 12, 134, 205
Bell, Derrick, 14, 25, 175, 205, 221
Bell, L. A., 94–95
Benavot, A., 157
Ben-Moshe, L., 132, 134, 135
Beratan, G., 19, 21, 38, 159
Bernal, D. D., 13, 14, 20, 113
Berry, T. R., 14, 29
Best, A. M., 17, 117
Bhopal, K., 36
Biklen, D., 10
BilDil, 209
Bilingual students, 16, 23
BillyJam, 132
Biological determinism, 177
Birchmeier, Z., 118
Bitch Media (magazine), 133–134
Black Lives Matter, 219
Blackorby, J., 15
Black power movement, 64
Black pride movement, 29, 64
Blacks
  low academic expectations of schools,
    42–43, 60–61
  middle-class racism and dis/ability in the
    United Kingdom, 3–4, 35–54, 214
  military service, 211
  observer identification process, 110,
    112–113
  overrepresentation as dis/abled, 2–3, 10,
    11, 12–13, 15, 16–17, 23, 90, 105,
    113–114, 115, 117–119, 122, 123,
    137
  police brutality, 59–60, 63–64, 131–132,
    133, 162, 184
  racial working identity in school-to-prison
    pipeline, 145–153, 217
  risk ratios for learning disabilities/special
    education, 30, 119, 123, 145, 146
  school segregation, 25, 51
  school suspensions, 65–66, 138, 146, 152
  secondary and higher education trends,
    153, 161, 162, 210
  slavery heritage, 10, 23, 26, 89, 134, 159,
    173, 206–209
  in the United Kingdom, 3–4, 12–13,
    35–54, 158–164
Blair, M., 43–44
Blair, Tony, 161–162